Revolutionary bodies

Manchester University Press

Revolutionary bodies

Homoeroticism and the political imagination in Irish writing

Michael G. Cronin

MANCHESTER UNIVERSITY PRESS

Copyright © Michael G. Cronin 2022

The right of Michael G. Cronin to be identified as the author of this work has been asserted by them in accordance with the Copyright, Designs and Patents Act 1988.

Published by Manchester University Press
Oxford Road, Manchester M13 9PL

www.manchesteruniversitypress.co.uk

British Library Cataloguing-in-Publication Data
A catalogue record for this book is available from the British Library

ISBN 978 1 5261 3542 1 hardback
ISBN 978 1 5261 7884 8 paperback

First published 2022

The publisher has no responsibility for the persistence or accuracy of URLs for any external or third-party internet websites referred to in this book, and does not guarantee that any content on such websites is, or will remain, accurate or appropriate.

Typeset
by New Best-set Typesetters Ltd

Contents

List of figures	*page* vi
Acknowledgements	vii
Introduction: Wilde Atlantic Ways: homoeroticism, Irish literature and revolution	1
1 Brendan Behan: Eros and liberation	37
2 John Broderick: perverse politics	63
3 Colm Tóibín: feeling neoliberal	91
4 Time and politics in Irish gay male fiction	117
5 Homoerotic and hopeful spaces in 'Celtic Tiger' fiction	153
Conclusion: 'After' equality	196
Select bibliography	214
Index	224

List of figures

1 Joe Caslin, 'The Claddagh Embrace' (2015). Image courtesy of the artist.   198
2 Joe Caslin, 'Ar scáth a chéile a mhaireann na daoine' ('We live protected under each other's shadow') (2016–present). Photo by Peter Grogan/Emagine.   199
3 Joe Caslin, 'The Volunteers – Collins Barracks' (2017). Image courtesy of the artist.   201

Acknowledgements

I am grateful to Maynooth University for facilitating sabbatical leave in spring 2019, which allowed me to work on this book.

More generally, I am glad to work in a university where the neoliberal reconstruction of higher education has, comparatively, been kept at bay, and where there is still freedom to teach and think. I am also glad to work with many good colleagues across the university, and especially those I work with most closely in the English Department led in recent years by Emer Nolan, Colin Graham, Stephen O'Neill and Lauren Arrington. I am particularly grateful for their practical support to Amanda Bent, Clodagh McDonnell and Tracy O'Flaherty. And many thanks also to my colleagues in the university library and the university bookshop. It is right to acknowledge the (grossly undervalued) work of our doctoral students and occasional teaching staff, on whose labour my freedom to research, and that of my permanent colleagues, depends; I am especially indebted to Thomas Connolly, Brenda O'Connell and Emma Roche. Many of the ideas in this book developed in classroom dialogue, and I am especially grateful for the thoughtful engagement of final year BA students and students on the English Department's MA programmes. And much thanks for their energy and enthusiasm to my colleagues in the MU SexGen Research Network, and especially to Patricia Kennon and Fergus Ryan.

For support, encouragement and solidarity, heartfelt thanks to: David Alderson, Julie Bates, Conrad Brunstrom, Denis Condon, Colin Coulter, Sharae Deckard, Treasa De Loughry, Dermot Dix, Bridget English, Ann Fogarty, Oona Frawley, Matthew Frost, Kevin Honan, Heather Laird, Chandana Mathur, Ed Madden, Mary McAuliffe,

Conor McCarthy, Donal Ó Drisceoil, Katherine O'Donnell, David Lloyd, Lionel Pilkington, Paul Ryan, Guy Woodward. The late Seamus Deane offered invaluable advice and encouragement.

For their time and assiduous care when reading chapter drafts, I am grateful to: Joe Cleary, Paul Delaney, Declan Kavanagh, Sinéad Kennedy, Emer Nolan. I am especially grateful to the readers for MUP for their thoughtful, sympathetic and encouraging response to the work.

A version of Chapter 1 was previously published in *Reading Brendan Behan* (Cork University Press, 2019); parts of Chapters 4 and 5 appeared in *The Oxford Handbook of Modern Irish Fiction* (Oxford University Press, 2020). For their supportive guidance many thanks to the respective editors: John McCourt and Liam Harte.

For permission to use photographs of his murals on the cover and in the book, many thanks to Joe Caslin.

I presented early versions of these chapters in various symposiums and guest lectures. Many thanks to warmly generous interlocutors on those occasions: John Brannigan, Maria DiBattista, Gavin Clarke, Tadgh Hoey, Naomi Michalowicz, Mary McGlynn, Barry McCrea, Ann Mulhall, Jamie O'Neill, Philip Roseman, Cherry Smyth and Eibhear Walshe. For generous hospitality thanks to the Irish Literary Society in London, the Columbia Irish Studies Seminar and to Notre Dame University in Rome.

I am especially grateful for the support and kindness of Joe Cleary, Sinéad Kennedy, Emer Nolan and Deirdre Quinn; sometime colleagues at MU, but, more importantly, very good friends.

Likewise, I am grateful for the support and love of family, friends and neighbours in Kerry, Carlow, Wicklow, Dublin, London, Berlin and Darmstadt. A special word of thanks to Sandra Godkin for encouragement and friendship.

This book is concerned with literature and politics, but also with imagining possibilities for freedom and love; Tony Broderick continues to teach me much about the latter.

Introduction

Wilde Atlantic Ways: homoeroticism, Irish literature and revolution

What the artist is always looking for is that mode of existence in which soul and body are one and indivisible: in which the outward is expressive of the inward: in which Form reveals.[1]

The best among the poor are never grateful. They are ungrateful, discontented, disobedient, and rebellious. They are quite right to be so.[2]

Across generations, literary styles and political perspectives, Oscar Wilde is a touchstone connecting the writers whose fiction this study addresses. To take just one example, the second quotation above, from 'The Soul of Man under Socialism' (1891), appears in Jamie O'Neill's historical romance *At Swim, Two Boys* (2001). Reflecting on this, I realised that Wilde's presence in the book was something more than that of a historical figure being cited or alluded to – something more than just a decorative pattern like the infamous wallpaper. In his writing, Wilde anticipated the constellation of literary and political concerns animating this book. In summary, that structuring problematic is the relationship between styles of writing homoerotic passion and styles of writing which cultivate a hopeful revolutionary imagination.

Some of those animating concerns are condensed in 'The Soul of Man under Socialism'. There Wilde affirms that a revolutionary transformation, rather than a reformation, of the existing social order is imperative. He grounds his commitment to this idea, and his sense of urgency about it, materially in his apprehension of how people's lives are blighted and distorted by want. 'The proper aim', he writes, 'is to try and reconstruct society on such a basis that poverty will be impossible.'[3] It is likewise a first principle of this book that the achievement of sexual liberation will, when it happens, be one essential element of the revolutionary transformation of capitalism into democratic socialism.

For Wilde, this revolution would proceed in two distinct spheres at once. In the sphere of social relations private property would be abolished and the means of sustaining human life collectivised. In our neoliberal society where the dismantling of socialised welfare is accompanied by the celebrated proliferation of philanthropy, Wilde's observations resonate: 'It is immoral to use private property to alleviate the horrible evils that result from the institution of private property. It is both immoral and unfair.'[4] This revolution in social relations would be accompanied by a revolution in human consciousness. In Wildean style the argument turns on a paradox; freedom for the individual can only be achieved when the means of sustaining human life are socialised – though, of course, this only appears to be paradoxical from within the prevailing bourgeois hermeneutic which sets 'individual' and 'collective' at odds.

Wilde nominates this revolutionary consciousness as 'Individualism', his use of capitalisation indexing its difference from the autonomous, separative and competitive individualism foundational to capitalist ideology. By contrast, the human subject Wilde anticipates in the figure of the 'Individual' will find the fullest expression of their self within a relational matrix with others, and, as Wilde's nature imagery suggests, with the ecosystem they inhabit. This anticipated Individualism will:

> grow naturally and simply, flower-like, or as a tree grows. It will not be at discord. It will never argue or dispute. It will not prove things. It will know everything. And yet it will not busy itself about knowledge … it will not always be meddling with others, or asking them to be like itself. It will love them because they are different. And yet while it will not meddle with others it will help all, as a beautiful thing helps us, by being what it is.[5]

Here Wilde anticipates a vital insight, and one of the most fertile philosophical currents, in twentieth-century radical feminist, anticolonial and Marxist thought. A revolution confined to institutions, to economic and political structures, is doomed to failure to the degree that it neglects to revolutionise human consciousness. As Kathi Weeks puts it, discussing the distinctive contribution of feminist standpoint theory, radical forms of thinking 'shift the focus to the position of subjects constituted by and constitutive of these systemic relations. It is the potential power of these subjects rather than just the effectiveness of the system that is the primary concern.'[6] From within that radical tradition, this study is particularly indebted to the work of Herbert Marcuse for coordinates towards conceptualising revolutionary forms of consciousness and the related task of reconceptualising sexual freedom. Below and in Chapter 1, I discuss some of his concepts which I have found most useful for thinking with. Here though we might just note that Marcuse follows Wilde in identifying a hierarchical binary between mind and body as an ideological cornerstone of modernity and of the alienation endemic to capitalism. Hence, for instance, when describing Individualism Wilde distinguishes between different forms of human understanding: between 'knowing', on one hand, and, on the other, 'knowledge' which insists on rational calculation. Here 'knowing' collapses the distinction, an iteration of the mind–body binary, between 'thought' and 'feeling'. In the chapters that follow we will be paying particular attention to styles of writing which undermine that thought/feeling distinction, and thereby challenge other politically operative ideological distinctions – notably: desire/need; identity/body; reform/ revolution.

Looking again at Wilde's prose when describing Individualism, we notice the repetition of 'it', which creates an abstract indistinctiveness. Wilde's prose indexes that this is an anticipatory projection of what subjectivity beyond alienation might be like in the conditions of a transformed and liberated future. In other words, we cannot, under current conditions, know, and we can only imagine what freedom will be like. Hence Art, as Wilde terms it, is indispensable to revolution since it cultivates the capacity to imagine the world as other than how it is. His essay includes a lengthy complaint about, and satire on, the philistinism of his contemporary English society. Leaving aside the local detail and characteristically witty epigrams, what remains most germane for our neoliberal times is his critique of the utilitarian demand that Art be purposeful – morally affirming the hegemonic values while also serving as commodified entertainment. Again, in his conception of the revolutionary uselessness of Art, Wilde foreshadows modernism and a signature insight of Marxist literary criticism. The least compelling form of political literary criticism approaches literature – and, in particular, the novel, the form with which this study is concerned – as a type of higher sociology: as a mirror 'reflecting' the society back to itself. As Raymond Williams argued, the problem with the reflection model is that it underestimates the dynamic capacity of art to shape reality. The reflection model 'succeeds in suppressing the actual work on material – in a final sense, the material social process – which is the making of any work of art. By projecting and alienating this material process to 'reflection', the social and material character of artistic activity – of that artwork which is at once 'material' and 'imaginative' – was suppressed.'[7]

While this book is concerned with 'history' – how we narrate, think and feel temporality, historical development and social change – it makes no claims to being *a history*: of the lesbian and gay movement in Ireland, or of the depiction of gay men in Irish writing, or of Irish gay writing. It is a work of literary criticism, in the precise sense that Joseph North defines, or more accurately advocates. North argues that two paradigms shaped the study of English literature in the twentieth century: criticism and scholarship. While the historical origins of the latter paradigm lie in philology, the most significant manifestation has been what North terms the 'historical-contextual' model of literary scholarship dominant since the 1970s. North identifies a central paradox about the emergence of this model. From the outset its political impetus was avowedly radical and leftist: to supplant the liberal-conservative style of literary criticism, associated with figures such as Lionel Trilling and F.R. Leavis, which largely defined the professional discipline of 'English literature' in its mid-twentieth-century nascence. In place of an idealist conception of literature as autonomous and transcendent, the object of analysis now was literature as a historical, discursive and political formation – the literary text as a route to understanding the society and its power dynamics. However, along with the radical political commitments motivating so much of this scholarship it also mutated, North claims, into a defensive adaptation to the increasingly hostile environment of the neoliberal university system. As North argues, 'if the turn to "cultural analysis" was a turn to the Left, it was also the moment at which the discipline agreed to transform itself into a discipline of observation, tracking developments in the culture without any broader mandate to intervene in it'.[8] Francis Mulhern glosses this as 'cultural symptomatology … the new paradigm is geared for the kind of output that the neoliberal academy can most easily handle: positive knowledge, sometimes even quantified; 'radical' maybe, but critical, no'.[9]

For this reason, North advocates revitalising a radical left style of literary criticism. This would develop a materialist rather than idealist conception of the aesthetic and actively intervene to 'enrich the culture directly by cultivating new ranges of sensibility, new modes of subjectivity, new capacities for experience'.[10] He finds useful historical coordinates for this materialist and politically radical mode of literary criticism as aesthetic education in the work of I.A. Richards; in a later revision he also finds inspiration for this style of literary criticism in Williams, a figure he earlier identified as central to the ascendance of historical-contextual scholarship.[11] I am crudely simplifying the historical range and complexity of North's argument; and since his book has something of the manifesto it too can veer towards the schematic, especially when compressing diverse political and theoretical positions into the category of 'historical-contextual' scholarship.[12] And evidently one of the defining conditions of possibility for this book, as for my political-intellectual formation generally, is the work of those who would, in North's categorisation, be exemplary of the 'scholarship' generation; for instance, Eve Kosofsky Sedgwick, Fredric Jameson and Alan Sinfield, to name just three.

Nevertheless, I have found it creatively energising to situate the formal, aesthetic and 'literary' qualities of these novels as foundational to this study, taking as axiomatic that novels stage their most powerful, compelling and effective political interventions less through representation than aesthetically and therefore affectively.[13] A related axiom is that the most politically interesting and radical literary affects are what Rachel Greenwald Smith terms 'impersonal feelings'. Greenwald Smith distinguishes between two modes of reading affect in literature. One, which she terms the affective hypothesis, focuses on personal feelings – feelings that are represented in the text as readily ascribable to a depicted character. The affective hypothesis so prevalent in contemporary literary culture demands that literature be therapeutic, by depicting feelings and thereby eliciting empathetic feeling from its readers. This, she argues, is symptomatic of our neoliberal culture: not only the utilitarian demand that literature be useful but, more crucially, the expectation that literature affirmatively naturalise hegemonic individualism – the 'person' who is the sacrosanct location of these 'feelings'. As Greenwald Smith observes, 'while neoliberalism casts the individual as responsible for herself, the affective hypothesis casts feeling as necessarily owned and managed by individual authors, characters, and readers'.[14] Against this style of reading Greenwald Smith poses an alternative interpretive mode, focusing not on the representation of an individual character's feelings, but on 'seeing felt literary effects as achieved through the play of formal surfaces rather than through representational depth'.[15] If the affective hypothesis buttresses individualism, the value of this alternative, Greenwald argues, is the posited relationship between aesthetics and feeling that destabilises the connection between the emotional and the personal, thereby 'reinterpreting feeling not as evidence of the primacy of the self but rather as evidence of the persistence of ecological interconnectedness'.[16]

In Wilde's writing political perspectives and aesthetic affects cluster with remarkable intensity around one type of artistic image: the beautiful male body, specifically the male body as object of a homoerotic gaze. 'The Portrait of Mr W.H.' and *The Picture of Dorian Gray* are hybrid texts. The first fuses literary scholarship and a short story; the second incorporates mythological, folk and Gothic archetypes into a realist novel that is also an essay on aesthetics. This textual *bricolage* is an expression of Wilde's intellectual technique of mobilising archaic or premodern cultural forms (Renaissance poetry; Hellenic art and philosophy) to challenge modernity's dominant ideology. It is an intellectual standpoint that is also a utopian style of temporal reasoning, grasping how the seeds of a transformed future can be nourished in the soil of the residual and archaic. This will be a recurring motif in the following chapters: novels generating their most startling, potentially radical, affects when novelists adapt artistic motifs and structures of feeling from outmoded, surpassed or discredited literary and cultural traditions – literary modernism; narrative forms such as the picaresque and the adventure tale; Christianity; Irish republican political writings and ballads.

In other words, Wilde understood that any potentially revolutionary critique of the bourgeois social order must challenge the developmental historicism that underpins it – that non-dialectical model of history as progress which situates capitalism, and the hegemonic norms of the present, as fixed and inevitable. In his writing, the portrait of a beautiful young man is a potent literary device for scrambling linear conceptions of time. The portrait freezes time. Three hundred years after inspiring Shakespeare, Mr W.H.'s beauty is unblemished. Basil Hallward's brushstrokes master time so that Dorian, in the portrait, will remain exactly as he is on that, symbolically suggestive, summer's day. Confronting this prompts Dorian to his rash bargain. The painting becomes human – mortal, vulnerable to the passage of time – while Dorian's human form takes on the objectivity and resilience to time of the artwork. Likewise, Mr W.H.'s portrait does not affirm the 'timelessness' of art, since it is not actually a record of Willie Hughes, the boy-actor, as he was but a retrospective creation to affirm Cyril's theory that he existed. These portraits do not so much freeze time then as distort it. In *Dorian Gray*, as Jed Esty argues, this temporal effect is embedded in the perversion of the *bildungsroman* plot and in the narrative rhythm of dilation and compression – the languorous narration of Dorian's unnaturally extended youth abruptly giving way to sudden, violent action (Basil's murder; the ending's reverse transposition of painting and body).[17]

If time is contingent and open – susceptible to the creative, speculative activity of Cyril and the unnamed narrator in 'Mr W.H.', for instance – so too is human subjectivity. This idea is powerfully mobilised around the homoerotic male body as a site for utopian speculation. *Dorian Gray* repudiates, through irony, those moralising, pathologising and juridical discourses casting homosexuality as sin and crime – discourses which would tragically ensnare Wilde four years later. The novel repeatedly hints towards an obscure vice corrupting Dorian's soul, leaving its grisly imprint on the painting but masked on his body by his preternatural beauty. But, it transpires, Dorian's most culpable 'vice' is actually his rigorous adherence to the hegemonic values of his society. To echo Wilde in 'Soul of Man', Dorian's most destructive vices are those intrinsic to the institution of private property: acquisitiveness – his collecting, to which, the novel's prose style implies, he is as addicted as he is to opium – and subordinating use value to exchange value. Thus, the first mark appears on the portrait after Dorian's rejection of Sybil because he insists on apprehending her as a reified object – the product of her labour as actress – rather than in the fullness of her potential and vulnerability as a human being.

In both texts a figure resembling the modern homosexual or gay man comes into view, and this figure takes most visible shape in the subject rather than the object of the homoerotic gaze: Basil and the unnamed narrator of 'Mr W.H.'. From both we hear a formulation of words prefiguring the confessional act of 'coming out' that would in twentieth-century culture – as still in our culture – reverberate with such volatile and contradictory emotions: abjection; sentimentality; politicised anger and pride. (In Chapter 4, we will examine the tonal, and thus affective and political resonances, of the literary form of the coming-out romance as it emerged in Irish writing after 1993.) Thus, Basil tells Harry that 'the reason I will not exhibit the picture is that I am afraid that I have shown in it the secret of my own soul ... there is too much of myself in the thing, Harry – too much of myself'.[18] Similarly, of his absorption in the sonnets, and in reconstructing Shakespeare's passionate relationship with Willie Hughes, the narrator of 'Mr W.H.' reflects: 'it seemed to me that I was deciphering the story of a life that had once been mine, unrolling the record of a romance that, without my knowing it, had coloured the very texture of my nature, had dyed it with strange and subtle dyes'.[19] Here the narrator identifies the affective potency of locating one's coordinates for negotiating the homophobic present in the historical traces of same-sex passion; as we will see, when discussing the gay historical romance in Chapter 4, this remained just as potent a century later. Moreover, as the narrator describes, this is a creative activity – creating compelling stories, as he realises he and Cyril have done, rather than uncovering facts – that ultimately creates rather than confirms structures of homoerotic feeling. It is not that the story of Shakespeare and Willie Hughes consolidates 'the texture of my nature' but leaves a creative imprint on it.

In both texts we are urged to read these avowals aesthetically and ethically rather than erotically and ontologically; not statements of identification but assertions of a political standpoint, and a commitment to those ideals that for Wilde cohered around Aestheticism and Hellenism. Thus, Basil asserts that Dorian 'unconsciously ... defines for me the lines of a fresh school, a school that is to have in it all the passion of the romantic spirit, all the perfection of the spirit that is Greek'.[20] And later, to reinforce this point, the narrator tells us that 'the love that he bore him – for it was really love – had nothing in it that was not noble and intellectual. It was not that mere physical admiration of beauty that is born of the senses, that dies when the senses tire. It was such love as Michelangelo had known, as Montaigne, and Winkelmann and Shakespeare himself.' In 'Mr W.H.' each of these historical allusions is developed at greater length to substantiate Wilde's conception of homosocial friendship as aesthetically and ethically purposeful.[21]

We could argue that Aestheticism and Hellenism function here as prestigious intellectual camouflage for the real intent – an intent which yet might have been perceptible to a minority of contemporary readers. In *Dorian Gray*, in this view, Basil tries to express the truth of his feelings but shields this truth behind avowals of artistic purpose. In other words, the novel strives to give expression to a homosexual or gay identity and sensibility but cannot yet do so. The tragic unfolding of Wilde's own life would demonstrate the depths of violent homophobia, as we would now conceptualise it, in *fin-de-siècle* British society, making such strategic caution in a novel entirely plausible. Arguably, the novel is itself disfigured by that homophobic culture, offering as it does the reassuring, to the homophobic imagination, image of eroticised male beauty punished, disfigured and destroyed. Firstly, in the disturbing disfigurement of the painting as it becomes gradually more hideous. Then in the closing description of Dorian's dead body beneath the magically restored painting; his disfigured corpse serves as a rebuke to the desires woven into the painting – a sign of the punishment that befits such desires.

Nevertheless, *Dorian Gray* and 'Mr W.H.' assert the idealised 'Hellenic' conception of male beauty and friendship with a rhetorical and lyrical force, such that the reader is obliged to consider them seriously and not merely as historical error or intellectual subterfuge. As Eve Sedgwick argued, for Wilde's generation 'the Romantic rediscovery of ancient Greece cleared out – as much as recreated – ... a prestigious, historically under furnished imaginative space in which relations to and among human bodies might be newly a subject of utopian speculation'.[22] It is not that we must accept or endorse the idealised conception of 'Greek love' – merging homoeroticism, homosocial friendship and artistic creativity with mentorship in ethics and citizenship.[23] Instead the point is to value this disconcerting encounter with alternative ways of imagining human relationships. Working to grasp that alterity can allow us to grasp our own discursive frameworks as contingent and mutable – understanding that organising ourselves into demarcated categories and identities is just one way of arranging ourselves as sexual and emotional subjects. In Chapter 2 we will explore a particularly difficult version of this in the novels of John Broderick. It requires some interpretive patience to locate the spark of radical potential in his depictions of perversity – depictions that it would be tempting to peremptorily diagnose as effects of homophobic repression.

In writing about the homoerotic male body then, our novelists were contending with a volatile and contradictory amalgam of modern discourses for framing male same-sex desire that has been operative in the capitalist world system since Wilde's lifetime. Wilde's writing registers a historical moment during which those discourses developed with particular intensity, just as, and not coincidently, that world-system was expanding with such ferocity in the era of high imperialism.[24] Likewise, his writing captures the width of the political spectrum across which these intertwined discourses ranged: from homophobic, oppressive and punishing to homophile, liberationist and utopian. While his writing expresses this historical dynamic, after his imprisonment and death it would cohere most spectacularly and lastingly around the figure of 'Oscar Wilde' as a cultural memory. As Alan Sinfield argued:

> For us it is hard to regard Wilde as other than the apogee of gay experience and expression, because that is the position we have accorded him in our cultures. For us, he is always-already queer – as that stereotype has prevailed in the twentieth century … But Wilde's typicality is after-the-effect – after, I believe, the trials helped to produce a major shift in the perception of the scope of same-sex passion. At that point the entire, vaguely disconcerting nexus of effeminacy, leisure, idleness, immorality, luxury, insouciance, decadence and aestheticism, which Wilde was perceived, variously, as instantiating, was transformed into a brilliantly precise image … The principal twentieth-century stereotype entered our cultures: not just the homosexual, as the lawyers and medics would have it, but the queer.[25]

We can see then why, in the work of these writers who, in various ways, identified or identify as bisexual or gay, Wilde's life and work will have strong resonances beyond the literary and intellectual. Here I might usefully digress to say something about the logic underpinning the choice of novelists and novels.

Firstly, it may seem counter-intuitive that the writers examined in a book critically interrogating the political valences of sexual identity should be selected on the basis of a shared identity. Thus, for instance, I do not address the depictions of gay men in recent Irish fiction by authors who do not identify as gay, lesbian or queer; for instance, Belinda McKeon's *Tender* (2015), Ann Enright's *The Green Road* (2015) and Sebastian Barry's *Days Without End* (2016) and *A Thousand Moons* (2020).[26] However, this apparent contradiction illustrates my standpoint on sexual identity, which is broadly that model of 'disidentification' advocated by José Esteban Muñoz and Rosemary Hennessey. Muñoz adapted his theoretical coordinates from psychoanalysis and focused on how late twentieth-century artists who were queers of colour navigated, through strategies of parody and subversion, between dominant and subordinate cultural identities – those of race and imperialism as well as of sexuality and gender. While not sharing Muñoz's attachment to psychoanalytic theory, I find his conception of performance as a creative strategy, and his emphasis on intersectionality, very useful for thinking about the recurrence of one trope in several of our novels: intertextual incorporations of Irish (Irish-language and Anglophone) ballads and political songs. Obviously, the convention of cross-gender identification in the Irish song tradition (male singers singing love songs from a woman's point of view, and vice versa) creates opportunities for homoerotic recoding, embedding into these 'traditional' texts subversive or alternate queer meanings legible to some but not all listeners. But, of course, coded meanings – Jacobite; republican; anticolonial; socialist – were already embedded in many of these songs. Thus, we can read these performances, and the recuring narration of such performances in the novels, as a subversive realignment of supposedly distinct (and, for liberal revisionist critics, opposed) subaltern identities. Alternatively, we can, as I argue, read these performances as dislodging identity with desire, and as bringing distinct forms of desire – homoerotic and revolutionary – into creative alignment.

Hennessy's reformulation of disidentification is more dialectical and materialist, and therefore closer in spirit to my standpoint. As she stresses, disidentification does not mean a simple renunciation or abandonment of identities. Instead, it requires a more challenging 'critical working on them to make visible their historical and material conditions of possibility ... this critical work does not replace the prevailing identities offered by capitalist culture but takes them as the place to begin to provoke the formation of a more comprehensive, collective agency'. As her recurring references to 'work' suggests, this is not an invitation to a ludic deconstruction of identity as such, but encouragement to a much more difficult task – recognising that the prevailing modes of organising sexual desires and identities are 'real sites of affective investment' while striving to 'unlearn' these investments but acknowledging that this unlearning is 'always an incomplete, unfinished business, and recognising this as an important lesson on the limits of one's historical position'.[27]

Likewise, the exclusive focus on literary depictions of homoeroticism and of gay men will seem counter-intuitive in a study aligned with a (Marxist) feminist standpoint on gender and capitalism. Certainly this study would be enriched and variegated by exploring the depiction of same-sex passion between women in Kate O'Brien's novels, for example exploring how in her fiction erotic passion is situated within a matrix of related but distinct types of relationships between women – a literary projection of Adrienne Rich's 'lesbian continuum' *avant la lettre* – and the political complexities flowing from that artistic choice (foregrounding potential feminist solidarity, for instance, while masking relations of power – notably class power – between women). Similarly, my discussion of the Irish coming-out romance in Chapter 4 is incomplete in so far as it lacks a comparative analysis of Mary Dorcey's and Emma Donoghue's contributions to that genre, and some consideration of how their divergent perspectives on the political legacy of lesbian feminism shapes their literary style.[28]

Since the 1970s the evolution of conjunctions and acronyms – gay and lesbian; LGB; LGBT – has been an important political semiotic. It registers symbolically what is apparent materially: that indispensable collective element in the creation of any movement for social change, and the creative pursuit of solidarity across different experiences, and across the various social positions individuals may occupy within the patriarchal, capitalist system. Nevertheless, this necessary political commitment to communality and solidarity can underplay or efface crucial variations and divergences in the affective, erotic and political experiences of transgender people, bisexual people, lesbians and gay men. Thus, for instance, this study is as concerned with the literary depictions of male bodies as with depictions of gay men. This is a reminder that in so far as modern gay male identity coheres around sexual object choice the idealised embodiment of that desired object hews closely to the idealised embodiment of cis-gendered masculinity valorised in patriarchal ideology – a discursive and embodied ideal to which lesbians and transgender people will have quite different, and diverse, responses. Moreover, Sedgwick's indispensable formulation of the homoerotic and the homosocial – opposed, violently policed but also proximate and interconnected structures of male–male relationships which reinforce the patriarchal domination of women in modern capitalist society – alerts us against eliding the different ways in which the oppressive effects of patriarchy are experienced.[29] Crucially, though, this book is not concerned with the historical and social *experiences* of gay men (or queer people). It is concerned with the circulation of images, ways of imagining homoeroticism and gay men, in the political imagination of late capitalism. It is precisely because, as we will explore further below, images of gay men – and the discourses of male homosexuality underpinning those images – have been so distinctive in late capitalism that I insist on the hermeneutic and political usefulness of focusing specifically on them. Moreover, this choice is motivated by the principle that a dialectical understanding of how images of gay men circulate in the political imaginary can potentially sharpen our capacity to imagine sexual liberation for all.

While Wilde's life and work will have resonated with them because of his sexuality, his nationality will also have been a point of fascination for this group of Irish novelists. For Brendan Behan and Jamie O'Neill particularly, Wilde is an insurrectionary figure; in his writing and in his life – as an Irishman convicted at the bar of British justice – he exemplifies for them a merging of political commitments that are gay affirmative and anti-homophobic with an anticolonial, socialist republicanism. For them, Wilde shares in that quality he ascribes to the 'ungrateful' poor – he is a rebel.

There are divergent views on the historical relationship between 'queer' and 'Irish' Wilde. This was sharply foregrounded in the disjunction between Eibhear Walshe's *Oscar's Shadow* (2011) and the late Brian Earls' response, a two-part essay in the *Dublin Review of Books* in 2013. Moving from the coverage of Wilde's three trials and imprisonment in the Irish press to writers, such as Colm Tóibín and Jamie O'Neill, imaginatively engaging with Wilde's memory a century later, Walshe identifies two currents in the Irish reception of Wilde. One is a literary and intellectual project to assimilate Wilde to the history of Irish nationalist, anticolonial struggle; iterations range across the twentieth century from Yeats and Joyce to Terry Eagleton. The second is gay- and lesbian-identified Irish writers foregrounding Wilde's queer sexuality and reclaiming him as a gay forefather. This, Walshe argues, was pioneered by Micheál MacLíammóir, and his hugely successful one-man show, *The Importance of Being Oscar*, in the 1960s, but accelerated after 1993. For Walshe, these currents are entirely at odds with each other. In his account, that second current is nuanced, progressive and politically sympathetic; for these writers, Wilde offered a richly productive route into imaginatively recreating a sustaining sense of gay history for contemporary lesbians and gay men. Towards the first current Walshe is sceptical and unsympathetic. The reclamation of Wilde as 'dissident Irishman', he argues, invariably proceeded through silencing and neutralising his sexual dissidence. The only useful lesson to be learned from that current is that Irish cultural nationalism – whether in 1895 or 1995 – was inherently and unrelentingly homophobic.[30]

Earls takes issue with this schematic binary. In a work of unusually rich archival density and range, he traces the Wilde family's nationalist and anticolonial commitments – from his mother's youthful immersion in the revolutionary energies around Young Ireland to the more staid support for Home Rule in young Oscar's family home.[31] More centrally, he locates discussion of Wilde's work as a recurring topic in Irish political and cultural debates throughout the early and mid-twentieth century. Far from Wilde being marginalised, as Walshe maintains, for a great variety of Irish writers and intellectuals writing about Wilde was a way of thinking about artistic and sexual freedom, about aesthetic innovation and anti-imperial commitment, and about the purpose of a national literature in decolonisation and liberation. For instance, Earls examines the salience of Wildean themes and allusions in Pádraic Ó Conaire's fiction and the critical engagement with Wilde's work in MacLíammóir's Irish-language journalism in the 1920s. He demonstrates how, for those two writers, Wilde informed their commitment to sexual transgression and freedom *and* their commitment to a cosmopolitan cultural nationalism characterised by linguistic and artistic experimentation.[32]

Surveying the variety of debates and positions, Earls notes the relative absence, in Irish political and cultural discourse, of homophobic condemnation of Wilde and, by contrast, a good deal of tolerant sympathy. He posits some hypotheses to explain this. One was popular admiration for 'Speranza', especially the cultural memory, still strong at the turn of the twentieth century, of her solidarity with the victims of the Famine. Another that the younger revolutionary Irish generation discovering Wilde in the years after his death 'would have brought their values and life histories to bear on their reading of his life and works' and for them 'the experience of prison, either for themselves or those whom they esteemed, was part of their generational landscape'. More speculatively, Earls detects 'a non-punitive attitude towards Wilde, shared by the Irish and French' which indicated, in both cultures, 'the survival at popular level of a moral order in which charity, in its social dimension, was what mattered, and lechery was seen as the least significant of the seven deadly sins'.[33]

If one difficulty with the 'queer Wilde/Irish Wilde' dichotomy is, as Earls demonstrates, that it does not entirely stand up to historical scrutiny, another is that it reduces politics to a zero-sum game of competing identities. The most persuasive refutation of that position is Wilde's writing. As we have seen, *Dorian Gray* is a 'queer' novel: an anxiously homoerotic structure of feeling, and critical perspectives on the homophile and homophobic sexual discourses circulating in Wilde's culture. Similarly, *Dorian Gray* is an 'Irish' novel in its literary and political perspectives, rooted in material historical experience, rather than in any identitarian sense. The narrative elements most disruptive of the novel's realism are adapted from Irish folklore and the Irish Gothic. As Maureen O'Connor observes, once Dorian and the portrait transmigrate, he enters a temporal equivalent of *Tír na nÓg*, the island of eternal youth in Irish mythology. In the nineteenth-century British imagination, O'Connor argues, '*Tír na nÓg* stands in for Ireland itself, an unreconstructed reservoir of soul, a land ever in its cultural youth.'[34]

More darkly, in trading his soul for perpetual youth Dorian makes a similar Faustian bargain as Charles Maturin's Melmoth, initiating a similar train of suffering and destruction, and he comes to inhabit a liminal, monstrous 'undead' subjectivity akin to Sheridan Le Fanu's Carmilla and Bram Stoker's Dracula. Irish Gothic fiction gives literary and symbolic expression to a complex structure of feeling. Essentially this is a combination of guilt and fear echoing the historical and political condition of a settler colonial class. Fear inculcated by being a minority at once powerful and precarious, and guilt, especially among more cultured or liberal members of that class who recognise that their privilege rests on a historical wrong (a primal act of violent expropriation) and recognise the contradiction between their commitment to modern progressive, democratic ideas and their anxiety that the historical realisation of those ideals will inevitably erode the power they enjoy.[35] In *Dorian Gray*, as Ellen Scheible argues, an Irish Gothic structure of feeling is subversively mobilised against the forms of epistemology and identity underpinning British imperialist ideology; as she demonstrates, 'symbols of Irish nationalism both moonlight in Wilde's text and take centre stage during scenes that underscore a degenerating British selfhood'.[36]

In other words, the 'Irishness' of *Dorian Gray* is most powerfully operative in its critical interrogation of imperialist and capitalist ideology. Dorian's hedonism – his cultivation of a stylised mode of living – balances on a fine line between the ethical ideals of aestheticism and a purposeless, insatiable consumption. As an aestheticist novel anxious about the ethics of aestheticism – the potential for those aestheticist ideals to be absorbed and resignified by bourgeois ideology, and to morph into the very values aestheticism sets out to challenge – *Dorian Gray* reiterates the difficulty of utopian thinking, of imagining the world differently, in the face of the dominant ideology. In this the novel prefigures the energetic capacity of late capitalism to absorb and resignify dissident and countercultural currents.

Moreover, as Jed Esty argues, Dorian's connoisseurship and acquisitiveness, the perpetual cycle of consumption he inhabits, is mapped spatially in the novel. Languorously unfolding descriptions of Dorian's objects are repetitively interspersed with references to places and cultures from which those objects originated. The prose luxuriates in the sensuous feel of the objects, with that sensuousness heightened by orientalist exoticism. In this way, the novel foregrounds how Dorian's aestheticized style of living depends on an imperialist mode of knowledge, in which metropolitan society is perceived as the global epicentre and the rest of the world as merely a source of resources to be extracted. As Esty argues, Dorian's 'long sensory bath requires – or at least unfolds most meaningfully within – the urban environment of the imperial metropolis where the wealth of dead nations and savage tribes filters in and remains available for consumption. Orientalism and metropolitan perception are cultural predicates for the ideas of pleasure, beauty and consumption: ideals such as Hellenism, hedonism, aestheticism and individualism.'[37]

At the same time, the novel offers a sensational, Gothic image of metropolitan society subjected to a devastation unleashed by the world-system it has created. Dorian, and the other sons of the British ruling class he is accused of corrupting, are destroyed by opium – historically the drug strategically used to propel mid-nineteenth-century British imperialism in Asia and to secure Britain as hegemon in that cycle of capitalist global expansion.[38] It is a powerful symbol of capitalism's rapacious exploitation of human and natural resources for profit wreaking vengeance on metropolitan society, and acutely captures our globalised reality more than a century later. For those of us living in the prosperous West, the psychic experience of late capitalism is not unlike having a decomposing portrait hidden in the attic; our suppressed knowledge about that enormity of human suffering and exploitation, and the unfolding ecological catastrophe, which enables our consumerist lifestyles.

Three points are useful to note here for our purposes. One is the significance of the spatial imaginary in interpreting Wilde's novel. The juxtaposition of Dorian's outward beauty and the corruption manifest on the hidden painting is repeated in the spatial juxtaposition of 'Society', located in London's West End, and the 'underworld', located in the East End. Moreover, in the novel the latter is populated by sailors, like James Vane, and foreigners, such as the opium sellers – the docks are the literal and symbolic point of connection between the imperial city and its colonies, and, in the novel's adaptation of sensationalist and Gothic moods, is felt as a particular point of anxiety and danger. In other words, the novel's critique of metropolitan perception takes shape in styles of writing social space. As we will see, I adapt this framework for reading the critical utopian impulses in those novels of the Irish 'Celtic Tiger' addressed in the final chapter.

Secondly, as Esty observes, Wilde insists on 'a strongly materialist understanding of even the most ethereal and aestheticized endeavours', and his exposure of the progressive logic of modernity is 'shot through with historical traces of Anglo-Irish colonialism and wider references to uneven development in the imperial world system'.[39] In the same way, in so far as this study specifically addresses the depiction of homoeroticism in Irish fiction the purpose is not to adumbrate the distinctiveness or peculiarity – positive or negative – of Irish historical experience and Irish sexual culture. Instead, the guiding purpose is that our critical understanding of one distinctive literary tradition is a useful leverage for gaining some radical critical purchase on the contradictory condition of sexual freedom in late capitalism. For that reason, as with Wilde, the critical analysis in the following chapters attends especially to the novels' receptivity towards, and critical engagement with, Irish anticolonial and anticapitalist political traditions, and their literary and cultural mediations.

Thirdly, while Dorian embodies an alienated and reified consciousness typical of consumerism, he is also insurrectionary and subversive – his 'vice' facilitates the avenging spectre of colonial exploitation and undermines the generational reproduction of the imperial ruling class. In this he prefigures the ambivalent and paradoxical position of the discursive homosexual/gay man in late capitalism; an ideologically mobile figure that is alternatively affirmative of and threatening to the hegemonic norms, and specifically the valorised form of consciousness that coheres around the dominant conception of liberal subjectivity.

Historically, the dialectical relationship between capitalism and sexual freedom for queer people is not in itself new. As John D'Emilio argued in his landmark essay, the development of industrial capitalism in the United States during the nineteenth and early twentieth centuries simultaneously created the conditions for inhabiting modern lesbian and gay identities and the conditions for the emergence of modern homophobia. The ascendency of wage labour, and the new centrality of the individual as a 'free' labourer, weakened the role of the family as the primary unit of production. These material and ideological developments also facilitated the gradual cultural differentiation of the imperative to procreate from sexual intimacy and pleasure. Moreover, the labour demands of industrialisation, accompanied by urbanisation, created a mobile labour force of young people making lives for themselves away from the connections and expectations of family. For those attracted to people of their own sex these developments facilitated a gradual, uneven, but decisive historical transition away from patterns of homosexual behaviour and towards emergent forms of consciousness and sexual identity.[40] As D'Emilio summarises, 'in divesting the household of its economic independence and fostering the separation of sexuality from procreation, capitalism has created conditions that allow some men and women to organise a personal life around their erotic/emotional attraction to their own sex. It has made possible the formation of urban communities of lesbian and gay men and, more recently, of a politics based on sexual identity.'[41]

This new style of political movement emerged in the mid- and late twentieth century out of new opportunities created by capitalism, while also being propelled by the pressure of new forms of oppression generated by capitalism. Centrally, D'Emilio argues, modern homophobia is an effect of capitalism's contradictory relationship with the family. On one hand, capitalism undermined the material basis of the family by replacing its economic functions with wage labour and weakening the dependency of individuals on family ties. At the same time, capitalist ideology has sanctified the family as a source of love, affection and nurture. Crucially, bourgeois gender ideology naturalised the physical and affective work of sustaining human life as the responsibility of women, making the family a privatised resource for the reproduction of labour.[42] Within this matrix of contradictory pressures, the discursive figure of the 'homosexual' came to embody, within the homophobic patriarchal imagination, a perceived 'threat' to the family, when that perception of threat was in fact an anxious effect of capitalism's endemic instability and alienation. As D'Emilio argues, 'while capitalism has knocked the material foundations away from family life, lesbians, gay men and heterosexual feminists have become the scapegoats for the social instability of the system'.[43]

In the twenty-first century this discursive image of the gay man, in particular as a threatening and subversive 'other', is still part of the conservative political imaginary. This is true within Western democracies but more viscerally so in countries such as Russia and certain Middle-Eastern and African states for instance, where this figure is being actively mobilised to incite legal persecution and violence against queer people.[44] But from within the perspective of the neoliberal world view now hegemonic in Western democracies, such as Ireland, this figure of the gay man as 'other' seems residual in two senses. Firstly, in this dominant world view homophobia is positioned as a residual phenomenon. That is, as an effect of pre-modern modes of thought and subjectivity – religion, nationalism, despotism, irrationalism – persistently infecting an otherwise rational, secular, democratic and cosmopolitan body politic. In other words, in this view homophobia is an epiphenomenon which it is unnecessary to conceptualise as a political problem within, or specific to, capitalism – unnecessary, for instance, to register that the most virulent political mobilisation of homophobia is currently located in states where extractive capitalism is most exploitative and kleptocratic.

Secondly, the idea of the gay man as threatening seems residual in a culture where the most familiar imagery of gay men appears to situate these figures at the definitional core, rather than the stigmatised periphery, of normative subjectivity – of what it is to be recognisably human. As you will have noticed, I am rather clumsily reiterating terms such as 'figure', 'discursive' and 'imagery' here. This is because, as David Alderson alerts us, we do well to proceed cautiously when thinking about the relationship between gay men and the phantasmagorias of contemporary consumer society. For one thing, we risk reactivating long-standing archetypes of purposeful, productive manly citizenship and wasteful, leisured effeminate consumption. These archetypes originated in eighteenth-century British debates about masculinity, citizenship, class and the rival claims to hegemony of landed aristocracy and commercial bourgeoisie.[45] In the nineteenth century these archetypes evolved into a variety of explicitly gendered figures – the woman shopper; the sex worker; the dandy; the aesthete; the homosexual – vibrating with misogyny and mobilised in European culture to articulate diverse critical and dissident responses to modernity: from conservative reaction to Romanticism to aestheticism and socialism.[46] In short, it is important to distinguish between, on one hand, the ideological effects of cultural imagery and narratives of 'gay men' and, on the other, actually existing men, who identify as gay, in all the variegated complexity of their lives and material conditions.

Moreover, in arguing that 'gay men' embody the alienating excesses of consumer capitalism we risk adopting those moralising and puritanical perspectives on consumerism to which critical analysis of capitalism – from the Left, alas, as much as from the Right – is prone. Such perspectives reactivate essentially theological categories – pleasure as sinful; the human body as fallen from grace – in the guise of political critique, while perpetuating an opposition between 'real' and 'false' needs that is hopelessly mobile and subjective. As

Alderson observes, 'the moralistic critique of the commodity that focuses primarily on conspicuous consumption suggests that other forms of consumption are more "natural" precisely because they accentuate a man's sense of his masculinity, or because they are family orientated ... hence, "gay" often signifies a decadent excess that serves to naturalize shifting heterosacremental norms of compatibility and absolve men in general of any sense of guilt for their own increasing narcissism'.[47] (In Chapter 4 we will explore this further when considering the depiction of that culturally ubiquitous figure of the sportsman as object of ambivalent desires in Jarlath Gregory's *G.A.A.Y.* [2005]). We must be alert then to how stories of contemporary gay men can become didactic parables illustrating how *some types* of people are especially susceptible to excess and the inauthentic satisfactions of consumerism – the latter construed as a kind of spiritual illness to which others are vulnerable.[48]

How then to steer between the twin pitfalls of celebrating the unalloyed freedom that late capitalism has delivered to gay men or denouncing the capture of gay men's souls by a wily, totalising capitalism that is ever and always homogenously oppressive? Firstly, by recalling Marx's dialectical conception of capitalism as contradictory and revolutionary. By sweeping away 'ancient and venerable prejudices and opinions' capitalism opens the possibility for new types of freedom; or, more precisely, the possibility for people to grasp their lack of freedom more distinctly and to actively mobilise collectively in response.[49] Capitalism is revolutionising, thus creating the potential to unleash the revolution that will overturn it. Secondly, by confronting the historical distinctiveness of neoliberal hegemony. Centrally we must recognise that the dominance of patriarchal familism has given way, as Alderson argues, to 'an uneven, incomplete and even contradictory diversified dominant that has accompanied the shift to neoliberalism and flexible accumulation'.[50]

As Alderson reiterates, to identify this diversified dominant as a chief characteristic of late capitalism is not 'to highlight an established and stable fact, since very little about this world is stable, but rather to indicate a general, sometimes contested, tendency for hegemonic legitimation to be achieved through such diversification as one indication of its sponsorship of an expanded freedom'. Moreover, confronting the contradictions underpinning the operations of this diversified dominant presents particular challenges for radical politics, since 'to speak of a diversified dominant is to highlight the extent to which a pluralism that might well be considered desirable in the abstract is nonetheless caught up in, and even determined by, vectors of class power and distinction. "Resistance" to it may take the ugly form of racism and *ressentiment*.' Those of us on the Left, Alderson concludes, 'who can be satisfied with neither diversified dominance nor the atavistic response to it often find ourselves wrong-footed by these dynamics'.[51]

While the diversified dominant takes shape through forms of pluralism which leave intact, and reinforce by securing consent for, the existing structures of capitalist domination, it likewise operates through the dispersal of repressive incitement. This concept is Alderson's revision, for the era of neoliberalism, of Marcuse's related concepts of 'repressive desublimation' and 'repressive tolerance' developed for the era of welfare capitalism. As we will discuss further in Chapter 1, in *Eros and Civilisation* (1955) Marcuse challenged Freud's view of repression. Formulated most vividly and tragically in *Civilisation and its Discontents* (1929), Freud saw repression as inevitable in the formation of human subjects and as potentially socially productive since it leads to the sublimation of libidinal drives into other aims such as scientific or artistic innovation. In this view, the sublimation of repressed drives is the indispensable element in the creation of human culture. In Freud's tragic paradox, human culture – 'civilisation' – is essential to preserve human beings from their aggressive drives, and yet submitting to the repressive demands placed on the psyche by that culture inevitably generates profound unhappiness.

While accepting that some repression might be an inevitable element of psychic formation, Marcuse argued that capitalism generated 'surplus repression' through the harnessing of our drives, energies and potentialities into the narrow objective of alienated labour. As Finn Bowring observes, 'the repressiveness of modern civilisation – which for Marcuse is embodied in the puritanical "performance principle" that demands endless toil – is no longer justified by a wild and merciless nature, but is instead perpetuated in the interests of domination. These interests are served by the manufacturing of needs, the hierarchical distribution of scarcity, and the imposition of unnecessary labour.'[52] In sum, the accumulation of surplus value requires surplus repression.

In *One-Dimensional Man* (1964) Marcuse identified the socially sanctioned release of repressed sexuality as an emerging phenomenon in welfare capitalism. For Marcuse, this liberalisation of sexual norms and relaxing of taboos was entirely different from sexual liberation as he conceptualised it; that is, the transformation of sexuality, as currently understood and lived, into the condition of freedom beyond alienation that Marcuse termed Eros, and which could only come about through the revolutionary transformation of social relations. Centrally, where liberation would create new forms of human freedom the sanctioned release of repressed sexuality integrated the creative potential of human erotic energies more securely into the dominant system, thus restricting human freedom. Marcuse characterised this as desublimation, since it entailed, as Bowring describes it, 'the paradox of a repressive reversal of repression'.[53] Or as Marcuse put it, these were developments in capitalist society which 'extend liberty while intensifying domination'.[54]

In the intervening decades those dynamics Marcuse identified have accelerated, with the demands of the performance principle extending beyond paid labour into every facet of the entrepreneurial subject's lifeworld. In 'Free Time' (1969) Adorno noted the paradox that those experiences marked as 'free time' were rigorously demarcated from 'work time' precisely to reinforce the disciplinary regimentation of labour. Free time 'must not resemble work in anyway whatsoever, in order, presumably, that one can work all the more effectively afterwards'. And yet, in consumer society leisure activity had come to resemble a form of work, since 'the contraband of modes of behaviour proper to the domain of work, which will not let people out of its power, is being smuggled into the realm of free time'.[55] While this is readily recognisable in the contemporary age of gym culture and Instagram, at the same time the suggestion that modes of work discipline are being surreptitiously smuggled into our leisure time seems quaint. Promising greater freedom – parasitically extracting positive value from terms like 'choice', 'flexibility' and 'creativity' – neoliberal culture quite explicitly undermines any distinction between 'free time' and 'work time', thereby also undermining the protections for paid labour secured by unionised workers during the twentieth century.[56] Invariably, resignifying 'work' and 'free' time like this entrenches class divisions – flexibility for the few is anxious precarity for the many.

In this context, Alderson argues, it is more useful to characterise the contemporary neoliberal equivalent of repressive desublimation as a form of repressive incitement. This has 'turned sex into fun, but fun is not as unproblematic as it imagines itself to be'.[57] While sex appears to have been desacramentalised, the aura of sex has been harnessed by the market. The widely dispersed incitement to sexual desire and pleasure as fun, such an indispensable element of contemporary culture, is repressive in so far as it reinforces the reification of human desires, pleasure and needs. Repression, in this context, refers to 'the specification and privileging of sex over other forms of sensuous experience' and to 'sexual desire's government by the performance principle'. As Alderson reiterates, repression in this sense should not be understood as a 'generalised subjective condition'; rather, 'experiences of desire and repression are separated out, often radically so, both in individual lives and depending on one's relative privilege within the system'.[58]

One way to conceptualise the ordering of this book is along this historical arc. Thus, we begin with noting Behan as a contemporary of Marcuse, but also of Jean Genet and Frantz Fanon. Behan's only novel, *Borstal Boy* (1958), unites two traditions of prison writing – Irish republican and queer male – which were already merged in Wilde's *De Profundis* (1897/1905). As in Wilde and Genet, in Behan's novel the humiliation and pain of imprisonment is transformative and radicalising – a central trope of Irish republican prison writing – and this radicalisation is given narrative and imaginative form through the narrator's erotic encounter with the male body as desirable and vulnerable; in Wilde the male body is that of Christ, in Genet and Behan it is that of youthful fellow prisoners (their youth taking on a symbolic significance as a rejection of development and 'mature' conformity to the performance principle). This style of writing homoerotic relations, as a bodily encounter of pleasure and solidarity rather than as an expression of identity, creates a literary space for imagining utopian possibilities. Echoing the narrative conjunction of two types of prison writing, we can conceptualise those utopian possibilities as a political conjunction of Marcuse and Fanon; the transformation of sexuality into Eros as a correlative of the transformative leap from decolonisation to liberation.

By contrast, in John Broderick's novels, published in the first half of the 1960s, the homoerotic male body gives way to the recognisably modern figure of the homosexual. Given the historical context of a postcolonial nation affirming its commitment to technological modernisation and economic subservience to the capitalist global order, we might reasonably expect this homosexual figure to be narratively and symbolically aligned with liberalisation. If nothing else, we might expect this abjected figure to present a 'social problem' to be progressively solved. Yet, as evidence from his critical reception demonstrates, Irish critics have found Broderick difficult to categorise and assimilate to the conventional modernisation narrative. His is just the type of critical realist aesthetic – eviscerating the pious hypocrisies of Catholic Ireland – that has long found a welcome home in Irish literary criticism. But the realist aesthetic of his fiction is ruptured by the irreconcilable presence of archaic structures of thought and feeling. One of these archaic forms is the homosexual reconfigured as a pervert; not necessarily, or not only, the homosexual as modern sexual pervert but as perverse in an older theological and political sense. In Broderick's fiction, the 'homosexual', the 'fallen woman' and the republican 'gunman' form an unholy trinity of unruly threatening perversity.

Moving to Colm Tóibín's fiction, and specifically a trio of gay-themed novels he published between 1996 and 2004, is obviously to go forward in time. Specifically, his fiction registers three significant historical developments. The most local is the decriminalisation of sex between men in the Irish Republic in 1993. But, as I discuss in Chapter 4, that punctual event envelopes within it a longer historical process – the emergence and evolution of the Irish lesbian and gay movement in the preceding two decades which, among other achievements, mobilised around the political objective of decriminalisation. This is the second significant historical development separating Broderick from Tóibín – or, more precisely, Broderick's fictional homosexuals from Tóibín's fictional gay men. That is the emergence of the modern lesbian and gay political movement in the 1970s – the historical moment that we now designate by the shorthand 'Stonewall', or, in its more radical incarnation, 'gay liberation' – and the new forms of consciousness, politicised identity and subcultural organisation initiated by that movement. The third historical development is depicted most explicitly in Tóibín's *The Story of the Night* (1996), in which the narrator participates in, and benefits from, the neoliberal reconstruction of the Argentinian state. As we will see, modern gay men in Tóibín's fiction embody, and experience as liberating, the political rationality and 'realist' 'common sense' characteristic of neoliberal subjectivity.

How does Tóibín respond imaginatively and politically to these intersected developments in his fiction? To answer that requires paying attention to Tóibín's style, and specifically the coexistence of different narrative techniques in his fiction. In one mode he uses the conventions of realism to construct gay male characters, and to incorporate those characters into inherited genres and plot types. In the other narrative mode – in which tone is more aesthetically and politically significant than plot – he sublimates homoerotic energies into the text to generate powerful impersonal affects and symbolic resonances. Approaching Tóibín's novels in this way we encounter a paradox. When their political imaginary is most closely in alignment with a progressive sexual politics is also when these novels are most fully in conformity with the hegemonic neoliberal norms. But when the concerns and obsessions of the fiction seems furthest removed from progressive sexual politics is when its political imagination is potentially most radical. In a particular way, when Tóibín writes about the male body the novels tonally generate affects which unsettle the hegemonic 'common sense' which the novels are otherwise committed to endorsing.

In the final two chapters we switch from authors to genres and plots. Surveying a group of novels published between 1993 and 2008 we can identify two key compositional principles: time and space. The first of these principles in turn informs two genres of gay writing: the coming-out romance and the historical romance, and these genres are our object of inquiry in Chapter 4. The novels under discussion there – by 'Tom Lennon', Jarlath Gregory, Denis Kehoe and Jamie O'Neill – give narrative shape to the forms of consciousness underpinning contemporary lesbian and gay politics and give imaginative expression to the dialectic of liberation and reformism inherent to that politics. Their manifest political perspectives are often critical and sometimes socialist in their sympathies. But, beneath these manifest commitments, the aesthetic form and texture of the fiction – plot; narrative and prose style; tone – generates varied affects. The chapter maps the variegated political valences of those styles and affects. As we will see, rather than assuming that 'Irish gay male fiction', to adapt Les Brookes' term, is by definition dissident, we will find that the political imagination of these novels could be radical, disruptive and utopian, or it could be in comfortable alignment with the hegemonic neoliberal conception of the individual and of social relations in 'boom-time' Ireland.[59] That difference in political perspective is most sharply discernible as a matter of literary style.

The contrast between the final two chapters illustrates that there are different ways of telling and interpreting fictional stories of contemporary gay men. One is to create heroic and, for the majority culture, redemptive narratives of an embattled minority staking its claim to recognition and representation; as we will see in Chapter 4, liberal values and neoliberal perspectives are especially buttressed by literary gay men as guarantors of personal authenticity and moral sincerity. The other is to create stories in which gay men's lives become typical or paradigmatic of the late capitalist condition as such. The question of whether, and in what way, stories of gay men can move us towards grasping this neoliberal condition sensuously and dialectically is primarily a matter of aesthetics – of how, not which, stories are told. The final chapter discusses novels by three authors (Keith Ridgway, Micheál Ó Conghaile and Barry McCrea) which facilitate this dialectical understanding, and do so primarily in two ways: through the creative fusion of realist and non-realist modes and generic conventions, and through the construction of plots foregrounding our apprehension of social space. These novels are examples of chronotopic writing in which styles of writing social space generate modes of temporal reasoning – moving us towards comprehending the contingent, dynamic, contradictory and revolutionary historical tempo of capitalist domination. Thus, these novels are also examples of hopeful writing – 'hopeful' in the politically utopian conception articulated by Ernst Bloch – and the primary symbolic location of hope is the male body as a site of desire and need, pleasure and vulnerability.[60]

Across these chapters I map contrasting styles of writing the homoerotic male body condensed around two contrasting affects: 'injury' and 'vulnerability'. In contemporary culture, narratives in which injury, rather than erotic desires and pleasures, is situated at the definitional core of what it is to be a gay man are ubiquitous. Such styles of writing implant pain and suffering as the existential horizon of gay male personhood. This structure of feeling is detectible across fiction and drama – from the 'high' literary style practiced by Garth Greenwell and Édouard Louis to the 'popular' forms of television and film drama – as well as the vernacular sphere of 'personal testimony' and 'memoir' so amplified by social media.[61] In the field of contemporary Irish literature, the dismaying nadir of such narratives was John Boyne's *The Heart's Invisible Furies* (2017), an overwrought farrago of cliché, implausible plotting, anachronism and historical inaccuracy – but characteristic too of the political tenor of contemporary Irish neoliberalism in the care Boyne took to restrict his outpouring of moral outrage to institutions and norms that had already been safely discredited.

The cultural ubiquity of injury, as an identity-defining affect, is more generally symptomatic of the contradictions each of us faces in late capitalism. On one side, we confront a capitalist world system where our lives are determined by deterritorialised and potentially cataclysmic processes that are difficult to apprehend let alone bring under democratic control: financialisation; outsourced production; ecological destruction and climate change. On the other, neoliberal political rationality imposes a relentless expectation that we exercise rigorous control over our fate while constructing well-managed lives as model entrepreneurial subjects. In Wendy Brown's critical analysis of politicised identity, which is outlined in more detail in Chapter 4, she argued that the principal limitation of such politics is that it mobilises people around injury and *ressentiment* – the fusion of powerlessness, abjection and anger which Nietzsche identified as intrinsic to modernity. Inevitably the political demands impelled by this mobilisation are restricted to recognition and redress, so that, paradoxically, achieving those goals means that suffering and injury are solidified, made permanent and congeal into citizenship. Politicised identity is a formation generated in opposition to the oppressive and alienating conditions of capitalism, which at the same time suppresses the possibilities of anticapitalist critique and politics. Those 'differences' which are an effect of the exploitative structural relations inherent within capitalism are neutralised as attributes inhering in individuals who aggregate as a minority in need of protection. Capitalism's endemic alienation is rescripted as a minoritarian and individualised question of inclusion and exclusion. Thus, in Brown's view, progressive movements predicated on identity unwittingly buttress the neoliberal hegemony they set out to challenge

– seeking 'inclusion' is after all to implicitly value and endorse that from which one is 'excluded'.

Nevertheless, as Judith Butler reminds us, this form of politics is strategically indispensable and powerfully operative for the feminist and lesbian/gay social movements, as it is for the political mobilisation of minorities defined by race, disability, ethnicity and sex/gender in the Western democracies and globally. It is politically essential to demand bodily integrity and self-determination, and to use the language of individual autonomy to secure legal protections and entitlements. In the Irish context the successful feminist-led campaign to repeal the constitutional ban on abortion, culminating in the 2018 referendum, is the most notable recent demonstration of the efficacy of mobilising around such claims.[62] Butler does not argue for an end to such politics. But she challenges us to simultaneously imagine a different form of politics; she challenges us to open up 'another kind of normative aspiration within the field of politics ... if I am struggling for autonomy, do I not need to be struggling for something else as well, a conception of myself as invariably in community, impressed upon by others, impinging on them as well in ways that are not fully in my control or clearly predictable'.[63]

Centrally that form of politics would not be premised on the autonomy and identity of the sovereign subject but on the condition of vulnerability intrinsic to the human body. As Butler observes, 'the body implies mortality, vulnerability, agency: the skin and the flesh exposes us to the gaze of others, but also to touch, and to violence, and bodies put us at risk of becoming the agency and instrument of all these as well. Although we struggle for rights over our own bodies, the bodies for which we struggle are not quite ever only our own.'[64] Writing in the wake of the 2001 attacks on New York and Washington, and the subsequent invasions of Afghanistan and Iraq by US-led forces, Butler was aware that this perception of vulnerability can be politicised in very different ways. One is the transformation of grief into rage, the urge to deny one's vulnerability by violently imposing that condition on others. On the other hand, Butler was also hopeful that 'mindfulness of vulnerability' can become the basis for a different type of politics.[65] Confronting our bodily vulnerability is a visceral reminder that 'we are all born in a position of radical dependency'.[66] Moreover it is not that we overcome or move beyond that radical dependency as we grow and develop. In every moment of our lives, we only survive because the resources necessary to sustain human life, and to create the conditions for human flourishing, are made available to us by the ecosystem we inhabit and the labour and love of other humans. It is not only that we are more dependent when newborn or aged, but also that the moments of our birth and our death are the most clarifying reminders of the vulnerability and dependency which we always inhabit.

This encounter with the material reality of our interdependence is a powerful solvent of the ideology of bourgeois individualism, since the disavowal of interdependence is essential to that ideology. As Butler puts it, 'we have become creatures who constantly imagine a self-sufficiency, only to find that image of ourselves undermined repeatedly in the course of life'.[67] To mobilise politically around human interdependence requires conceptualising our consciousness and sense of self as relational rather than separate. But not relational in the conventional aggregative understanding of relationality as two autonomous selves entering into relationship with each other; not 'I' relating to 'you', but the profoundly unsettling realisation that there is in fact no 'I' prior to, or independent of, that relationship with 'you'. This Butler describes as 'another way of imagining community ... which affirms relationality not only as a descriptive or historical fact of our formation, but also as an ongoing normative dimension of our social and political lives, one in which we are compelled to take stock of our interdependence'.[68]

To recognise vulnerability as ontological, as intrinsic to human existence as such, is also, as Butler reminds us, to recognise vulnerability as political. In the capitalist world-system the distribution of corporeal vulnerability – degrees of exposure to violence, exploitation and want – is, to put it mildly, starkly inequitable. And to recognise that we are radically dependent on the world's resources and on the labour of others is to confront how, in our current system, the extraction of those recourses is often recklessly destructive and that labour is invariably alienated and punitively exploited. To figure the human body as vulnerable is therefore to figure that body dialectically; vulnerability is the visceral mark of capitalist exploitation, and also the visceral source of potential revolt against it.

To shift our literary critical optic for framing the symbolic homoerotic male body, from the isomorph 'injury/identity' to the isomorph 'vulnerability/body', generates a shift in political register. It is to gesture beyond the minoritarian demand for recognition and reform and towards a universal mobilisation around the desire for liberation and revolutionary transformation. It is a literary critical correlative of the political practice of disidentification, as Hennessy defines it – the critical work of radically historicising our identities, confronting their imbrication in material conditions and class relations while acknowledging their affective power. Through this dialectical practice we can, Hennessy argues, 'replace the narrow resentment of identity politics with the potentially much more powerful and monstrous collective opposition of all of capitalism's disenfranchised subjects'.[69]

Notes

1. Oscar Wilde, *De Profundis, The Ballad of Reading Gaol and Other Writings* (London: Wordsworth Classics, 1999), p. 65.
2. Oscar Wilde, *The Decay of Lying and Other Essays* (London: Penguin, 2010), p. 238.
3. Wilde, *Decay of Lying*, p. 236.
4. *Ibid.*
5. Wilde, *Decay of Lying*, pp. 243–4.
6. Kathi Weeks, *Constituting Feminist Subjects* (London: Verso, 2018 [1998]), p. 90.
7. Raymond Williams, *Marxism and Literature* (Oxford: Oxford University Press, 1977), p. 97.
8. Joseph North, *Literary Criticism: a concise political history* (Cambridge, MA: Harvard University Press, 2017), p 12.
9. Francis Mulhern, 'Critical revolution', *New Left Review*, 110 (2018), 39–54, p. 43.
10. North, *Literary Criticism*, p. 6.
11. Joseph North, 'Two Paragraphs in Raymond Williams', *New Left Review*, 116/117 (2019), 161–87.
12. The tensions and problems are evaluated by Mulhern, and by Lorna Seaton in 'The ends of criticism', *New Left Review*, 119 (2019), 105–32.
13. My evolving thoughts about the practice and politics of literary criticism have also been inspired by the reflective mediations, and illustrative practice, of Peter Boxall, *The Value of the Novel* (Cambridge: Cambridge University Press, 2015) and Vincent Quinn, *Reading* (Manchester: Manchester University Press, 2020).

14 Rachel Greenwald Smith, *Affect and American Literature in the Age of Neoliberalism* (Cambridge: Cambridge University Press, 2015), p. 2.
15 Greenwald Smith, *Affect and American Literature*, p. 13.
16 Greenwald Smith, *Affect and American Literature*, p. 19.
17 Jed Esty, *Unseasonable Youth: modernism, colonialism and the fiction of development* (Oxford: Oxford University Press, 2012), pp. 104–15.
18 Oscar Wilde, *The Picture of Dorian Gray*, ed. Joseph Bristow (Oxford: Oxford University Press, 2006), pp. 8 and 13.
19 Wilde, *Decay of Lying*, p. 220.
20 Wilde, *Dorian Gray*, pp. 12–13.
21 Wilde, *Dorian Gray*, p. 102; Wilde, *Decay of Lying*, pp. 185–93.
22 Eve Kosofsky Sedgwick, *The Epistemology of the Closet* (London: Penguin, 1990), p. 136.
23 Wilde, along with contemporaries such as Walt Whitman and Edward Carpenter, took inspiration from Hellenism, while merging this with their commitment to radical democratic and socialist politics. As we will see in Chapter 4, Jamie O'Neill is a modern writer fascinated by the radical potential of that imaginative concatenation. Nevertheless, the 'Greek love' ideal was inevitably elitist, taking at least some of its historical inspiration from Athenian 'democracy' and a misogynistic, oligarchic conception of masculine citizenship defined by the exclusion of women and slaves. For a textured investigation of 'Greek love', see David Halperin, *One Hundred Years of Homosexuality* (London: Routledge, 1990), pp. 15–40.
24 Distilling insights from Lukács's *History and Class Consciousness* and Foucault's *History of Sexuality volume one*, Kevin Floyd connects the reification of the labouring body and of the gendered and erotic body at the turn of the twentieth century. These were intertwined elements central to an epochal transition in the capitalist mode of production. In their different spheres, 'Taylorism' and psychoanalysis effected a similar abstraction and objectification of human capacities and affects, and also generated a similar reifying of consciousness into forms of identity: 'the worker', 'the homosexual' and so on. Kevin Floyd, *The Reification of Desire: towards a queer Marxism* (Minneapolis, MN: University of Minnesota Press, 2009), pp. 39–78.
25 Alan Sinfield, *The Wilde Century* (London: Cassell, 1994), pp. 2–3.
26 McKeon's fiction, including *Solace* (2011), which remains the most searching literary response to the 2008 crash, has been unduly neglected in Irish literary studies. Barry's pair of historical novels has not yet received much attention, though when that critical work arrives it will probably conform to the hagiographical tone evident in reviews.

And it is a reasonably safe bet that this critical work will remain inattentive to the political conservatism, and moral vacuity, of Barry's signature redemptive aestheticising of violence. Enright's novel has received sustained critical analysis in Emer Nolan, *Five Irish Women: the second republic, 1960–2016* (Manchester: Manchester University Press, 2019), pp. 181–92.

27 Rosemary Hennessy, *Profit and Pleasure: sexual identities in late capitalism* (London: Routledge, 2000), p. 230. See also José Esteban Muñoz, *Disidentifications: queers of colour and the performance of politics* (Minneapolis, MN: University of Minnesota Press, 1999). One especially interesting aspect of Muñoz's approach is exploring the dynamic relationship between paired (white and non-white) artists, such as Jean-Michel Basquiat and Andy Warhol, or Isaac Julien and Robert Mapplethorpe. This is useful for thinking about the creative affinities, identifications and disidentifications with Irish cultural and literary traditions (ballads; writers – Wilde, but also Joyce and others) which is, as we will see, a characteristic of the more politically radical, as I argue, of our novels.

28 For some further elaboration of these points, see my '"Our nameless desires": the erotics of time and space in contemporary Irish lesbian and gay fiction' in Liam Harte (ed.), *The Oxford Handbook of Modern Irish Fiction* (Oxford: Oxford University Press, 2020).

29 Eve Kosofsky Sedgwick, *Between Men: English literature and male homosocial desire* (New York: Columbia University Press, 1985).

30 Eibhear Walshe, *Oscar's Shadow: Wilde, homosexuality and modern Ireland* (Cork: Cork University Press, 2011).

31 Brian Earls, 'Oscar and the Irish' and 'Oscar Wilde and the Irish', *Dublin Review of Books*, www.drb.ie/essays/oscar-and-the-irish and www.drb.ie/essays/oscar-wilde-and-the-irish. Accessed 5 July 2021.

32 As Earls notes, Ó Conaire's critics have 'discerned stylistic traces' of *The Picture of Dorian Gray* in his novel *Deoraíocht* (1910), translated as *Exile*. Stylistic and intertextual connections with Wilde's work are further amplified in *An Chéad Chloch* (1914), a collection of short stories translated as *The First Stone*. Most notably, Ó Conaire's 'Teatrarc na Gailili' ('Tetrarch of Galilee') draws on the same biblical tale as *Salomé*, while echoing the play's themes – sexual obsession; the homoeroticised male body; political rebellion in a colonial state – and its expressionist style.

33 Earls, 'Oscar and the Irish'.

34 Maureen O'Connor, 'The Picture of Dorian Gray as Irish national tale' in Michael Patrick Gillespie (ed.), *The Picture of Dorian Gray (Norton Critical Edition)* (New York: W.H. Norton, 2006), pp. 475–6.

35 On Wilde's engagement with the political aesthetics of the Irish Gothic literary tradition, see Jim Hansen, *Terror and Irish Modernism: the Gothic tradition from Burke to Beckett* (Albany, NY: SUNY Press, 2009), pp. 59–86. My reading of Irish Gothic is also informed by Terry Eagleton, *Heathcliff and the Great Hunger* (London: Verso, 1995), pp. 145–225 and Luke Gibbons, *Gaelic Gothic: race, colonialism and Irish culture* (Galway: Arlen House, 2004).

36 Ellen Scheible, 'Imperialism, aesthetics and Gothic confrontation in *The Picture of Dorian Gray*', *New Hibernia Review*, 18,1 (2014), 131–50, 137.

37 Esty, *Unseasonable Youth*, p. 106.

38 Giovanni Arrighi, *The Long Twentieth Century: money, power and the origins of our time* (London: Verso, 1994), pp. 247–77.

39 Esty, *Unseasonable Youth*, pp. 109–10.

40 More recently the late Christopher Chitty developed his theory of 'sexual hegemony' as intrinsic to the development of the capitalist world system, from its origins in late-medieval northern Italy. Drawing on Gramsci and on Arrighi's model of the historical cycles of capitalist development – each stabilised by a hegemonic state; successively expanding in global scope – Chitty examines archival evidence of the policing of homosexual behaviour in the successive urban centres of the global hegemon (Florence; Amsterdam; London; New York; he also includes nineteenth-century Paris). His analysis situates the social regulation of same-sex behaviour as intrinsic to the emergence of capitalist class relations – an indispensable element in the recruitment of a property-less peasantry into a modern proletariat, the contested consolidation of property rights and the assertion of bourgeois hegemony. Christopher Chitty, *Sexual Hegemony: statecraft, sodomy and capital in the rise of the world system*, ed. Max Fox (Durham, NC: Duke University Press, 2020). My thanks to Sinéad Kennedy for alerting me to this work.

41 John D'Emilio, 'Capitalism and gay identity' in H. Abelove, M. Barale and D. Halperin (eds), *The Lesbian and Gay Studies Reader* (London: Routledge, 1993), p. 470.

42 This is one of the central insights of Marxist-feminism. Two of its most sustained formulations are Lise Vogel, *Marxism and the Oppression of Women: toward a unitary theory* (Chicago, IL: Haymarket Books, 2014 [1983]) and Silvia Federici, *Caliban and the Witch: women, the body and primitive accumulation* (London: Autonomedia, 2004).

43 D'Emilio, 'Capitalism and gay identity', p. 473.

44 Lucas Ramon Mendos, *State-Sponsored Homophobia 2019* (Geneva: ILGA [International Lesbian, Gay, Bisexual, Trans and Intersex Association], 2019).

45 David Alderson, *Sex, Needs and Queer Culture: from liberation to the post-gay* (London: Zed Books, 2016), pp. 127–8. See also Declan Kavanagh, *Effeminate Years: literature, politics and aesthetics in mid-eighteenth-century Britain* (Lewisburg, PA: Bucknell University Press, 2017).
46 Rita Felski, *The Gender of Modernity* (Cambridge, MA: Harvard University Press, 1995). Alan Sinfield, *The Wilde Century* (London: Cassell, 1994), pp. 52–83.
47 Alderson, *Sex, Needs and Queer Culture*, p. 128. I discussed the contradictory operation of these distinctions in millennial Irish culture, specifically around the gendered cultural valuations of 'sport' and 'fashion', in 'Clubs, closets and catwalks: GAA stars and the politics of contemporary Irish masculinity' in C. Holohan and T. Tracy (eds), *Masculinity and Irish Popular Culture: tiger tales* (Basingstoke: Palgrave Macmillan, 2014), pp. 13–26.
48 For some inspiring reflections on how we might radically reconceptualise pleasure, need and consumption, see Kate Soper, 'Alternative hedonism, cultural theory and the role of aesthetic revisioning', *Cultural Studies*, 22,5 (2008), 567–87.
49 Karl Marx and Friedrich Engels, *The Communist Manifesto* (1848) in Karl Marx, *Selected Writings*, ed. Lawrence H. Simon (Indianapolis, IN: Hackett Publishing, 1994), p. 161.
50 Alderson, *Sex, Needs and Queer Culture*, p. 104.
51 Alderson, *Sex, Needs and Queer Culture*, pp. 90–2.
52 Finn Bowring, 'Repressive desublimation and consumer culture: re-evaluating Herbert Marcuse', *new formations*, 75 (2012), 8–24, 12.
53 Bowring, 'Repressive desublimation', 16.
54 Herbert Marcuse, *One-Dimensional Man* (London: Sphere Books, 1968), p. 72.
55 Theodor W. Adorno, *The Culture Industry*, ed. J.M. Bernstein (London: Routledge, 2001), p. 190.
56 On the capture of the concept of creativity for the purposes of legitimising contemporary modes of domination and unfreedom, see Oli Mould, *Against Creativity* (London: Verso, 2018). On the uses of creativity for reconfiguring work practices and intensifying precarity, see especially pp. 17–54.
57 Alderson, *Sex, Needs and Queer Culture*, p. 147.
58 *Ibid.*
59 Les Brookes, *Gay Male Fiction since Stonewall: ideology, conflict, and aesthetics* (London: Routledge, 2009). See Chapter 4.
60 Ernst Bloch, *The Principle of Hope*, 3 volumes, trans. Neville Plaice, Stephen Plaice and Paul Knight (Cambridge, MA: MIT Press, 1986; original German-language publication, 1959). See Chapter 5.

61 Garth Greenwell, *What Belongs to You* (London: Picador, 2016) and *Cleanness* (London: Picador, 2020). Edouard Louis, *The End of Eddy*, trans. Michael Lucey (London: Vintage, 2018) and *History of Violence*, trans. Lorin Stein (London: Vintage, 2019). In Louis's writing there is a fascinating oscillation between the literary modes of 'injury' and 'vulnerability'. The abjection and pain suffered by the gay child and young man is contained within a biographical narrative, but also framed as indicative of, as an occasion for grasping, the exploitative violence endemic to late capitalism – and especially the violence endured by the labouring and migrant body. The latter political impulse is especially strong in *Who Killed My Father*, trans. Lorin Stein (London: Vintage, 2019). The original French-language publication dates are: 2014, 2016 and 2018.
62 For an insightful Marxist-feminist analysis of that campaign see Sinéad Kennedy, 'Ireland's fight for choice', *Jacobin* (25 March 2018), www.jacobinmag.com/2018/03/irelands-fight-for-choice. Accessed 29 July 2021. See also Sinéad Kennedy, '"#Repealthe8th": Ireland, abortion access and the movement to remove the Eighth Amendment', *Anthropologia*, 5,2 (2018), 13–31.
63 Judith Butler, *Precarious Life: the powers of mourning and politics* (London: Verso, 2004), pp. 26–7.
64 Butler, *Precarious Life*, p. 26.
65 Butler, *Precarious Life*, p. 22.
66 Judith Butler, *The Force of Non-Violence* (London: Verso, 2020), p. 41.
67 Butler, *Force of Non-Violence*, p. 42.
68 Butler, *Precarious Life*, p. 27.
69 Hennessy, *Profit and Pleasure*, p. 229.

1

Brendan Behan: Eros and liberation

Brendan Behan's only novel, *Borstal Boy* (1958), elicits a certain style of reading, which has an aesthetic and a political element. The first-person narrator and central protagonist is a teenage boy named Brendan Behan, and the experiences he narrates accord closely with those of Brendan Behan, the author. In December 1939 Behan, then aged 16, was arrested in Liverpool, having just arrived there from Dublin. He was found guilty of possessing explosives and sentenced to three years detention in borstal. In all he spent just under two years in custody before being deported from Britain in October 1941. In the months before his arrest the IRA, of which young Behan was a member, carried out a series of bomb attacks in English cities, several of which resulted in fatalities and high numbers of causalities. According to Michael O' Sullivan, his biographer, it is most likely that Behan was impulsively acting on his own initiative rather than participating in a planned IRA attack; Behan's 77-year-old grandmother, along with her two daughters, had been imprisoned earlier in 1939 after being arrested in Birmingham in similar circumstances, and likewise acting independently of the IRA.[1]

The novel begins with the narrator's arrest in Liverpool and ends with his journey to Dublin after being deported. Unsurprisingly then, readers have tended to respond to *Borstal Boy* as an autobiography rather than as a work of fiction. This began with the earliest reviews – Derek Hand cites some examples in his analysis of this style of reading the novel – and it continues decades later.[2] Thus, for instance, O'Sullivan, in his carefully researched, sympathetic and nuanced biography, draws extensively on *Borstal Boy* when writing about Behan's life during 1940 and 1941. In this way the novel functions as another archival document, equivalent in kind to the personal and official correspondence, newspaper reports, court records and official documents Sullivan also cites.[3] The difficulty with framing the text through the prism of the life is that it underestimates Behan's creative work, over a decade and a half, on the given material of the life, and the degree to which the meaning of the text is determined by this act of sculpting the life story.[4] As Bernice Shanks argues, the novel is deliberately crafted as a work of 'autofiction'.[5] Behan created a contrapuntal play of first-person narration, dialogue and oscillation between perspectives (Brendan's interior thoughts and the performed self he presents to the world), registers (the proliferation of Irish and English slang; the phonetic reproduction of accents) and tenses. This produces a persona, 'Brendan', that is intimately an aspect of, yet distinguishable from, 'Brendan Behan' the author – a narrative consciousness simultaneously immersed in the immediacy of his youthful experiences and retrospectively evaluating them. Moreover, the text is characterised by an energetic linguistic playfulness and a dense intertextual palimpsest; the range of intertextual quotations and allusions is wide ranging – Wolfe Tone to Virginia Woolf – as is the tone in which they are framed; sincere or parodic, and sometimes both at once. In other words, this text energetically draws attention to its textuality. The reader of *Borstal Boy* actually encounters this idea before they begin on the novel proper, reading the epigraphic quotation from Woolf's *Orlando* (1928) – a novel offering a model of how playfully subverting the conventions of biographical realism for serious ends can be aesthetically and politically compelling.

If this style of reading underplays Behan's aesthetic creativity, it also revises his political standpoint. Framing *Borstal Boy* as a biographical narrative rigidly situates individual consciousness as central to our interpretation, which in turn determines the meaning of the novel as the liberation of the individual from the inhibiting constraints of the collective. In this view, prison provides Brendan with the opportunity to achieve a more authentic self, away from the burdensome, ensnaring and inauthentic demands of familial, political and national commitments. Given that young Brendan's political commitment to socialist republicanism is central to the plot, this framing of the novel as a developmental narrative, moving from immaturity to maturity, is also cast as a salvation narrative in which our hero transcends the fallen state of political activism and moves into the light of redemption that is liberal humanism. A key element of this interpretive mode is to replace politics with identity; Brendan starts out conceptualising himself through a crude binary of national identities – 'Irish' versus 'English' – but through his experiences learns to self-identify in less rigidly narrow and more humane terms.

Fintan O'Toole's reading of the novel illustrates the conservative political destination to which this style of reading can lead. O'Toole boldly asserts that 'Behan was not a revolutionary. He was something much more interesting and relevant: a terrorist and a child soldier.'[6] For this reason, the novel tells 'a story of our times'. The import of that story is that Behan's 'fanaticism' – which O'Toole characterises as a mindlessly confused 'Catholic communism' while also conflating it with fascism, declaring that 'Behan was in effect a Nazi collaborator'– was defeated by 'kindness' rather than by coercion. In this reading of the novel, Brendan's expectation of English cruelty – and his desire for 'the glory of martyrdom' – is confounded by individual acts of generosity and, more crucially, by the focus on rehabilitation rather than punishment in the British borstal system. The message for our times is that Western liberal democracies will defeat 'fanatics' and terrorists by showing their best face to that threat. In O'Toole's view, Behan's novel reminds us that the worst thing you can do to a terrorist is 'not to execute him or to waterboard him or to render him to Guantánamo. It is not to tear up democratic ideals. It is to preserve your own better values.'[7] Leaving aside the queasiness induced by this neoliberal utilitarianism – the objection to state-sanctioned execution and torture is inefficiency not ethics – we might wonder in amazement at the depth of O'Toole's faith in the liberal fantasy that systematic violence and torture are inherently alien to capitalism and liberal democracy, that we could strive to remove these from the neoliberal state's administrative repertoire and our 'democratic ideals' and 'better values' would remain intact.

But, as David Lloyd points out, the increased visibility of state-sanctioned torture, and discussion about its legitimacy, in Western democracies after 2001, developments signalled in O'Toole's allusions to waterboarding and Guantánamo, emphatically undermined the notion that such practices are exceptional or anomalous, and has done so in two ways. The new visibility of torture has drawn our attention to the indispensable centrality of such violence in the historical development of modern capitalism; for the colonised and enslaved these forms of violence were always the rule rather than the exception. At the same time, the visibility and normalisation of state-sanctioned torture registers a distinctive shift in contemporary politics, where that condition of being subjected to biometrical surveillance and coercion is now generalised to all citizens, transforming the relationship between the neoliberal state and its citizens as well as the conception of human subjectivity as such. As Lloyd describes it, 'the enclave of private space has succumbed to the penetration of new modes of biopower that unfold the subject in its desires and fantasies out into what was once a distinct public realm. Increasingly the subject becomes familiar with inhabiting a realm of routinized torture that makes of the citizen not the autonomous subject but one whose identifications are split between being the one who might torture and the one who might be subjected to torture.'[8]

For Lloyd, British policy in Northern Ireland during the 1970s and 1980s – internment and the policy of criminalising sections of the population; the coercive regime in the H-blocks and in Armagh Women's Prison – was a key colonial laboratory for this now generalised mode of neoliberal biopower. At the same time the strategies adopted by republican prisoners protesting the policy of criminalisation from the mid-1970s to the hunger strikes in 1981, especially those 'on the blanket' during the 'dirty protest', illuminate a potential mode of resistance. Centrally, Lloyd argues, these resistance strategies did not reaffirm the autotomy of the sovereign subject but transformed the vulnerability of the body exposed to violence into a medium of community – most literally the body, and its orifices, used to transmit communications – and a source of radical political formation. 'For the prisoners in Northern Ireland', he observes, 'the extreme experience of interrogation and torture, and their corollary, the abusive deprivation of the prison block, could be converted through their deliberate assumption of "the body in pain" into a means, temporary and resistant, of life in common, a way of living that even from the most extreme conditions could shape an alternative collective ethic.'[9]

Restoring the body to our interpretation of Behan's novel reclaims the novel's political radicalism from the conservativism of readings such as O'Toole's. As Maria DiBattista observes, through the procedures of being processed as a prisoner, Brendan confronts 'his own creatureliness'. This bodily abjection, reinforced by 'the all-pervading, sickening smell of jailhouse shit and soap against which there is no effective barrier or available palliative', teaches Brendan 'what the body is, what it can suffer and what it alone knows'.[10] However, along with being prone to suffering the imprisoned male body in Behan's novel is also a location of homoerotic pleasure. For O'Toole, this aspect of the novel can also be converted into the hermeneutic of subjective and national identities – Brendan 'falls in love with an English fellow inmate' – thus bolstering his recruitment of the novel's politics for a defence of liberal values; it is yet another element in the confounding of Brendan's expectations of English cruelty. As O'Toole rightly observes, Brendan's relationship with Charlie, an imprisoned young sailor, is 'at the heart of the story'. But, as we will see, Behan's style of writing homoeroticism dwells on affects and bodies, so that this relationship cannot be so easily confined to an individualised romance narrative. Instead it becomes Brendan's impetus towards a sense of solidarity and collectivity that enriches his anticolonial and anticapitalist perspective; encountering the homoerotic pleasure of the male body prompts him towards an expansive and radical vision of liberation and what, in a different context, Lukács terms a 'revolutionary humanism'.[11]

To access these liberationist strands in the novel's political imagination requires restoring the novel's aesthetics to our interpretation. Centrally, the novel's plot presents a paradox. By adopting the conventions of the *bildungsroman*, the novel conforms to the temporal logic of maturity, thereby symbolically affirming the progressive historicism of modernity; the maturity of the individual reconciling to the reality principle, overcoming the naivety of political idealism, as metaphor for the society adjusting to the reality principle of capitalism. At the same time, the novel's style undermines its own narrative logic. Stylistically this is most apparent in the final section, where the plot's tightly ordered pattern descends into a looser episodic sequence. Colbert Kearney offers a convincing historical and biographical explanation for Behan's loss of control when reworking this section; the IRA's bombing campaign in 1956 gave Behan a sense that this was an inauspicious time for such a work and made him reluctant to part with the manuscript; the London success of *The Quare Fellow* and *The Hostage* brought the distractions of celebrity.[12] Nevertheless we can, I think, also read this resistance to narrative as such as a compositional correlative of the novel's queer temporality – Behan's melancholic faithfulness to his younger self and his resistance to the developmental imperative of the reality principle. Or, to express this in generic terms, the novel dislodges the *bildungsroman* with an alternative type of formation plot, adapted from two traditions of prison writing – Irish republican and homoerotic.

In that final section of the novel, which describes his time in the more progressive and benign regime at Hollesley Bay, Brendan recounts an incident that takes place in the institution's library. He finds a fellow borstal inmate reading Frank Harris's *Life of Oscar Wilde*. This prompts Brendan, as narrator, to admit to the reader that in his childhood he had conflated the story of Wilde's imprisonment with the heroic tales of Irish rebels at the bar of British justice in which, as the child of a republican family, he was steeped. Even when he began to suspect that it had something to do with sex, and asked his mother why Wilde was jailed, he remembers her replying vaguely 'his downfall – they brought him down the same as they did Parnell'.[13] His mother's reply thus concedes that Wilde's was a sexual scandal, like Parnell's, while still insisting on the interpretive framework of British injustice towards an Irish patriot. In the prison library, in the narrative present, Brendan is now told exactly why Wilde was imprisoned, albeit elliptically in the text itself. He responds with studied insouciance – 'every tinker has his own way of dancing' – keen to stymie his worldly fellow inmate's satisfaction at shocking 'Paddy'.

Brendan also tells us that the first fact he knew about Wilde was that his mother was 'Speranza', whose poetry he learned in school. This leads into a lengthy digression, in which Brendan recounts what he knows of Frank Harris, whose books his father read and who was another 'Irish rebel' sympathetic to the Fenians, along with his and his father's critical anti-sectarian views on the Catholic Church's anathematizing of Fenianism. In characteristic style, this narrative digression is framed as a series of rhetorical questions ('Didn't old Bishop Moriarty condemn the Fenians[?]') and culminates in an extract from 'Down by the Glen', which plaintively salutes the memory of 'the Bold Fenian Men' and was, as Brendan reminds us, written by Behan's uncle.[14] Through his mother, and her association with the Young Irelanders, as well as the younger Brendan's naive assumption that Oscar must also have been a rebel, Wilde is associated in the novel with that tradition of prison writing – from Wolfe Tone's *The Autobiography* (1826) to Thomas Clarke's *Glimpses of an Irish Felon's Prison Life* (1913) – that was a key vehicle for the articulation of Irish anticolonial and republican ideas from the 1790s onwards. *Borstal Boy* contains a dense web of intertextual references to these Irish republican prison writings, and to other significant modes of nationalist discourse such as ballads, poetry, speeches from the dock and Irish mythology.

As John Brannigan has delineated, Behan's novel takes its form from this current in Irish writing – it is, on the surface, another account of an imprisoned Irish republican – while also offering an ironic and subversively parodic commentary on that tradition.[15] Thus, when Brendan gives his own speech from the dock his earnest declaration of commitment to 'the Irish Worker's and Small Farmer's Republic' is undercut by a policeman comically mistaking the Hibernicism 'small farmer' as a commentary on the stature rather than the status of these farmers.[16] Moreover, Brendan's commitment to the content of his statement sits alongside his sharp awareness that this is a performance rather than a spontaneous expression of ideals. His performance has been honed through immersion in notable examples of the genre. In a dense sequence of references and quotations, Brendan parades his knowledge of this tradition – from Robert Emmet to the Manchester Martyrs (he explicitly links his use of 'God save Ireland' at the end of his speech to a ballad about them which he quotes) to Roger Casement (disparagingly referred to by a prison officer a few paragraphs later).[17] In marked contrast with O'Toole's crude characterisation of a 'child soldier', Brendan is acutely conscious of his diverse audiences. The most significant audience is not in the courtroom but at home in Ireland, where the left and right wings of the republican movement will respond very differently to the speech; contemplating the anger of the right wing, which they will be required to suppress and publicly support him, accentuates Brendan's pleasure in his performance. In addition, the adolescent Brendan excitedly reflects on how the reports of his speech will, he believes, burnish his heroic, sexy manly image.

At the same time, the narrative captures an undertone of sincerity in Behan's declaration. As Colbert Kearney observes, 'he believes in his vision of himself'.[18] Moreover, creatively sustaining that vision, through singing 'Dark Rosaleen' and 'Kevin Barry', extracts of which are incorporated into the text, to Charlie in a neighbouring cell, is a source of comfort to Brendan amid the initial terror, humiliations and isolation of prison life.[19] The dialogism of Behan's text, and the interwoven perspectives of Brendan the protagonist, Brendan the narrator and Brendan Behan the author retrospectively moulding his youthful experiences into a narrative, has multiple political effects – in which, for instance, Brendan's speech from the dock is simultaneously a cynical performance, and source of comedy, and the distillation of a revolutionary vision. The tissue of intertextual allusions to the various modes and styles of Irish republican discourse emphasises how young Brendan is sustained by, but also entangled in and struggling to make his own, this cultural and political inheritance. This textual vibrancy – the pattern of quotations and illusions and the proliferation of perspectives and tones – encodes a dynamic narrative of self-formation; rather than an inert national identity being overcome the novel's style conveys a creative, dialectical process of identification and disidentification with an open, plastic political tradition.

We noted Brendan's apparent indifference to the revelation of Wilde's 'crime', and this is reinforced by the way in which he draws a distinction between himself – and implicitly his relationship with Charlie – and the 'Wildean' character who gleefully retails this information. This figure is identified as 'the novelist's nephew' and Brendan is 'not surprised' to see him reading Harris's biography of Wilde in the library because of his mannered and dandified appearance: 'a cigarette holder and a civilian tie of rose colour'; 'a languid elegant accent'. As Brendan magnanimously observes, 'he was altogether as decadent as our frugal means allowed. He was doing his best anyway, and not badly under the circumstances'.[20]

This friendly but anxious demarcation between the dandified Wildean queer and Brendan's self-identity is more directly addressed in an unpublished manuscript Behan prepared in the early stage of developing *Borstal Boy*. There he writes:

> I loved Borstal boys and they loved me. But the absence of girls made it that much imperfect. Homosexuality (of our sort) is not a substitute for normal sex. It's a different thing, rather similar to that of which T.E. Lawrence writes in *The Seven Pillars*. The youth of healthy muscle and slim wrought form is not the same as the powdered pansy

> (who I hasten to add, as good as anybody else, has every right to be that and a bloody good artist or anything he wants to be). Our lads saw themselves as beautiful and had to do something about it ... As I say however, without women it could not be a pattern of life, only a prolonging of adolescence – it was as beautiful as that.[21]

With its unsteady combination of bold assertion, parenthetical equivocation and unstable taxonomic categorisation – 'our sort' of 'homosexuality' as distinct from the sort embodied by the 'pansy' – Behan's prose indexes that 'radical and irreducible incoherence' which, as Eve Sedgwick argued, has structured modern concepts of sexual identity since the end of the nineteenth century.[22] According to Sedgwick's influential and still compelling model, the epochal *fin-de-siècle* shift from a hermeneutic of legitimate and illegitimate *acts* to a hermeneutic of normal and deviant *identities* was distinguished by two internally contradictory axes of thought. One is the difference between a minoritising view that 'there is a distinct population of people who "really are" gay' and a universalising view that 'sexual desire is an unpredictably powerful solvent of stable identities ... that apparently heterosexual persons and object choices are strongly marked by same-sex influences and desires'.[23] The other is the difference between viewing same-sex object choice as a matter of gender transitivity or gender separatism. Does same-sex object choice situate one in a liminal position between genders, and necessitate some form of cross-gender identification, or does same-sex object choice situate one even more centrally at the definitional core of one's own gender? The implications of this incoherence for the social production of masculinity were intensely volatile. A distinct and historically devalued category of (queer/homosexual/gay) masculinity was identified against which normative heterosexual masculinity is defined – a category which must be repudiated, even to the point of violence. At the same time, there is the ever-present anxiety that this devalued masculinity is not in fact a distinctive type at all but a tendency or potentiality internal to normative masculinity and against which one must be internally vigilant.

Excising this passage when creating the finished version of *Borstal Boy* may reflect Behan's caution about addressing this topic so directly, and since the novel was banned by the Irish censorship board such caution was not unfounded. At the same time, we could also read its removal as indicating Behan's impatience with these schematic rigidities, and indicating too the incompatibility between this style of reasoning and the style of writing homoerotic pleasure that characterises the novel – in which 'prolonging adolescence' is narratively and symbolically key. Between writing 'The Courteous Borstal' and finalising the novel Behan published a short story, 'After the Wake', in *Points* in January 1951. In contrast with the former's earnest tone the story comically burlesques the cultural categories of sexual definition. In a queer inversion of the 'love triangle' a friendship develops between the male narrator and a newly married couple, his neighbours in their Dublin tenement building. Contrary to their neighbours' suspicions, and to the apparent amusement of the wife, the narrator is not infatuated with the wife but with the husband. But, doubtlessly dashing the expectations of his contemporary readership, Behan did not write a tragic tale of a lonely homosexual abjectly pining for an unattainable 'real' man. Instead the narrator describes his 'campaign' of seduction, in which he strategically deploys all the available stereotypes and contradictory concepts to persuade and coax his friend. Thus, he begins by encouraging his friend to 'think it manly, ordinary to manly men, the British Navy, "Porthole Duff", "Navy Cake", stories of the Hitler Youth in captivity … to remove the taint of "cissiness", effeminacy, how the German Army had encouraged it in Cadet Schools'. The loose prose indexes that ironic distance the narrator perceives between these ideas and his own self-conception. He also opens up a second 'front', as he puts it, in the campaign by 'appealing to that hope of culture – Socrates, Shakespeare, Marlowe'.[24] In a grotesque denouement, the story ends just as the narrator is about to secure victory in his campaign. Unexpectedly the wife dies, and on the night of her wake he is about to go to bed with his friend while her corpse is in the other room; the narrator imagines her face 'looking up from the open coffin'. Behan's use of ambiguity and tonal ambivalence is daring. The first-person narration situates the 'predatory' homosexual as the point of sympathetic identification; we share his perspective on his strenuous and heroic campaign. But then the unsettling ending, fusing sex and mortality, seems to reveal his true nature as the vampiric grotesque of the homophobic imagination. But in addition to sympathy and revulsion Behan may be deliberately cultivating another emotion – fear. Rather than striving for sympathetic recognition of his humanity, Behan's homosexual embraces his monstrosity – gleefully and provocatively becoming one with the figure of threatening Dionysian destruction projected onto him.

By contrast homoeroticism in *Borstal Boy* is more allusive and elliptical, and idealised as erotic friendship. Brendan's relationship with Charlie has its beginnings in the physical intimacy of the washroom when he is first on remand. Brendan stands behind the young sailor 'innocently admiring the back of his neck' before describing his 'brown hair and long dark eyelashes' for us. At Charlie's request, Brendan helps him back into his uniform and 'wiped, carefully, the back of his ears' – the parenthetical emphasis on 'carefully' reiterating the tenderness of the gesture. When Charlie gives Brendan a gift of tobacco, matches and a newspaper he points out that Brendan's hands are wet and insists on, rather elaborately, placing the tobacco in his pockets and the newspaper inside his shirt, 'next my skin, putting his hand around me'.[25] This physical intimacy continues when they are back in their cells and communicate by placing their 'lips to the spyhole'. At Charlie's instigation – he explains to Brendan that he attended a Catholic school in London and learnt Irish songs from his schoolfellows – they sing to each other. Along with 'Dark Rosaleen' and 'Kevin Barry', Brendan sings an Irish-language song he does not name but describes, to the reader, as 'Ireland crying for the Bonnie Prince, not that him or his old fellow or anyone belonging to him ever did anything for us, but it was a good song'. Some of the lyrics are then reproduced on the page:

A bhuachail aoibhinn aluinn-ó,
Ba leathan do chroí is ba dheas do phóg...
    ...beautiful lightsome, awesome boy,
Wide was your heart, and mild was your eye,
My sorrow without you, for ever I'll cry,
...Is go dteíghidh tú, a mhuírnín, slán,
Walk my love, walk surely
White as new lime, your thighs and hips,
Your clustering hair, and your sweet-bitten lips.
My last blaze of strength would die well in,
                their kiss...
Is go dteíghidh tú, a mhuírnín, slán,
Walk my love, walk surely...[26]

Characteristic of the controlled and ordered pattern of Behan's prose – beneath the ostensibly free-flowing sequential biographical narrative – these lyrics echo the sensuous clustering of bodily description in the washroom episode while also cohering around an admiring gaze – and, of course, typical of Behan's sly humour the male object of admiration and desire in both instances is named 'Charlie'. As Ríona Ní Fhrighil notes, Brendan's singing echoes a similar episode in 'After the Wake', where the narrator sings an Irish-language song to the couple, exploiting 'the ambiguities of the oral song tradition in Irish where men sang women's songs and vice versa, the narrative of songs being free enough to allow for reinterpretation from various perspectives'.[27] It is also notable that Behan's textual medium for surreptitiously expressing homoerotic desire is political allegory – a medium for surreptitiously expressing dissident anticolonial political desires. Around the body of Charlie, as of his historical namesake, desire that is erotic is interwoven with desire that is political; the longing that is evoked, or called forth, by the male body merges with the longing that is evoked, or called forth, by utopian visions of a transformed future. Contrary to those readings of *Borstal Boy* which figure the sexual and political as opposed 'identities' – where Brendan's encounter with homoeroticism facilities overcoming his politics to reconcile with the reality principle of modernity – Behan's resignification of this fragmentary residue of a 'lost' cause suggests another possibility: that all politics is inherently sexual and that desire, like hope, is the ambient state of all transformative political mobilisations.

Though Brendan's younger self mistook the reasons for Wilde's imprisonment, Wilde's post- prison writing, *The Ballad of Reading Gaol* (1898) and *De Profundis* (his letter-memoir-essay, originally written in 1897 but not published in complete form until 1962) is where his work comes into closest alignment with the Irish republican prison-writing tradition. Centrally Wilde's prison writing shares with that tradition a conception of the prison experience as politicising and transformative; narrating the prison experience is to narrate the transformation of human consciousness and the emergence of, or potentiality for, a less alienated, less individualistic and more relational subjectivity. In a characteristic trope of republican prison writing, Wilde aligns prison and pedagogy; thus 'the two great turning points in my life were when my father sent me to Oxford and when society sent me to prison'.[28] As in Behan's deployment of Jacobite poetry, as coded expression of his erotic desire for Charlie which simultaneously translates Charlie into a symbol around which the political desire for transformation also adheres, Wilde too writes about the desirable male body to figure the radical transformation of consciousness.

Two men, both of whom had a difficult relationship with their father, are defining presences in *De Profundis*: Alfred Douglas and Jesus Christ. The letter is addressed to Douglas, and the first part is an anguished and desolating anatomy of their relationship. Wilde recounts, in painful detail, numerous instances of Douglas's selfishness, carelessness and cruelty towards him – culminating in the fatally reckless decision to sue for libel to placate Douglas's pathological hatred of his father. But Wilde does not just accuse and reprimand Douglas for his conduct; he also seeks to understand it. Bosie, he realises, loved, or tried to love, him but his upbringing had left him incapable: 'you loved me far better than you loved anybody else. But you, like myself, have had a terrible tragedy in your life, though one of an entirely opposite character to mine ... in you Hate was always stronger than Love. Your hatred of your father was of such stature that it entirely outstripped, o'erthrew and overshadowed your love of me.'[29] Since, to borrow one of Wilde's aphorisms, 'All art is at once surface and symbol', we need not confine ourselves to interpreting this purely biographically – as personal and familial dysfunction – but might also read Douglas as, another favourite Wildean term, a 'type': that is as a figure embodying the political-affective category of injury.

By contrast, Wilde's characterisation of Christ echoes 'The Soul of Man under Socialism'; as Wilde claims, 'above all, Christ is the most supreme of Individualists'.[30] Why, for Wilde, does Jesus figure so powerfully in his conception of a revolutionised consciousness – that relational mode of being in which freedom for one is only achieved as freedom from necessity for all? For one thing, Jesus did not exist; even from the perspective of an orthodox believer his existence in historical time is enfolded within the temporality of what Walter Benjamin terms 'messianic time'.[31] Wilde captures this in a quip; while there were some Christians before Christ 'the unfortunate thing is that there have been none since'.[32] Like the artist then, Christ allows us to imagine that mode of being which is not yet realisable or possible; 'his whole conception of Humanity sprang right out of the imagination and can only be realised by it'.[33] Moreover Christ was a 'rebel' who rejected the governing orthodoxies, the common sense, which upheld the structures of power and property in his society; he scorned 'respectability', 'worldly success' 'wealth' and 'the cold philanthropies, the ostentatious public charities, the tedious formalisms so dear to the middle-class mind'.[34] Finally, Christ embodies that revolutionary consciousness because he exposed his human body to suffering, making himself vulnerable in his 'terrible death by which he gave the world its most eternal symbol' and 'took the entire world of the inarticulate, the voiceless world of pain ... and made of himself its eternal mouthpiece'. For Wilde then, the transformative potential of prison is that the suffering endured by the prisoner might bring them imaginatively closer to grasping that form of consciousness figured in Christ; a form of consciousness in which pain is not experienced as the inwardness of injury, precipitating the destructive narcissism embodied by Bosie, but as the outward orientation of vulnerability, precipitating solidarity and collectivity.

Narrating prison as radically transformative and figuring such transformation around the male body, *De Profundis* stands at the nexus of those two distinctive prison-writing traditions – Irish republican and homoerotic – in which we can situate *Borstal Boy*. And, like the Irish republican tradition, the homoerotic tradition has had remarkable longevity in both 'high' and 'low' cultural registers.[35] Of the former, Manuel Puig's *The Kiss of the Spider-Woman* (1976) is a notable late twentieth-century instance which attained greater prominence in the Anglophone world as a film adaptation in 1985. Like Brendan, one of its protagonists, the Marxist revolutionary Valentín, is imprisoned because of his politics. Similarly, the novel is susceptible to a narrowly biographical reading, because Molina shares Puig's cross-gendered fascination with the aesthetics and stylised femininity of 1930s and 1940s cinema. And, as David Alderson outlines, Puig's novel has been subject to a depoliticising style of reading – similar to the tendency we noted in Behan criticism – in which the inhuman rigidity of revolutionary political commitment is subordinated to the humane reformation of the self, and by extension of the culture, promised by postmodern queer desire and gender subversion. By contrast, Alderson develops a dialectical reading more sympathetically alert to the revolutionary potential in the novel's political imagination.³⁶

In 'low', less culturally prestigious, culture, the erotics of incarceration still flourishes as a staple *mise en scène* of gay porn. Not unlike Behan's 'After the Wake', the tonal and political ambivalence of such scenes encodes and parodies the 'radical incoherence' still characterising our culture's sexual and gender categories. In the 'policeman/prison officer' figure an ideal of masculine identity – and by extension normative subjectivity – in its most unashamedly authoritarian and violent form is, apparently, abjectly desired and fetishized as the acme of authentic masculinity and personhood. But in fulfilling the presumed gay viewer's fantasy of being fucked by – or indeed fucking – that brutal figure, the inevitable narrative denouement affirms homosexuality as that 'universal' potential internal to normative masculinity; even the 'straightest' of men is sexually available. Interestingly then, perhaps the viewer's pleasure is not, or not only, derived from the fetish of 'real' masculinity, but also, in the style of Behan's narrator in 'After the Wake', from the deliberate provocation of the fearful anxiety instilled in men about that potential. Moreover, the performance of desirably authentic masculinity by the 'policeman/prison officer' figure is just that: a highly stylised performance displaying many aesthetic attributes of drag. And, as Judith Butler famously argued, there is no drag performance, or gender parody, that uniformly subverts or reconsolidates gender norms: subversion and reconsolidation are present simultaneously in each performance.³⁷

Jean Genet's *Miracle of the Rose* (first published in French in 1946; in English translation in 1965) is an example from the homoerotic prison-writing tradition chronologically and aesthetically closer to Behan's work, while incorporating formal elements from pornography. Like *Borstal Boy*, *Miracle* is a fictionalised autobiography, structured as Genet's memoir of his imprisonment as an adult in Fontevrault prison and, woven through this, memories of his youth in the Mettray Reformatory.³⁸ Despite these generic similarities Behan and Genet write in a very different style and register. Where *Borstal Boy* is a comic, realist, linear narrative, *Miracle* is a highly stylised, lyrical narrative, characterised by a shifting, unstable temporal fluidity. Moreover, where *Borstal Boy* idealises erotic friendship between similarly aged adolescent boys, and stigmatises as perverse any suggestion of sexual attraction between adults and boys, *Miracle* eroticises power. In Genet's fictional carceral world, erotic attraction between men is invariably pederastic and propelled by hierarchies of age, status and physical strength. As Alan Sinfield observes, Genet insists 'that our sexual fantasies depend on the power structures in our societies'.[39] Genet politicises the erotic, but does so through an existentialist hermeneutic in which abjection and masochism paradoxically generate a radical freedom, and in which, through the medium of erotic fantasy, the norms and morals of bourgeois society are turned on their head: the criminal is the hero; the sinner is the saint. In almost all respects this transgressive sexual vision is entirely uncongenial to the *Weltanschauung* of contemporary, post-Stonewall, lesbian and gay culture, with its political vocabulary of identities and civil rights and, as Kadji Amin puts it, its 'historically recent ideal of the coupled relationship as an authentic, consensual, contractual encounter of equals'.[40] In a similar way, Genet's modernist aesthetic, with its pervasive recourse to imagery drawn from Catholic religious devotion, is in many ways uncongenial to a secular sensibility.

The homoeroticism of *Borstal Boy* is not characterised by the heightened emotional pitch and sadomasochistic fantasies we find in Genet. Nevertheless there is a common structure of feeling, what Amin, writing about *Miracle*, characterises as 'a distinct pre-Stonewall queer sodality characterised less by a shared sexual identity than by a queer fusion of pleasure and pain, togetherness and exile'.[41] Both works resist enveloping desire between men within a hermeneutic of identity, but we must be wary of reading that resistance as bad faith, as a manifestation of psychic and political 'denial'. As Amin argues, we must strive to avoid reading these earlier styles of writing same-sex passion as 'retrograde resistance to "progressive" politics or compensation for the impossibility of same-sex desire in the novel's present'.[42] In particular we must avoid reading them teleologically, as artefacts from an earlier stage in the evolution of a progressive narrative of sexual liberation that reached its apotheosis with the emergence of the modern lesbian and gay movement. Homoeroticism in Behan and Genet is striated by masculinist and misogynistic currents, but it is precisely that which is most disturbingly irreconcilable to our conception of sexual freedom in this writing that may most productively trouble our complacency about the regulatory frameworks that shape our lives. As Heather Love observes, in *Feeling Backward*, 'paying attention to what was difficult in the past may tell us how far we have come but that is not all it will tell us; it may also make visible the damage we live with in the present'.[43] Centrally, Behan's and Genet's eroticised idealisation of youthful delinquency – youth irreconcilable with the demands of productive and reproductive mature masculinity – offers a symbolic critique of the dominant temporality of capitalist modernity.

Along with Wilde and Genet, a third coordinate for grasping the radical potential of Behan's style of writing homoeroticism is Herbert Marcuse's *Eros and Civilisation* (1955). There, as we saw in the Introduction, Marcuse argued against Freud's view that repression is an essential and necessary component of human culture. On the contrary, Marcuse argued that in modern 'Western civilisation' the persistence of repression was ideologically sustained in the interests of domination; rather than being 'necessitated by the "struggle for existence"', as Freud argued, it is 'surplus-repression'.[44] This surplus-repression was not intrinsic to human culture as such but to the historically specific reality principle of modern capitalist society, which Marcuse termed the 'performance principle'. Moreover, Marcuse's conception of repression is not narrowly psychological – avoiding Freud's ahistorical pneumatic model with its tragic calculus of perversion (too little repression) and neurosis (too much) – but holistic, historical and materialist. Rather than being internal to the individual psyche, repression is endemic to the social and economic structures of capitalism, structuring not just the relations of gender and sexuality but those of labour, property and power. As the reality principle of modern capitalist society, the performance principle describes a distinctive form of unfreedom characteristic of 'an antagonistic and acquisitive society in the process of constant expansion' where 'domination has been increasingly rationalised'. In that society, the majority of people 'while they work do not fulfil their own needs and faculties but work in alienation … labour time, which is the largest part of the individual's life time, is painful time, for alienated labour is absence of gratification, the negation of the pleasure principle'.[45] Above all, Marcuse's conception of the performance principle is, in contrast with Freud's ahistorical fatalism, dialectical. The potential for greater human freedom which modern society has created is also that which most powerfully sustains those structures of domination and unfreedom:

> the repressiveness of the whole lies to a high degree in its efficacy: it enhances the scope of material culture, facilitates the procurement of the necessities of life, makes comfort and luxury cheaper, draws ever-larger areas into the orbit of industry – while at the same time sustaining toil and destruction. The individual pays by sacrificing his (*sic*) time, his consciousness, his dream; civilisation pays by sacrificing its own promises of liberty, justice, and peace for all ... the rationality of progress heightens the irrationality of its organisation and direction.[46]

In such a society, what we term sexuality is the human capacity for pleasure and intimacy subordinated to the performance principle. 'Sexuality', in Marcuse's conception of the term, describes a human instinct narrowly inhibited and confined to genital activity and reproduction, and confined to a socially and morally sanctified realm of marriage and the patriarchal family.[47] This conceptualisation of sexuality has been inseparable from those rigid binaries underpinning bourgeois subjectivity: between the body as productive instrument and the creative soul or mind; between labour and leisure; between a masculine public sphere and a feminine private sphere; between political and moral actions; between individual relations and social relations. In other words, sexuality, in Marcuse's usage, is inseparable from the reification of human consciousness, affects and relationships under capitalism. The 'organisation of sexuality' – the centralisation of the libidinal instincts into one object of desire, embodied in a member of the opposite sex, which defines the formation of healthy 'normal' subjectivity in the Freudian narrative – requires the 'desexualisation of the body: the libido becomes concentrated in one part of the body, leaving most of the rest free for use as instrument of labour'.[48]

Central to Marcuse's utopian vision of a 'non-repressive civilisation' – a human culture freed from the domination of the performance principle – that we might strive to imagine and create, is the distinction he draws between 'sexuality' and 'Eros'. In a non-repressive culture, Eros would describe a state where the human body 'no longer used as a full-time instrument of labour would be resexualised ... the body in its entirety would be an object of cathexis, a thing to be enjoyed – an instrument of pleasure'. For Marcuse, the transformation of sexuality into Eros should not be thought of simply in terms of individual psyches throwing off the shackles of repressive morality, 'sexual liberation' as the 1960s counterculture understood it, but of a revolutionary reordering of social relations. This will require, he reiterates, 'not simply a release but a transformation of libido; from sexuality constrained under genital supremacy to eroticisation of the entire personality'. This transformation will be the result of 'a societal transformation that released the play of individual needs and faculties'.[49]

Without citing him, Marcuse echoes Wilde's insistence on the importance of imagination and fantasy when striving to fulfil the potential to create revolutionised forms of consciousness and social relations. Hence the aesthetic is indispensable as the medium for facilitating imaginative projections of a freedom that can only yet exist in potential, not realised, form. Again, Marcuse's conception of the political valences of art is dialectical, the artwork at once reconciling us to the reality of life as it is while discordantly alerting us to the potential for it to be other. To formally represent our repression and lack of freedom, art must give to that unfreedom the 'semblance of reality' and, moreover, all art forms, even the most uncompromising and tragic, must invest its representation of that reality, no matter how critical, with the quality of enjoyment. Thus, people 'read and see and hear their own archetypes rebel, triumph, give up or perish. And since all this is aesthetically formed, they can enjoy it – and forget it.' Nevertheless, 'within the limits of the aesthetic form, although in an ambivalent form' art expresses 'the return of the repressed image of liberation'.[50]

In a further echo of Wilde, Marcuse deploys artistic images and narratives of the male body, and specifically the cultural figuration of the male body as simultaneously vulnerable and beautiful in Christ, Orpheus and Narcissus, as figures for envisioning the potential of Eros and a non-repressive culture. In Marcuse's interpretation, Christ articulated a 'message of liberation: the overthrow of the Law (which is domination) by Agape (which is Eros)'. The most powerful symbol of this message was becoming human and bodily. Conversely, the subsequent betrayal of that message by his followers was symbolically manifest in the narrative of transubstantiation and deification – 'the denial of the liberation in the flesh'.[51] If the orthodox Christian version of Christ gives narrative shape to the damaging hierarchy of body subordinated to mind/soul, the received version of the Narcissus myth likewise reiterates that binary – in the translation of an image of sensuous male beauty into a moral tale of fatal, self-destructive vanity. Again, Marcuse revises the tale, noting that Narcissus did not know that the image he admired was his own. Thus, rather than an image of the self-absorbed separative self, Narcissus's pleasurable contemplation of his own beauty depicts a relational standpoint – an openness to the other and to the natural world he inhabits. Marcuse observes the 'striking paradox that narcissism, usually understood as egotistical withdrawal from reality, is here connected with oneness with the universe ... beyond all immature autoeroticism, narcissism denotes a fundamental relatedness to reality which may generate a comprehensive existential order'.[52]

As Marcuse's reference to 'immature autoeroticism' reminds us, the Narcissus myth, as with its *fin-de-siècle* reworking in *Dorian Gray*, centres on an image of male youth abruptly frozen in time. For Marcuse, imagining the utopian possibility of Eros requires an alternative style of temporal reasoning to the progressive historicism demanded by submission to the performance principle. In other words, the difference between sexuality and Eros can also be formulated temporally. The Freudian narrative of self-formation is stadial and teleological. For the subject to come into being, perverse desire must be brought under control, diverted into genital procreative – (re)productive – sexuality and polymorphous perversity left behind.[53] For Marcuse, by contrast, the temporality of perversity is prophetic rather than progressive. Like fantasy, to which it is closely aligned, perversity is a 'revolt against the performance principle in the name of the pleasure principle' and thus a residue of the presocial consciousness offering a glimpse of what sexuality transformed into Eros might look like in the future.[54]

Returning to the originary scene of Brendan and Charlie's first meeting, in the washroom with its pools of water and mirror, Charlie, the unselfconscious object of Brendan's admiring gaze, becomes at once character and symbol – embodying that fusion of desire and vulnerability (he is physically less strong than the other boys, and Brendan protects him from their aggression) that Wilde and Marcuse identify as exemplary of the potential relational self. The Narcissus imagery, and a visceral reminder of the human body's vulnerability to the violence of modernity, returns with shocking poignancy towards the end of the novel when Brendan learns that Charlie, recently released, has been drowned aboard a torpedoed ship.[55] As we have seen, from the beginning of their relationship physical intimacy – touching, singing to each other, whispering through the spyhole of their cells – is woven through acts of generosity, care and kindness. Moreover, as the novel unfolds, Brendan's relationship with Charlie is one intensified link in a web of such nurturing and sustaining relationships within the group of boys who form Brendan's closest friends – in prison rhyming slang, 'chinas'. In this way, we could argue that the homoerotic is figured in the novel less as a site of identity than as a source of solidarity, and less as a distinctive current of sexual desire than as one component on an elastic continuum of bodily needs, affects and potentialities.

The erotic and affective intensification of his and Charlie's bodies is the indispensable first step in Brendan's growing solidarity with the other boys in the prison. One crucial feature of this growing solidarity is Brendan's gradual appreciation of the working-class culture he shares with boys from Liverpool, Glasgow and London. Here again, as with the question of same-sex passion in the novel, the temptation is to resort to a hermeneutic of identity; to project a distinction between a confected, politically problematic 'national' identity and a more authentic, properly political 'working-class' identity, and then to interpret the novel's *bildung* narrative in terms of Brendan's movement from one to the other.

However, we might profitably interpret his growing awareness of that shared working-class culture in different terms, as Brendan reformulating his cognitive map of empire. Rather than the relatively straightforward exploitation of colony by coloniser he can now begin to grasp those imperial currents and flows of capital and labour in which his native Dublin and these other port cities are interconnected in a much broader global system, and where the distinction between those who profit and those who are exploited must be conceptualised much more rigorously than any distinction between 'Irish' and 'English' would allow. (In this it might be said the novel is prescient of our own 'globalised' world, where formal colonialism has largely ended but the exploitative structures of the capitalist world system are stronger than ever.) In this view then, the trajectory of Brendan's emotional and political development can be understood less as a movement from a 'national' to a 'post-national' identity than the difference between the nativist and liberationist stages of anticolonial consciousness charted by Franz Fanon; as with Eros, liberation, as Fanon describes it, requires a transformation of social consciousness beyond national consciousness.[56]

Borstal Boy ends with Brendan's arrival at Dun Laoghaire port, arriving back to Ireland having served his time and been deported. Specifically, it ends with this exchange between Brendan and an immigration officer:

> I handed him the expulsion order.
> He read it, looked at it and handed it back to me. He had a long educated countryman's sad face, like a teacher, and took my hand.
> 'Cead mile failte (*sic*) sa bhaile romhat.'
> A hundred thousand welcomes home to you.
> I smiled and said, 'Go raibh maith agat.'
> Thanks.
> He looked very serious, and tenderly inquired, 'Caithfidh go bhuil sé go hiontach bheith saor.'
> 'Caithfidh go bhuil.'
> 'It must be wonderful to be free.'
> 'It must,' said I, and walked down the gangway, past a detective and got on the train for Dublin.

Brendan appears to affirm the custom officer's complacent certainty that the conservative, repressive, bourgeois nationalist regime of the post-independence 'Free State' constitutes 'freedom', while actually asserting the direct opposite. Here we see something like the coded language (the open secret; the signal or gesture that can be read quite differently, but equally plausibly, by different audiences) that was part of the communicative repertoire of same-sex subcultures in the twentieth century. One of the conditions of possibility for such subcultures was that they could be simultaneously recognisable and unrecognisable. For instance, while Wilde's dandified performance was read by some London contemporaries as disclosing his same-sex desires, others, including those close to him such as his biographer Frank Harris, were apparently genuinely shocked by the revelations at the trials.[57] But Behan's authorial decision to have this exchange take place in Irish, and to present it bilingually, as it were, with 'original' and 'translation' woven together on the page is also striking. In this way he reiterates how the grammatical structure of the Irish language makes possible this coded gesture of defiance. The novel ends with an expression of utopian aspiration – 'it must be wonderful to be free' – that is a sudden and unexpected eruption into a text that otherwise seems committed to a more reformist reconciliation with reality. This momentary utopian aspiration is made possible by the conjunction of a queer expressive strategy and an Irish linguistic register.[58] This conjunction mirrors the book's twin generic legacies in the Irish republican and homoerotic prison-writing traditions, and also mirrors that symbolic conjunction where Charlie's body, as a location of homoerotic desires and affects, sparks the fusion between the revolutionary possibilities of Eros and liberation.

As Marcuse and Fanon each remind us so compellingly, and as the history of the twentieth century so painfully insists, neither Eros nor liberation will be easily achieved. *Borstal Boy* offers us a powerful emblem of this in the contrast between the beauty of Charlie's body in the washroom where Brendan first meets him – lustrous with the promise and potential of a transformed future – and the drowned body of the young sailor in the seas off Gibraltar, destroyed by the present reality of war. The novel's ending also reiterates that we can only grasp the idea of freedom in the conditional tense. Under our present conditions, we cannot know in advance what exactly Eros or liberation will look like; we can only speculate, and hope, about how 'wonderful' they might be.

Notes

1 Michael O'Sullivan, *Brendan Behan: a life* (Dublin: Blackwater Press, 1997), pp. 41–3.
2 Derek Hand, 'Brendan Behan's *Borstal Boy*: the public persona and the delicate art of deceit' in John McCourt (ed.), *Reading Brendan Behan* (Cork: Cork University Press, 2019), p. 16.
3 O'Sullivan, *Brendan Behan*, pp. 45–73.
4 The earliest published sketch for what would become the novel was published in the Irish literary periodical *The Bell* in June 1942. See Brendan Behan, 'I become a Borstal Boy' in Sean McMahon (ed.), *The Best from The Bell* (Dublin: O'Brien Press, 1978), pp. 83–8. A version of the novel's opening was published as 'Bridewell revisited' in *Points*, a Paris-based avant-garde literary magazine, in winter 1951–52. On the significance of Behan's working relationship with *Points* see John Brannigan, 'Bohemian Behan: late modernism, sexual politics and

the "great awakening" of Brendan Behan' in McCourt (ed.), *Reading Brendan Behan*, pp. 58–60.
5 Bernice Shrank, 'Brendan Behan's *Borstal Boy*: politics in the vernaculars', *Irish University Review*, 44,1 (2014), 129–48, 129.
6 Fintan O'Toole, 'Brendan Behan: playwright, novelist, terrorist', *Irish Times* (6 September 2014), p.B8.
7 *Ibid.*
8 David Lloyd, *Irish Culture and Colonial Modernity 1800–2000: the transformation of oral space* (Cambridge: Cambridge University Press, 2011), p. 194.
9 Lloyd, *Irish Culture*, p. 196.
10 Maria DiBattista, 'Lessons of detention' in McCourt (ed.), *Reading Brendan Behan*, p. 34.
11 Georg Lukács, *The Historical Novel*, trans. Hannah and Stanley Mitchell (Lincoln, NE: University of Nebraska Press, 1983 [1937]), p. 266.
12 Colbert Kearney, *The Writings of Brendan Behan* (Dublin: Gill and Macmillan, 1977), p. 95.
13 Brendan Behan, *Borstal Boy* (London: Corgi, 1958), p. 254.
14 *Ibid.*
15 John Brannigan, *Brendan Behan: cultural nationalism and the revisionist writer* (Dublin: Four Courts Press, 2002), pp. 126–50.
16 Behan, *Borstal Boy*, p. 13.
17 Behan, *Borstal Boy*, p. 29.
18 Kearney, *The Writings of Brendan Behan*, p. 92.
19 Behan, *Borstal Boy*, pp. 24–5 and 34–5.
20 Behan, *Borstal Boy*, p. 253.
21 Cited in Kearney, *The Writings of Brendan Behan*, pp. 84–5. The twelve-page manuscript, entitled *The Courteous Borstal*, is now held in the Morris Library at Southern Illinois University. Kearney believes Behan wrote it at some point in the two years after his deportation.
22 Eve Kosofsky Sedgwick, *The Epistemology of the Closet* (London: Penguin, 1990), p. 85.
23 *Ibid.*
24 Brendan Behan, *After the Wake*, ed. Peter Fallon (Dublin: O'Brien Press, 1981), p. 48.
25 Behan, *Borstal Boy*, pp. 18–20.
26 Behan, *Borstal Boy*, p. 24. Ellipses in original.
27 Ríona Ní Fhrighil, 'Brendan Behan's Irish-language poetry' in McCourt (ed.), *Reading Brendan Behan*, p. 106.
28 Oscar Wilde, *De Profundis, The Ballad of Reading Gaol and Other Writings* (London: Wordsworth Classics, 1999), p. 60. Reflecting on the formal affinities between *De Profundis* and republican prison writing, it

is worth noting Wilde's explicit assertion there, unusual in his writing, of his family's politics; his parents 'bequeathed me a name they had made noble and honoured ... in the public history of my own country in its evolution as a nation' (pp. 45–6).
29 Wilde, *De Profundis*, p. 30.
30 Wilde, *De Profundis*, p. 73.
31 Walter Benjamin, 'These on the Philosophy of History' in *Illuminations*, trans. Harry Zohn, ed. Hannah Arendt (New York: Shocken Books, 2007 [1969]), p. 263.
32 Wilde, *De Profundis*, p. 83.
33 Wilde, *De Profundis*, p. 70.
34 Wilde, *De Profundis*, p. 81.
35 For instance, Lloyd explores Bobby Sands's imaginative engagement with, and continuation of, this tradition in his prison writing; this includes establishing Wilde's *Ballad of Reading Gaol* as a significant model for some of Sands's poetry, and for its imaginative exploration of the political potential of vulnerability. Lloyd, *Irish Culture*, pp. 178–80.
36 David Alderson, *Sex, Needs and Queer Culture: from liberation to the post-gay* (London: Zed Books, 2016), pp. 207–23.
37 Judith Butler, *Bodies That Matter: on the discursive limits of 'sex'* (London: Routledge, 1993), pp. 124–8.
38 Jean Genet, *Miracle of the Rose*, trans. Bernard Frechtman (London: Faber, 1973).
39 Alan Sinfield, *On Sexuality and Power* (New York: Columbia University Press, 2004), p. 54. Sinfield develops his argument in critical dialogue with Leo Bersani's celebration of Genet's homoerotic transgressive – his 'scatological aesthetic' – as radically self-negating and revolutionary in *Homos* (Cambridge, MA: Harvard University Press, 1995), pp. 113–84. For a provocative comparative reading of Behan's and Genet's drama, see Frank McGuinness, 'Saint Behan', *Irish University Review*, 44,1 (2014), 78–91.
40 Kadji Amin, 'Anachronizing the penitentiary, queering the history of sexuality', *GLQ: a journal of lesbian and gay studies*, 19,3 (2013), 301–40, 303.
41 Amin, 'Anachronizing', 307.
42 Amin, 'Anachronizing', 305.
43 Heather Love, *Feeling Backward: loss and the politics of queer history* (Cambridge, MA: Harvard University Press, 2007), p. 29.
44 Herbert Marcuse, *Eros and Civilisation* (New York: Vintage, 1962), p. 118.
45 Marcuse, *Eros and Civilisation*, p. 40.
46 Marcuse, *Eros and Civilisation*, p. 91.

47 Marcuse, *Eros and Civilisation*, p. 187.
48 Marcuse, *Eros and Civilisation*, p. 44.
49 Marcuse, *Eros and Civilisation*, p. 184.
50 Marcuse, *Eros and Civilisation*, pp. 131–2.
51 Marcuse, *Eros and Civilisation*, pp. 63–4.
52 Marcuse, *Eros and Civilisation*, p. 153.
53 However while rehearsing his established narrative of self-formation in *Civilisation and its Discontents* Freud qualified his conception of development through stages with a model of accretion. No part of the psyche is lost or discarded; hence the sense of 'oceanic feeling', as he describes it, to which humans are susceptible is a residue of the preconscious state of overwhelming immersion in libidinal pleasures. Characteristically, though, this leads him to a typically pessimistic – not to say reactionary – conclusion. Since our primal drive to aggression can never be fully overcome we must submit to the repressive control of civilisation for our own survival. Sigmund Freud, *Civilisation and its Discontents*, trans. David McLintock (London: Penguin Modern Classics, 2002).
54 Marcuse, *Eros and Civilisation*, p. 45.
55 Behan, *Borstal Boy*, pp. 373–4.
56 Frantz Fanon, *The Wretched of the Earth*, trans. Constance Farrington (London: Penguin, 1991), pp. 119–49.
57 Alan Sinfield, *The Wilde Century* (London: Cassell, 1994), pp. 1–3.
58 In *Languages of the Night*, Barry McCrea discusses Behan's decision to write and publish primarily in the Irish language at the beginning of his career, between 1945 and 1950. For McCrea the apparent irrationality of this decision, to write in a second language that was also a minor language which would severely limit his potential readership, expressed a desire that was both queer and utopian for Behan, as it did for Pier Paolo Pasolini who, around the same time, made a similar decision at the beginning of his career. See Barry McCrea, *Languages of the Night: minor languages and the literary imagination in twentieth-century Ireland and Europe* (New Haven, CT: Yale University Press, 2015), pp. 64–7. And in the context of our discussion here it is also worth noting that Behan's relatively small number of Irish-language poems published in his lifetime includes an elegy for Wilde. See Ní Fhrighil, 'Brendan Behan's Irish-language poetry', pp. 107–9.

2

John Broderick: perverse politics

Since the turn of the millennium there has been some modest incorporation of John Broderick, who died in 1989, into the ubiquitous Irish literary/heritage industry. The 'John Broderick Weekend' was held in his native Athlone in 1999 and 2001, and the John Broderick Writer-in-Residence scheme was initiated by the Arts Council of Ireland and Westmeath County Council in 2018.[1] Broderick published nine novels between 1961 and his death (another was published posthumously). He also reviewed extensively for Irish newspapers and periodicals from the late 1950s to the 1980s, the stylishness of his reviewing work overshadowed by his rather ugly and misogynistic vendetta against Edna O'Brien.[2] The quality of his fiction is certainly uneven, within each novel but more sharply between the novels published in the 1960s and his subsequent work. Sadly, the primary reason for the latter decline was alcoholism and associated poor health. But, according to one of his editors, even when he was still well and active Broderick hated editing and revising his manuscripts and refused to do more than perfunctory proofreading.[3] Interestingly, this might be an unusual instance of leisure afforded by unearned income hindering rather than facilitating literary work. At a young age Broderick inherited a successful bakery business in Athlone, which gave him a handsome income without requiring much of his attention, and so he did not rely on the income from his writing.

This unevenness of his output notwithstanding, it is striking how little critical interest Broderick's fiction has received in Irish literary studies. The only sustained engagement has been from a liberal Catholic perspective. Eamon Maher sought to read Broderick's fiction as an Irish equivalent to the early and mid-twentieth-century French

'Catholic novel', exemplified by the fiction of François Mauriac. Characteristically, such novels were shaped around narrating the modern individual's frustrated quest for spiritual authenticity in a secular world. While broadly sympathetic to Broderick's critical perspective on the dominant values of mid-twentieth-century Ireland, Maher concludes that the fiction does not actually conform to the style of the 'Catholic novel', notwithstanding Broderick's intellectual engagement with that French tradition and his personal friendships with Mauriac and others. In Broderick, Maher concludes, 'we find someone who is more comfortable when attacking complacency than when exploring the nuances of inner turmoil'.[4]

The lack of critical interest is all the more surprising given that excoriating portrayal of Irish society Maher notes in the fiction, and that Broderick's first novel was banned.[5] Viewed together, his novels doggedly expose the hypocritical piety, ruthless materialism and sexual neurosis that is, in this view, so pervasive among a specific faction in Irish society – Catholic middle-class families, prosperous business owners living in a 'provincial town' that is a daguerreotype of Broderick's Athlone. A newspaper account of a public event in 1970 quotes Broderick asserting that 'my Ireland, which I write about, is purse-proud, narrow-minded, bigoted to an extent, rather hypocritical and sexually frustrated. I write about the Catholic bourgeoisie … nobody really believes that the two million or so members of the Irish Catholic bourgeoisie exist.'[6] However, it can be difficult to gain much critical purchase on the political perspectives underpinning this fiction. The narrative voice is acutely sensitive to the gradations and microdynamics of class politics in the society depicted, but the hegemonic ideas underpinning the structure of those class relations remain unquestioned. At most, within the novel's world view, this bourgeoisie is satirised and condemned for being, as it were, insufficiently bourgeois – for being philistine, inauthentic, illiberal and conformist. Moreover, the tightly restricted social setting leaves us unsure if these failings are specific to the 'Irish Catholic' bourgeoisie, in contrast with some normative bourgeoisie elsewhere, or characteristic of modern bourgeois life as such.

However, the principal obstacle to critical interpretation is not so much political as aesthetic. To read Broderick as deploying the conventions of realism – or, more precisely, naturalism – to imaginatively depict the forces and contradictions shaping Irish society requires overlooking the fiction's persistent deviation from those conventions. In his overview of Broderick's career, Patrick Murray identifies a curious paradox about Broderick's writing. Broderick's literary journalism demonstrates that he was deeply engaged with twentieth-century fiction, and the significant modernist innovations of narrative technique from James and Conrad to Joyce and Woolf. Yet he wrote his fiction as if these developments had never taken place. As Murray observes, 'he was happy to be the traditional omniscient narrator ... never willing to let his story or his characters develop of their own momentum, he must always be at the reader's elbow, nudging him (sic), enlightening him, prompting his responses'. Thus, Murray concludes that Broderick's oddly 'old-fashioned technique' situates his fiction in a 'safe if unadventurous tradition'.[7]

In this chapter I want to develop an alternative view of Broderick's uneven style, through a reading of three of his early – and strongest – novels: *The Pilgrimage* (1961), *The Fugitives* (1962) and *The Waking of Willie Ryan* (1965). Rather than thinking of Broderick's style as cautious and outmoded we might think of it as a type of failed realism, where the failure gives most critical traction – wrinkles and tears in the textual fabric providing glimpses into its political unconscious. What is of most critical and political interest in this fiction, I will argue, is a perverse structure of feeling.[8] Rather than reading Broderick's fiction as novels with characters, we could read the fiction as parables composed of archetypes. Specifically, we can identify two salient archetypal categories in these novels – converts and perverts. The latter are not, or not just, perverse in their sexual transgressions, but also in their adherence to anachronistic values; they are religious and political as well as sexual heretics animating the insurrectionary potential immanent to the bourgeois social order.

The epigraph to *The Waking of Willie Ryan* is from Saint Paul: 'And where there is no law, neither is there transgression.' This idea expresses a central concept in the genealogy of perversion unearthed by Jonathan Dollimore in *Sexual Dissidence*. Dollimore argued that the modern category of sexual perversion, inherited from late nineteenth-century sexology and twentieth-century psychoanalytical theory, has compacted within it older theological and political connotations. In its simplest theological meaning 'pervert' functions as an antonym of 'convert' – that is, turning towards or away from God. From this sense of directional activity derives a teleological conception of perversity as a wilful deviation from an established and natural trajectory. But why, as Dollimore asks, should deviation from the right path in itself be considered evil? One answer, Dollimore suggests, is that such deviation is politically subversive as it demystifies what is ideologically framed as 'natural'. Deviation from orthodoxy moves us towards grasping the fixed reality of social and ideological structures as dynamic and contingent, a potential insight that Dollimore describes as, 'the path we thought we were on naturally, or by choice, we are in fact on by arrangement'. Glimpsing that possibility opens the potential to reveal 'alternative ways to the future'.[9]

Along with being teleological the concept of perversity is also dialectical, which, Dollimore argues, is also derived from Christian theology. If perversion is a deviation *from* the natural and the good, then perversion must also originate *within* the natural and good. In Augustine's theodicy – the justification of the existence of evil within a divinely created order – evil is at once the antithesis of God, and yet intrinsic to our fallen human nature which was created in God's likeness. As a wilful turning away from God, and from good, perversity is above all a perversion of the free will with which God endowed human beings. As with Milton's charismatic Lucifer in *Paradise Lost* – God's favoured among the angels before his rebellion – evil originates within that which is closest to, not most distant from, God. As Dollimore observes, in Milton: 'evil is absolutely and clearly contrary to good, and yet in fallen practice barely distinguishable, or only arduously so, or perhaps not at all'.[10]

As Dollimore summarises: 'in the Western tradition indebted to Augustine we find evil conceptualised simultaneously as, on the one hand, a foreign force or agency, at once alien, antithetic and hostile; on the other, as an inner deviation, the more insidious for having departed from the true, its point of departure from *within* the true being also its point of contact for the perversion *of* the true'.[11] This theological conception of perversion is at one and the same time a political conception of perversion as insurrectionary, and doubly so since it poses 'a threat from outside in, and inside out'. The perverse, Dollimore observes, 'not only departs from, but actively contradicts the dominant in the act of deviating from it, and does so from within, and in terms of inversion, distortion, transformation, reversal, subversion'.[12]

This perverse paradox – perversity as intrinsic rather than extrinsic to the dominant order, and thereby subversive of that order – has found a modern form in theories of sexual perversion. For Freud, the preconscious, and thus presocial self, is in a state of polymorphous perversity where instincts and desires are aimed at undifferentiated objects. For the subject to come into being, positioned within sexual difference and within the social order, perverse desire must be brought under control and its energies sublimated into other activities which are essential to the creative reproduction of human culture. Perversity threatens civilisation, and yet civilisation depends on perversity's transformed energies. Later in the twentieth century that idea was reformulated within Foucault's critical revision of Freud. Foucault rejects any notion of some originary or presocial polymorphous perversity; rather than an energy that is repressed and sublimated by modern culture, the perverse is implanted in human subjectivity by modern culture. Nevertheless, the conclusion is remarkably similar; the perversity which is abjected and stigmatised by modern culture inheres within the structural dynamics of that culture.

Dollimore identifies three discursive figures that have in modernity powerfully instantiated the threat of perversity, where perversity is understood as this volatile amalgam of the religious, sexual and political. One such figure is the heretic, the figure who repudiates the existing conventions of Christian faith from within rather than from without, and thus from a position of claiming access to a more profoundly authentic faith rather than asserting a lack of faith. The etymology of the term 'bugger', deriving from an eleventh-century Bulgarian sect which practiced the Manichean heresy, illustrates how sexual deviance was also imbricated with the religious conception of perversions well in advance of sexology.[13]

As a scholar of Renaissance drama, Dollimore regularly turns to the early modern period in *Sexual Dissidence* to illuminate his late twentieth-century contemporary moment. Thus, his second figure of perversion is the 'wayward woman'. As Dollimore outlines, the expansion of capitalism, and particularly the intensified commercialisation of agriculture, created a large 'surplus' population of the unemployed and dislocated in early modern England. In Tudor and Jacobean political and religious discourse, 'social and economic dislocation were often refigured as the evil of aberrant movement'.[14] Hence, there was intense political and cultural concern with what was termed vagrancy and with controlling 'masterless men' and 'wayward women'. One effect was legislation and innovative developments in state control over the population. Another was a cultural emphasis on instilling self-discipline, exemplified most obviously in puritanism, and a 'strategy of ideological control conceived in ethical and religious terms'.[15] The threat posed to the social order by the 'wayward woman' was represented as greater than that presented by the masterless man. Her perversely aberrant status challenged the rights of property and patriarchy, but, more than this, her uncontrolled sexuality threatened to lead others astray with her. Thus the 'wayward woman', dispossessed by immediate material circumstances, was discursively conflated with the archetypal biblical 'harlot' and 'fallen woman' and, above all, with Eve, the woman whose disobedience was instrumental to that primal 'Fall' into sinfulness – and, in the paradoxical Augustinian world view, into death but also into human subjectivity, or, in other words, life.

Conventionally, the terms 'pervert' and 'sexual pervert' are now synonymous. But, as Dollimore points out, that usage of the word is not cited in the *Oxford English Dictionary (OED)* until the 1933 supplement, and then only with a single instance – the religious and political connotations predominate. This reminds us that historically our conception of sexual perversion is relatively novel. The original functionalist meaning in nineteenth-century medicine, as a deviation from the sexual instinct for reproduction, was superseded by the sexological taxonomic categorisation of types of sexual behaviour, and thus types of people. And while this style of reasoning remains strongly with us in the concept of sexual identity, Freudian psychoanalysis unwittingly undermined it by suggesting that perversity may not be a quality of some types of people but the substratum on which consciousness as such rests.

Sexology's paradigmatic sexual pervert was the male homosexual, a figure crystallised most vividly in the popular imagination by the media coverage of Oscar Wilde's trials in 1895. While Dollimore broadly assents to Foucault's argument that a historical transition took place during the late nineteenth century between two sexual epistemes – sexual behaviours to sexual types; sodomy to homosexuality – he also argues for stronger continuities between the discursive figures of the sodomite and the homosexual. In particular, and as with the other two archetypes of perversity, he stresses the conflation of religious, political and sexual concepts in the figuration of the sodomite. In early modern England, for instance, sodomy 'was associated with a whole range of evils including insurrection and heresy', and at the end of the eighteenth century the number of prosecutions for sodomy increased as the sodomite's association with evil, rebellion and insurrection meant that he 'was perceived as an internal deviant who figured a foreign threat', in this case the threat from France and republicanism.[16]

In Broderick's fiction there are characters who conform to aspects of the mid-twentieth-century literary stereotype of the male homosexual, and specifically the repressed homosexual.[17] As we will see below, these characters are caricatured and stigmatised as neurotic, effete and 'unmanly', while being relatively marginal to the plot. By contrast, I argue that Broderick's protagonists, around whom narrative consciousness is focalised, are archetypes conforming to Dollimore's historical figures of perversion – modern versions of 'wayward women', religious heretics and political insurrectionists. A homoerotic structure of feeling adheres to the latter two types of character particularly: that is, the male figures of queer perversion. It is there, rather than in the naturalist depiction of homosexuality as psychic or social 'problem', that we can locate the most politically interesting, and potentially radical, currents in Broderick's fiction. What creates this radical affect is that these queerly perverse figures do not invite sympathy or identification from the reader; in other words, no affect that can be translated into a liberal politics of compassion for a minority. Rather, they incite feelings of disquiet and perplexity; this is because they are not figures of identification but figures of insurrection.

Broderick's first two novels are principally focalised around two 'wayward women'. At the beginning of *The Pilgrimage*, Julia Glynn is married to the older Michael, now invalided by arthritis, while having an affair with his nephew and doctor, Jim. In a retrospectively narrated chapter, we learn of her casual relationships with men as a younger woman, and how, after the abrupt ending of her most sustained relationship with Howard, a wealthy American, she had married Michael. Her primary motivation for this decision was the wealth and security the marriage offered, and she quickly discovered that his motivation was equally mercenary – to disguise his precariously repressed homosexuality.

The Fugitives opens with the arrival in an Irish midlands town of Lily Fallon from London. She has returned to the town after a five-year absence to help her brother, Paddy, who is now hiding in his family home from the authorities having taken part in the IRA's assassination of a British politician in London. On the night of the murder her panicked brother came to Lily, who is having an affair with a married man and living as a 'kept woman'. Along with Lily, Hugh Ward, an older member of Paddy's IRA squad, also arrives at the family home to watch over Paddy. Over the following days these three live with the sibling's widowed step-mother, Hetty, and their aunt, Kate, a former nun. Lily and Paddy have a difficult relationship with the cold and sanctimonious Hetty, and the two older women live in a grim state of silent hostility and enforced dependence. When Hugh, Lily and Paddy realise that the police have identified Paddy's location, they move to an abandoned house in the bog some miles from the town, but Paddy is captured. Not unexpectedly, in concluding the novel Broderick makes much of the hypocrisy and double standards of a society which savagely condemns a woman's sexual transgression – Lily's secret affair is revealed at Paddy's trial – while remaining tolerantly ambivalent about her brother's murderous violence.

As we've noted, perhaps the least interesting perverse figures in Broderick's fiction are versions of the modern sexual pervert, or more precisely the repressed homosexual. Michael Glynn, in *The Pilgrimage*, and Michael Ryan, in *The Waking of Willie Ryan*, are identical in this regard. Though successful, wealthy and middle-aged, neither wields the expected patriarchal power within their family. Michael Glynn's illness has left him anxious, fearful and dependent on his servant, Stephen. In the novel's conventional gender schema such weakness and dependence are marked as feminine; thus 'when he was excited Michael fell into a cosy, spinsterish way of speaking which ordinarily embarrassed Julia'.[18] Likewise, Michael Ryan is depicted as vague, insubstantial and ineffectual. Though not ill, he is evidently descending into alcoholism. This is precipitated, we are led to assume, by his guilt at conspiring with his wife to incarcerate his younger brother, Willie, in an asylum twenty-five years before. Again, his weakness and dysfunctionality are symptomatic of a reversal of 'normal' gender relations and the dominant position of his more astute, manipulative and powerful wife, Mary, who dominates their business and home. In both instances, the reversal of gender norms is aligned with the repression and perversion of sexual desires. As Julia recalls from their infrequent sexual encounters when they were first married, Michael Glynn was a violent and sadistic lover and this, the narrator tells us, was because he was 'trying to reform his nature'.[19] From Willie Ryan's recollections of his childhood, we learn that he was sexually abused by his older brother.[20]

More interesting in Broderick's fiction are those figures who are deeply immersed in homoerotic feelings and relationships, but whose homosexuality is complexly overlaid with older theological and political notions of perversity: Stephen in *The Pilgrimage*, the eponymous Willie Ryan and Hugh in *The Fugitives*. Having established the rhythm of Julia's life – luxury, security and respectability guaranteed by marriage; freedom from the sexual demands of her now incapacitated husband; some sexual pleasure from her easily managed though passionless affair – the plot of *The Pilgrimage* is initially precipitated by the disruption of this stability. Julia begins to receive anonymous letters containing pornographically detailed accounts of her sexual encounters with Jim. Her anxious suspicions about the source of these letters settle, rightly it turns out, on her husband's servant, Stephen. At the same time, she learns that Jim is engaged – a highly respectable marriage that will be advantageous for his career – and their sexual liaison ends; this repeats what happened with Howard, and in both cases she first knows about the engagement by reading about it in a newspaper.

While surreptitiously following Stephen through the local town, to find out if he is posting the letters, Julia sees him meet a young man whom she recognises as one of Jim's neighbours in Dublin. Subsequently, Julia learns from Jim that this young man, Tommy Baggot, has committed suicide because he was being investigated by the police after propositioning a man on the street. She also learns that her husband had funded Tommy's move to Dublin and, until his illness, paid his rent there. Moreover, as Jim reveals, the police had taken possession of letters from Stephen to Tommy. However, we later learn that Mitchell, Tommy's flatmate and the source of Jim's information, lied about this. In fact, Mitchell has the letters and blackmails Stephen with them; we also assume, though it is not confirmed, that Mitchell lied to Jim about being Tommy's flatmate and was in fact his lover. By this time Stephen and Julia have become lovers and so she gives him the money to get the letters back.

The narration is centrally focalised around Julia, and the unfolding of these events is reported to her in conversation with Jim or Stephen. Moreover, the dominant mood is intensely claustrophobic and, like Michael, we are mainly confined within his house. Characteristically then, the novel gestures towards different genres and perspectives: suspense and mystery of crime fiction (suicide; sexual scandal; blackmail); a critical realism, exposing 'social problems' (the homosexual underworld; police harassment; injustice). But the action unfolds at something of a distance from us and resolves itself rather precipitously. In other words, the novel's commitment to the tension of the thriller or the naturalist excavations of critical realism is not really sustained. Instead, the plot takes shape as a study of human types through mapping a pattern of repetitive or mirroring action. As the narrator observes in typically pseudo-philosophical mode, 'life is a series of recurring patterns, each a little more blurred than the ones which have gone before'.[21]

This patterning can be heavy-handed and not averse to cliché in its deployment of symbolism. Thus, Julia and Stephen's first sexual encounter takes place while the funeral bell for Tommy Baggot can be heard tolling in the distance; crude psychologising – Stephen impelled by grief and anger rather than actual desire for Julia – merges with the symbolic and overly literal insistence on the Augustinian connection between sex, sin and death. More grimly, this first encounter is narrated in grotesquely Gothic fashion. Julia has been drinking heavily and is incoherent, delirious and helpless. In a darkened room, a figure she is unable to identify aggressively attacks her.[22] This mirrors her last sexual encounter with Jim, when he was drunk and raped her.[23] In their subsequent consensual sexual encounters Stephen also reminds Julia of her husband, since he exhibits the same desperate sexual aggression towards her. Lest we are not convinced by Julia's reading of this behaviour we must also be subjected to comically portentous observations from the narrator: 'the truth was that Julia was turning the situation to her own advantage with the supreme adaptability of the highly sexed woman. She doubted if Stephen ... would ever be able to dissociate lovemaking from the furtive, the sordid and the unclean. Few Irish men, she knew, ever were. The puritanism which was bred in their bones, and encouraged in their youth by every possible outside pressure, was never entirely eradicated.'[24] This is Broderick's most severe stylistic weakness: authorial interventions which repackage ludicrous generalisations as philosophical aphorisms. It is the primary reason why it is unprofitable to read his fiction for sociological verisimilitude or historical and political insight, and why attending to his style and distinctive structure of feeling is more enlightening.

While Stephen is threatening, devious and aggressive, he is simultaneously shown to be profoundly unworldly and naive. He idealises Tommy Baggot and insists to Julia that their relationship was platonic and too pure to be sullied by sex. While Stephen mirrors Michael, he also mirrors Julia. His attraction to Tommy was precipitated by being reminded of a young man from his youth; Tommy is a reflection of this platonic ideal, just as Jim and Stephen are diminished copies of the lost Howard for Julia. But there is also a gendered reversal here. While Julia maintains a realistic perspective on the limitations, squalid compromises and inherent desperation of her and Stephen's relationship, he succumbs to romantic idealisation. Again, in the novel's conventionally gendered schema his volatile, emotional and hysterical responses are marked in stereotypically feminine terms. Thus, when Julia offers the money to buy back his letters, 'he began to weep. There was something infinitely pathetic about the way he turned from her to conceal the tears which rolled down his cheeks. His shoulders were shaking and he put up his hand and knuckled his eyes like a child.'[25]

Overall, Stephen is an amalgam of contradictory attributes which do not add up to a conventional fictional character. Beneath the veneer of an impeccably dutiful, loyal servant and nurse there is a pattern of brutal and sinister behaviour – terrorising Julia with the letters; assaulting her – that is puzzlingly motiveless. Sending the letters, for instance, is vaguely presented as a plea for attention and a declaration of his devotion to Julia, but never properly explained. And yet, as the image of him hiding his tear reiterates, he is childlike and innocent and entirely unworldly in his dedication to the romantic ideal of non-sexual communion with an idolised 'friend'.

With the eponymous Willie Ryan, Broderick creates a similar figure to Stephen while placing him more centrally in the narrative. The novel begins with Willie returning to his family farm, Summerhill, having escaped from the asylum where he was incarcerated twenty-five years before. His nephew, Chris, is restoring the house and has taken up farming; his parents had moved into a much grander house in the nearby town years before and concentrated on running the prosperous business inherited by his mother. Chris ignores his parents' objections and welcomes Willie. However, Willie's health is poor and within a few months he dies; the title refers to the gathering on the day of his burial with which the novel ends.

The plot revolves around revealing the story behind Willie's incarceration by Michael and Mary, his brother and sister-in-law, but mainly around the effects of Willie's return in the present. Stylistically, Broderick makes substantial use of dialogue in this novel. The narration is composed of a series of episodes featuring conversation between two or more characters, interspersed with descriptive prose marking the passage of time from autumn to winter through lyrical evocations of the landscape. This structure gives a degree of dialogical complexity to this novel in contrast with the other two novels. The authorial interventions are minimised, and in so far as there is a perspective that accords with the narrator it is given to a minor character. Halloran, an attendant from the asylum, regularly visits Willie to whom he listens sympathetically – their conversations are crucial for giving us Willie's account of what happened years before – while offering righteously angry and cynically disenchanted denunciations of the family's, and the society's, pious hypocrisy.

Through the various conversations, we gradually acquire a picture of what happened. In the version offered by Mary and Michael they had to act because of Willie's worsening drunkenness and volatile behaviour, culminating in an attempted assault against Mary in the Summerhill kitchen. In addition, Willie had stopped practicing his religion, which, they claim, was a further symptom of his potentially dangerous disconnection from society. However, Halloran, and some of their neighbours, detected a material motivation; with Willie in the asylum Michael would be the sole heir of the farm. In his account Willie confirms that this was partly Michael's motivation, along with 'being afraid of me', presumably because of what Willy could reveal about the childhood sexual abuse.[26] More significantly though, Willie reveals that his incarceration was propelled by an unspoken conspiracy to hide a sexual scandal. In his early twenties Willie had become close friends with his middle-aged neighbour, Roger Dillon, a widowed 'gentleman farmer'. Willie describes the first five years of their relationship as idyllic. In Roger he found the affectionate father figure he had never known, along with access to the culture and social life – books, music and conversation – lacking in his own home. But then Roger insisted on their relationship becoming sexual and Willie reluctantly acquiesced, though, notably, he presents this as a repetition of his childhood abuse rather than consensual or pleasurable – 'just like Michael'.

It was then that Willie, in despair about this relationship which he needed and yet could not endure, began to drink heavily. He also began to bring young men from the local pub with him to Roger's house. One of these young men told his mother about having sex with Roger and she went to a local priest, Fr Mannix. However, since Roger had always diligently maintained his respectability and religious conformity – as well as being a generous Church benefactor – a potential scandal was averted. Indeed, Roger and the priest became good friends. Though their relationship became increasingly bitter and angry, Roger and Willie continued to meet in secret. But in reaction to this sordid hypocrisy Willie's despair and erratic behaviour worsened, along with his relationship with Mary. Trying to make amends for his behaviour one day he rashly embraced Mary and kissed her on the cheek. However, Mary 'got hysterical and accused me of trying to rape her'.[27] Looking back now, Willie assumes that the police knew 'something about me in the town' but had wanted to avoid a public scandal because of the Church and Roger's status. Mary and Michael's accusations now gave them the opportunity to punish him without such a scandal.

In recounting this story to Halloran Willie pays particular attention to an encounter with Mannix, after the priest had discovered his relationship with Roger. Willie describes 'hating' the priest for what he had done – facilitating Roger's hypocritical masquerade of respectability – and responding angrily to his friendly overtures about resuming his religious practice. In response, Willie 'told him exactly what I was and that I would never be any other way'. Mannix told Willie that he must never see Roger again, to which Willie angrily responded that 'in his heart' Mannix 'didn't care what went on so long as nobody knew about it and that his religion was nothing but a fraud and a humbug'.[28] Willie blames Mannix for not speaking up later when Mary made her accusation. Indeed, he is angrier at Mannix than his own brother, whom he dismisses as weak: 'but

Mannix could have helped. He also knew that I would never try a thing like that. But he never lifted a finger. I didn't fit into the scheme of things and so I was got rid of.'[29]

In the narrative present, Willie's return makes Michael and Mary anxious, though we never precisely understand what threat they perceive from Willie. In their conversations with other characters, we only hear of their concern for others: that Willie will not 'settle' and would be happier back in the asylum; for Chris having to care for Willie when he gets older; above all, for Willie's 'soul'. However, Willie never confronts them about the past and seems disinterested in demanding any explanation or exacting any retribution. When he goes through the motions of religious observance and takes Communion at a mass held at Summerhill it is, he later admits to Mannix, a strategic submission to conformity – the price he is willing to pay to be allowed to live out his life comfortably in his home. Mary and Michael's spiritual concerns – in so far as we can assume any substance to them – are thus assuaged, as, more importantly, are their pragmatic concerns that he will refuse to adhere passively to social conventions. And, of course, his death soon after provides an even more definitive solution to this disruptive presence.

Strikingly, the plot is centrally focused on the relationship between Mannix and Willie, and much of the present narrative, especially in the latter part of the novel, consists of a series of conversations between the two, now elderly, men. Confronted by Willie's unsettling tone – gentle friendliness lapsing abruptly into camp frivolity or gnomic opaqueness – the priest finds his authority and self-assuredness undermined. In response he lurches from self-exculpatory apology to violent anger to resignation; there are even shared moments of humour and friendly conviviality, as when they sit down to play chess. At the core of this series of conversations is the priest's impassioned pleading with Willie to consider reconciling with his religion, and Willie's sometimes camp, but nevertheless implacable, refusal to do so. In an earlier conversation Willie says he has forgiven Mannix. But then, in their culminating encounter after the mass, he exacts his revenge. Willie lets the priest know that he received Communion that morning without attending Confession, and his sacrilegious reason for doing so – to secure the family's compliance to his wish to stay out of the asylum. Moreover, he confronts Mannix with the fact that years before Roger continued to meet Willie, while maintaining to the priest that he had stopped doing so, and that Roger's religious conformity was entirely insincere. Thus, Willie undermines Mannix's conception of what unfolded: that Roger had been 'reformed' and given up his 'vice'; that it was Willie who had led Roger into 'sin', when in fact Roger had 'seduced' Willie, who 'hated it; but I did it because I loved him'.[30] Mannix had earlier recalled his deathbed conversation with Roger, but now Willie challenges him to consider that even this was part of the charade. Mannix maintains that this makes no sense: 'it wouldn't have been necessary to keep it up to the bitter end. There was no more acting to do'. But Willie persists with his attack: '"How can you be sure, Father?" Willie went on inexorably, "Roger hated you. You wrecked his life. You made him live a lie. You took from him the only person he loved ... and in the end he defeated you and your kind of religion. Holy water and pious aspirations! They didn't save you from being mocked at the edge of the grave. You believe what you want to believe about Roger. But you can't be sure now, can you?"'[31]

Aside from the concluding chapter after the funeral, the novel ends with Mrs Whittaker, Roger's sister, visiting the ailing Willie. She tells Willie that before he died her brother had confided in her about their relationship, that he 'wasn't lying in the end ... the only thing he worried about was you', and that Willie was the last person he spoke about.[32] Receiving this affirmation of his and Roger's love leaves Willie weeping but peaceful; we find out that he died that night. However, while the story ends there the plot reaches its dramatic climax earlier in Willie's confrontation with Mannix, and the dismaying, shattering effect it has on the priest. The shape of the plot – the focus and method of Willie's retribution – provokes questions about how to interpret this novel.

One possible approach is to view the novel as work of critical realism. Viewed from a historical-sociological perspective we could investigate what the story tells us about the use of institutional incarceration in mid-twentieth century Ireland to enforce a rigid code of respectability, conformity and sexual repression, but also to secure ownership of property in a society where the rights of property dominated just as much as the demands of sexual morality. As Willie's story demonstrates, such incarceration involved the explicit or tacit collaboration of family, state and Church. Nevertheless, it is not entirely clear how much the novel deepens our understanding of the familial, social and political dynamics underpinning the widespread incarceration of those deemed as sexual dissidents – most numerously the women incarcerated in Magdalene Laundries – at this time. As we have seen, the emphasis of the plot is on Willie's confrontation with Mannix, rather than with his family, even though he concedes that Mannix's role involved passively failing to intervene rather than actively conspiring to incarcerate him. In contrast with the diminished Mannix – our final sight of him is a character commenting on his strange behaviour, 'swaying and muttering like he was going to fall in', while conducting Willie's burial service – the family's equilibrium and complacency is restored.[33] Mary and Michael are not forced to account for their conduct, and there is no sense of justice being achieved, or even sought, by Willie.

The climax of the plot turns on a sharp reversal of perspective – from disenchanted rational critique of social hypocrisy to unselfconscious assent to a divinely ordered numinous universe. Or, in aesthetic and narratological terms, there is a sudden movement from the characteristic irony of literary realism to the literal truth of received tradition. For the reader to fully grasp the dismaying effect of Willie's revenge on Mannix they must sympathetically inhabit – however provisionally – a religious, and specifically Catholic, world view. From a secular perspective, Willie's orchestration of his confrontation with the priest is rather perplexing and Mannix's reaction hysterically overwrought. To grasp the emotional depth of Mannix's dismay we must 'believe' that taking Communion as Willie does is profoundly sacrilegious – to read it, in a secular mode, as hypocrisy or conformity cannot explain how shattering it is to Mannix. *The Pilgrimage* ends with a similar reversal of secular and religious perspectives, though even more dramatically achieved. The final chapter is just one sentence: 'In this way they set off on their pilgrimage, from which a week later Michael returned completely cured.'[34] That ending requires the reader's emotional assent to a religious structure of feeling and to the 'fact' of a miraculous cure. Thus, the reader is forced, as it were, to recognise a definite distinction between religion as a worldly institution, indistinguishable from the social infrastructure of bourgeois capitalism, and religion as a structure of thought and feeling. (This contrast is reiterated in *The Pilgrimage*; Michael Glynn made his fortune constructing religious buildings and a bishop, acting like the manager of a corporation rather than spiritual leader, comes to discuss tenders for a new school.)

In enacting his retribution on Mannix, and in the way which he achieves this, Willie does not stake a claim to justice, much less to any recognisable conception of sexual freedom. As we have noted, he repeatedly distances himself from the sexual desires and demands of his brother and Roger. Like Stephen in *The Pilgrimage*, he is profoundly committed to an ideal of homosocial friendship, in which emotional and spiritual connection merges with cross-generational, and cross-class, transmission of cultural capital: male friendship combining *agape* and apprenticeship, but without Eros. In other words, Willie is not a pervert in the modern sexual sense, and his story cannot easily be interpreted within any homophile or post-Stonewall narrative of homophobic oppression. At most we could read his stated aversion to sexual intimacy and his self-portrayal as someone coerced into sex through a psychological lens as a symptom of repression and internalised self-hatred. But, as with the historical-sociological mode of reading the novel in light of later revelations about incarceration and abuse, such a psychological or 'case study' style of reading requires muting the characteristic tone and simplifying the idiosyncratic world view of Broderick's fiction. Paradoxically, we might say that it would require straightening out rather than queering the novels.

Instead, Willie stakes a claim to authenticity – to an unalienated form of life, imaged in that ideal of male friendship – rather than to justice. He strikes at Mannix's faith from the perspective of a more authentic form of faith rather than from the perspective of secular unbelief. In short, his perversion is closer to that of the heretic than the homosexual. Indeed, Willie is figured through various forms of religious iconography: martyrdom – suffering for fidelity to his beliefs (that personal credo of honesty and friendship); resurrection – returning inexplicably from the death-in-life of the asylum; prophecy – uncannily foretelling his own death, as he does a number of times. Moreover, religion merges with Romanticism, as the figuration of Willie as saint or holy man is emphatically registered through his instinctive connection with the landscape and with animals. Thus, our first view of Willie, through the eyes of Mrs Whittaker, is of a solitary figure standing contemplatively beneath a large beech tree. Unaware of her presence, he was 'holding out his hand to catch a leaf … fluttering to the ground, changing colour in the dappled shade from red to purple, until it rested on his palm, light and yellow as a brimstone butterfly. The stranger covered it with his other hand, touching it as gently as a blind child fondling a doll.'[35]

Again, as with Stephen, we notice the recurrence of the image of the child, thereby evoking the innocence conventionally imputed to childhood. Moreover, the image is of a 'blind child', associating Willie with dependence, vulnerability and powerlessness, while simultaneously gesturing to his empowering rage against hypocrisy and sharper perception of the truth hidden beneath the simulacrum of appearance and respectability; his 'blindness' to convention allows him to 'see' more clearly. The lyrically aestheticised evocation of the leaf – movement; colour; simile evoking a creature of decorative beauty beyond any obvious necessity – contrasts with a description of Mary's tea table in the next chapter: 'the Crown Derby cups, the silver kettle, the Carrickmacross lace'.[36] This list, in prose that is functionally devoid of imagery, indexes how, in this household, the spontaneous, instinctive human gesture of hospitality is subordinated to ostentatious consumerism, and to the display and performance demanded by social respectability. Human relations are hollowed out by utilitarianism – Michael notes the objects indicate 'an important visitor' – and alienation.

Obviously, there is nothing especially original about this literary deployment of childhood and 'nature' as symbolic guarantors of authenticity and moral integrity, and as a rebuke to the artificiality and hypocrisy of society and 'culture'. It is, after all, almost everywhere in English literature since Romanticism, while having earlier antecedents in the pastoral. What is striking in Broderick's fiction is that those figures embodying childlike and natural innocence are at the same time malevolent; vulnerable, like a child, and yet also threateningly sinister like Stephen or capriciously cruel like Willie. Halloran's disturbed response to hearing Willie's account of his final confrontation with Mannix encourages us to feel that Willie, though hardly without motive, was needlessly ruthless in exacting his revenge. Likewise, while Broderick's 'wayward women' – Julia and Lily – are shown to be ensnared by the deep-seated misogyny and sexual double standards of their society, and subject to the hypocritical strategizing and sexual violence of men, they are never entirely sympathetic.

Unlike the male figures of perversion they are more 'realistic', lacking in idealism and cynically willing to compromise to gain sexual pleasure and material security.

Of Broderick's pervert figures the most explicitly political is Hugh Ward in *The Fugitives*. In many ways, he conforms to various generic types. He is the type of literary terrorist familiar since Joseph Conrad's *The Secret Agent* (1907): a psychopathic criminal, spouting clichéd political slogans to mask his actual motivation. Likewise, the novel's dominant tone is determined by proliferating Gothic tropes: the Fallon home is a claustrophobic house hiding secrets; Hetty, a usurping, unloving step-mother; Aunt Kate, the nun-like figure shut away from the world. Within this frame Hugh becomes a disturbingly charismatic and manipulative Gothic villain who embodies a motiveless evil. Thus, after a conversation with Kate, which has left her deeply upset but which serves no plot function and from which Hugh has nothing to gain, we have this description: 'his eyes were sparkling with excitement in the dim light of the landing and he was laughing quietly to himself'.[37] From Kate's perspective Hugh's motivation for his political activity is a profound emotional and psychological lack which instinctively draws him towards those, like Paddy and Lily, who are vulnerable and susceptible to his manipulation: people like Hugh 'coil around others, knowing exactly their weak spots where eventually they will tighten their hold and strangle their prey. Because in the end they always destroy ... they're bloodsuckers, vampires.'[38]

In a familiar convention of the popular romance, Lily's deep hostility towards Hugh mutates into, or, more accurately, perversely merges with sexual attraction. At the same time, Lily believes that she has uncovered the psychosexual motivation that is the 'real' spur to Hugh's involvement with the IRA. Unlike the other two novels, here the narrative is discreetly imprecise about the relationship between the older and younger man. Thus, Lily hears from Paddy's room 'the murmur of voices and the sudden gurgle of intimate laughter'.[39] Adult emotions and sensuality, 'intimate', are jarringly juxtaposed with 'gurgle', a sound associated with infants. More directly we see Paddy drunkenly telling Hugh how much he depends on him – 'I don't know what I'd do if you weren't here' – but then recoiling when Hugh goes to comfort him. Hugh angrily accuses him of being repressed, fearful and manipulative: '"You're afraid aren't you? ... there are too many people like you", Ward went on passionately, "too many hypocrites. They want to be admired without giving anything in return. They recognise something with their bodies and their skins, that they want, but they won't commit themselves because they are afraid."'[40] Hugh's exasperated claim that 'this has gone on too long' lets us know that this is not just a drunken incident but part of an ongoing relationship. By the end of the novel Lily has intuited this aspect of their relationship and interprets the motivation for Hugh's political commitments as entirely sexual, while positioning her brother as his prey. As the police close in and Paddy is about to be shot, she tells her brother to run because 'you could have bought your freedom anytime if you had given him the filthy thing he was looking for ... do you know what he thought you were, do you, Paddy? He doesn't give a damn for Ireland, or freedom, or martyrs or all the rest of that nonsense. He only wanted you.'[41]

Reading Broderick's fiction as realism would require approaching these figures as characters – that is, motivated by unconscious needs and desires shaped, or determined, by history. Thus, we might, for instance, consider Lily and Paddy as orphans, and how the loss of their parents at a young age left them emotionally vulnerable to manipulative men. Like Paddy's dependent relationship with Hugh, Lily's relationship with a married man in London has left her with no independent life of her own. Moreover, we might wonder, to what degree did the piety, hypocrisy and snobbery of their native town – indexed by the choric conversations between Hetty and Mrs Lagan, dripping with bitterness, spite and assertions of pious conformity – contribute to the loveless childhood that has so disabled them? Entombed in a self-willed living death in reaction against the religious faith of her younger self, Kate's fate might be considered a chilling indictment of this society. Likewise, we could consider the effects of those repressive gender and sexual norms that produced Paddy's conflicted performance of masculinity, alternating between overwrought machismo and 'effeminate' hysteria and coquetry.

But how are we to incorporate the figure of Hugh into this style of reading? The novel offers us various routes towards grasping his motivations. The evidence of his encounter with Paddy, along with Kate and Lily's judgement on him, implies that he is primarily impelled by thwarted homosexual desires, merely abusing involvement in politics to possessively control a vulnerable younger man. Yet whenever the omniscient narrator is, so to speak, 'alone' with Hugh, and we might expect some focalised narration giving us insight into his consciousness, all we encounter are puzzling and bizarre images. Thus, his 'sparkling' eyes and devilish laugh as he stands alone on the landing, for instance. Most strangely, one episode narrates Hugh leaving the Fallon house, going to a hotel room and sitting in the dark to play with an expensive set of toy soldiers he has brought from London. At no point in the novel are we given any explanation for this or any way to assimilate it into the plot. Along with being narratively confusing the episode is tonally disconcerting. On one hand, the tension of a 'gunman' and 'criminal' evading the police – 'Ward walked quickly through the narrow, rain-lashed streets of the town' – and the disconcerting reversal of time, adulthood to childhood, heightened by the Gothic distortions of this figure in the gloom: 'the naked bulb threw down a harsh glare in front of the looking-glass and for a moment he could not see his reflection'. On the other, Hugh innocently absorbed in child's play: 'neatly, delicately ... he arranged and re-arranged the soldiers in different patterns, now placing them in a single line across the carpet to the bed, now forming them into squares, carts, cart-wheels'.[42]

To confuse our perception of Hugh further, near the end of the novel – as the police close in on the abandoned house in the bog where Hugh, Paddy and Lily are hiding – he unexpectedly asserts his political beliefs.

> The dim shape did not move; but the voice rolled out, rich and persuasive.
>
> 'What do you know of this country? And what do you care? Have you ever really given it a thought in the last ten years? Have you ever thought about it at all in the whole of your life? There hasn't been enough bloodshed and it must always be like this until we get what we are fighting for. Forty years ago men died in this country for an ideal. The ideal was a free and undivided Ireland. They have been betrayed. We are not free. We are still divided. And what is being done about it? Nothing. Who cares about the forty thousand people who are exported from this country every year like cattle? A few pious platitudes and then silence. That's all that's done about it. What have those men died for? A smug little corporation, run by professional politicians who have no interest except self-interest.

> They have canonised the men of Nineteen Sixteen; written them up like plaster saints in the schoolbooks because every racket needs its martyrs. Not a day passes but one of the racketeers makes a speech about the Border. Nobody believes what they say; they don't even believe it themselves anymore. Is it any wonder that Ireland today is the most cynical country in the world? It is, you know. I've been around and I know. None of these racketeers want the Border removed. What would happen if we had a large and powerful Protestant minority? Has anything ever really been done about a united Ireland? Aren't they only playing with words? That and a few border posts blown up, a few policemen shot. Who cares about policemen? They don't count with politicians. But now that something has really been done, what do we find? The whole of Scotland Yard working over here with the Irish Government because we dared to do the same thing that put most of the racketeers or their fathers in power. Because for the first time something irreparable has been done. Something they can't blow away with words.'
>
> The beautiful disembodied voice went on…[43]

As with the ending of *Borstal Boy*, here the reader is challenged to revise their understanding of twentieth-century Irish history. Where Behan's concluding dialogue used linguistic playfulness and comic irony to subvert the self-conception of the Irish 'Free' State, Broderick deploys a blunt, interrogatory style of political rhetoric to confront the verities of the Irish 'Republic'. Despite the divergence in tone, in both instances the political effect rests on a series of conceptual reversals: independence is actually dependence; freedom is actually continued unfreedom; a transformative rupture with the imperialist world-system is actually continued conformity with its hegemonic logic. In Broderick this effect is amplified through various rhetorical permutations on the category of epistemological and political realism. Hugh contrasts the idealism of the revolutionary generation with their descendants' cynical adaptation to reality, a historical declension figured by the dynamism of the Easter 1916 leaders now calcified in the inert substance of 'plaster'. Yet it transpires that the idealists – and their heirs in the present – are actually the more thoroughgoing realists. It is they, Hugh implies, who can honestly confront the material and human consequences of underdevelopment – 'exported … like cattle' – or think through the actual demographic, cultural and political consequences of Irish unity. But the conceptual energy of the idealist's subversive challenge ultimately rests not on the unavoidable solidity of the real but on the performative capacity of imagination: on the call to imaginatively supplant the prevailing telos of Irish history with an alternative narrative where partition and the counter-revolution of the 1920s and 1930s never happened. Thus, for instance, Hugh's reminder about the demographics of reunification can be read as a practical – realistic – reminder that the institutional and ideological conformity of the Irish State with the Catholic Church would invariably be sundered by the end of partition. At the same time there is a more far-reaching challenge embedded in Hugh's reference to Protestantism. Imagining what Ireland would look like without partition requires confronting the gap between the 'Irish Republic' as it exists in 1962 and the model of secular, democratic Irish republicanism that had historically developed from the eighteenth century onwards – a political tradition to which Irish Protestants, such as Tone and Henry Joy McCracken, notably made a formative contribution.

This odd disruption into the narrative of Hugh's extended monologue – playing, like Behan, with a political genre: the 'speech from the dock' – challenges the reader to respond to him less as villain or psychopath than as rational political actor. The evidence of his speech implies that he is motivated by sincerely held political ideals. But again, as so frequently in Broderick's fiction, tone and perspective are unstable and confusing. Within quotation marks, the speech is clearly distinguished from those authorial interventions that, as we have noted, mar Broderick's fiction. As such Hugh's position is susceptible to subversion, irony and satire. Most obviously, it is potentially undermined by the perspectives of Kate and Lily – the view that this is all bluster and 'nonsense', in Lily's phrase, to mask his psychosexual motivations and his predatory, vampiric manipulation of Paddy's vulnerability. The prose style too contributes to undermining Hugh's perspective. Reiterating again that Gothic mood, the subject of the introductory sentence is a disembodied 'dim shape' and 'voice', which is then repeated: 'the beautiful disembodied voice went on'. Instead of a character expressing ideas we have language emanating from an apparitional or ghostly presence. As the hectoring and interrogatory tone – the unrelenting series of questions leaving no space for answer – suggests, this figure is not concerned with communicating but with exerting control. Yet the voice is also 'beautiful' and so not just threatening but seductive. In a queer echo of the Irish literary tradition, as with the Jacobite *spéirbhean* or Cathleen ni Houlihan (as reimagined by James Clarence Mangan or by Lady Gregory, Yeats and Maud Gonne) the erotic allure of the speaker, that the voice is 'beautiful' and thus 'persuasive', reinforces the performative impact – the call to political consciousness and action. In addition, while author and narrator may be sceptical about Hugh's republicanism, his emphasis on 'realism', as an epistemological category and the excoriating political critique such realism facilitates, aligns with the novel's aesthetic. Throughout the novel we see Hugh confronting other characters – Kate, Lily, Paddy – with unpalatable truths, just as he confronts the reader here – and just as confronting the 'Irish Catholic bourgeoisie' with the truth about its hypocrisy is central to Broderick's style.

As we have seen, the radical potential of Broderick's novels is not to be found in its manifest aesthetic and political commitments: to the descriptive and critical capacity of naturalism; to the subversive potential of satire and irony; to the liberal ideal of freedom of action and conscience for the individual; to the value of personal integrity and authenticity. Rather that potential is to be found in the fiction's abrasive aesthetic effects on the reader. The sources of these effects include: an unstable hybrid of generic plot types, narrative figures and tropes; narrative linearity yielding to patterns of recurrence; disjunctive coexistence of narrative modes (realism of the social novel; anti-realism of the tale or parable), narrative moods (satirically comic; tragic) and epistemologies (secular; religious). These aesthetic effects cluster most acutely around Broderick's perverts, and more specifically the homoerotic male body as perverse.

We could read the novels as staging a recurring conflict between perverts and converts. And in a characteristic reversal, the converts are revealed as perverts – cynical deviants from the ideals of their religion, national history and social class – while the perverts are the real converts – steadfast adherents to the true and the authentic. In this way, the oddness of the perverse figures could be accommodated to more reassuring liberal political commitments by buttressing our conception of individual integrity pitted against social conformity and hypocrisy. But, as we have seen, such a reading founders on the inscrutable ambiguities and paradoxes of Broderick's perverts – their perversity as it were – so that they resist incorporation into any of the reassuringly heroic historical narratives beloved of the liberal imagination. Rather than forming points of comforting identification for the reader these perverts form points of potential disidentification.

Reviewing *The Pilgrimage* in the *Irish Times*, on its publication, the journalist Maurice Kennedy observed of its terse concluding chapter – 'In this way they set off on their pilgrimage, from which a week later Michael returned completely cured' – that 'the climax could depend as easily on an operation at the Mayo Clinic as a pilgrimage to Lourdes'.[44] That humorous dismissal and studied cosmopolitan tone suggests some embarrassment about Broderick's uncompromising ending, with its refusal of any sheltering irony for the secular imagination. Clearly his fiction was an irritant to the still dominant conservative and reactionary post-independence political formation – it was banned by the Irish censorship board – but that did not mean that it could easily be assimilated to the emergent modernising political formation either. Likewise, as a writer who dissented from the dominant Catholic middle-class culture of the mid-century, and, moreover, addressed dissident sexual and gender identities along with sexual repression and shame, one would expect Broderick to be ripe for recovery by contemporary Irish literary studies. That this has not happened suggests something intractable to current critical modes about Broderick's fiction, making it difficult to assimilate to contemporary political positions – across the spectrum – and difficult to assimilate to contemporary gender and sexual politics.

But perhaps this is what is most valuable about Broderick's fiction. The content of the political imagination in these novels is of limited interest. After all, identifying another liberal, but in substance conservative, bourgeois writer committed to the satiric mode and naturalist aesthetic is unlikely to significantly alter our understanding of Irish literary history. Of more substantial critical interest are the political amplifications of that perverse structure of feeling in this fiction. Broderick created pervert figures animating the subversive potential immanent to the social order and embodying the threat posed by religious and political heretics who perversely adhere to anachronistic values. Perhaps what makes this fiction so intractable for contemporary literary criticism is that perversity is not the substratum for a politics of identity – as readers we are not required to *identify with* these figures – but of insurrection. Broderick's queer perverts leave us feeling unsettled and ambivalent. But then again, whatever threatens to radically undermine the social order – in contrast with any reformist politics to modify it – must, by definition, be frightening and unsettling.

Notes

1. Lectures delivered at the 2001 event were published in Gearoid O'Brien (ed.), *Proceedings of the Second John Broderick Weekend* (Athlone: The John Broderick Committee, 2001). On the residency scholarship see Eamon Maher, 'John Broderick: "a fugitive from a superior civilisation"', *Irish Times* (23 February 2018).
2. On Broderick's life and work see Madeline Kingston, *Something in the Head: the life and work of John Broderick* (Dublin: Lilliput Press, 2004). Accessible and informative, this biography is nevertheless written from the appreciative perspective of a friend; the absence of a scholarly critical biography indicates the limited interest Broderick's work has attracted in Irish literary studies. A selection of Broderick's reviews is available in Madeline Kingston (ed.), *Stimulus of Sin: selected writings of John Broderick* (Dublin: Lilliput Press, 2007).
3. Kingston, *Something in the Head*, p. 64.
4. Eamon Maher, 'John Broderick (1924–89) and the French "Roman Catholique"', in E. Maher, E. O'Brien and G. Neville (eds), *Reinventing Ireland through a French Prism* (Frankfurt: Peter Laing, 2007), p. 261. See also Eamon Maher, 'Representations of Catholicism in the twentieth-century Irish novel' in L. Fuller, J. Littleton and E. Maher (eds), *Irish and Catholic?: towards an understanding of identity* (Dublin: Columba Press, 2006), pp. 111–15.
5. See the interview with Broderick in Julia Carlson (ed.), *Banned in Ireland: censorship and the Irish writer* (London: Routledge, 1990), pp. 39–51.
6. David Nowlan, 'Novelists speak about writing: realists without realism', *Irish Times* (28 August 1970), p. 10.
7. Patrick Murray, 'Athlone's John Broderick', *Eire-Ireland*, 27:4 (1992), 20–39, 24. Murray's essay offers a comprehensive and rigorous assessment of Broderick's fiction, with some perceptive critical judgements. But Murray's critical skills abruptly desert him when he tries to respond to Broderick's only developed and humane depiction of same-sex passion between men in *The Trials of Father Dillingham*

(1982). Murray abandons analysis for inanely vacuous moralising; the precipitous intellectual decline is registered by the descent of his prose into comically Victorian clichés about 'vice' and 'sodomy'.

8   In what follows, I use 'perverse' where I could just as effectively use 'queer' – or, more precisely, 'quare' in Noreen Giffney's innovative and suggestive Hibernicisation of that term – not to denominate a taxonomic identity but an insurrectionary practice, at once sexual, cultural and political. As should become clear, I choose 'perverse' and 'pervert' primarily because their anachronistic undertone suits the characteristic structure of feeling in Broderick's fiction. See Noreen Giffney, 'Quare theory' in W. Balzano, A. Mulhall and M. Sullivan (eds), *Irish Postmodernisms and Popular Culture* (Basingstoke: Palgrave Macmillan, 2007), pp. 197–209.
9   Jonathan Dollimore, *Sexual Dissidence* (Oxford: Oxford University Press, 1991), p. 106.
10 Dollimore, *Sexual Dissidence*, p. 126.
11 Dollimore, *Sexual Dissidence*, p. 143. And here we might note the similarity between this dialectical relationship between perversity and orthodoxy and Sedgwick's characterisation of the relationship between homosexuality and heterosexual masculinity, defined by that contradictory tension between minoritising and universalising logics.
12 Dollimore, *Sexual Dissidence*, p. 125.
13 Dollimore, *Sexual Dissidence*, p. 237.
14 Dollimore, *Sexual Dissidence*, p. 119.
15 *Ibid.*
16 Dollimore, *Sexual Dissidence*, p. 273.
17 For a useful discussion of the political valences of the literary homosexual in contemporaneous British fiction see Alan Sinfield, *Literature, Politics and Culture in Post-War Britain* (London: Continuum, 3rd edn, 2004), pp. 68–96.
18 John Broderick, *The Pilgrimage* (London: Weidenfeld and Nicolson, 1961), p. 51.
19 Broderick, *Pilgrimage*, p. 18.
20 John Broderick, *The Waking of Willie Ryan* (London: Weidenfeld and Nicolson, 1965), pp. 66 and 112.
21 Broderick, *Pilgrimage*, p. 50.
22 Broderick, *Pilgrimage*, pp. 71–2.
23 Broderick, *Pilgrimage*, pp. 37–8.
24 Broderick, *Pilgrimage*, p. 126.
25 Broderick, *Pilgrimage*, p. 96.
26 Broderick, *Waking*, p. 115.
27 *Ibid.*

28 Broderick, *Waking*, p. 114.
29 Broderick, *Waking*, p. 115.
30 Broderick, *Waking*, p. 158.
31 Broderick, *Waking*, p. 160.
32 Broderick, *Waking*, p. 185.
33 Broderick, *Waking*, p. 187.
34 Broderick, *Pilgrimage*, p. 140.
35 Broderick, *Waking*, p. 11.
36 Broderick, *Waking*, p. 12.
37 John Broderick, *The Fugitives* (London: Weidenfeld and Nicolson, 1962), p. 87.
38 Broderick, *Fugitives*, p. 126.
39 Broderick, Fugitives, p. 43.
40 Broderick, *Fugitives*, p. 90.
41 Broderick, *Fugitives*, p. 167.
42 Broderick, *Fugitives*, p. 93.
43 Broderick, *Fugitives*, pp. 163–4.
44 Maurice Kennedy, 'Middle-class morality?', *Irish Times* (28 January 1961), p. 6.

3

Colm Tóibín: feeling neoliberal

Colm Tóibín's trio of gay-themed novels – *The Story of the Night* (1996), *The Blackwater Lightship* (1999) and *The Master* (2004) – poses two questions. One question concerns literary style and the aesthetics of representation. How should a writer incorporate the distinctive social and psychic experiences of gay men in the twentieth century into the novel form? Or, in an alternative formulation, how might a writer use the conventions of realist fiction to give expression to those modern forms of consciousness – homosexual; queer; gay – that evolved during that time? The other question is interpretive and political. What are the political valences of the different artistic choices a writer might make to achieve this end? What are the symbolic and cultural resonances of these decisions about literary style?

To that aesthetic question Tóibín's fiction offers two distinctive responses. One is to use the conventions of realism to construct gay male characters, and to incorporate those characters into inherited genres and plot types: specifically, the *bildungsroman* (*The Story of the Night*) and the family or generational narrative (*The Blackwater Lightship*). In this way, Tóibín strives to depict, directly and frankly, the lives of modern gay men – embedded in identifiable historical conditions – in fiction. But Tóibín also pursues a different style and narrative mode, in which erotic, specifically homoerotic, energies are sublimated into the text to generate powerful effects and symbolic resonances. These effects are particularly condensed around ways of writing the male body as a location of pleasure and pain. In short, we could summarise the distinction between these two styles in terms of the salience of different narrative figures in each: 'characters' and 'bodies'.

Assessing the various political and symbolic resonances of these two literary modes we encounter a paradox. When the political imaginary of Tóibín's fiction is most closely in alignment with a progressive sexual politics – concerned to depict the lives of modern gay men as richly complex through creating compelling, resonant stories about their lives – is also when it is most conservative; not illiberal or reactionary but most fully in conformity with the hegemonic norms and values of its historical times. And when the concerns and obsessions of the fiction seem furthest removed from progressive sexual politics – when the novels are most absorbed with the tragic and with the melancholy erotics of the closet – is also when the political imagination of this fiction is potentially most radical and disruptive to those hegemonic norms.

Generically, the *bildungsroman* and the family/generational plot have a common structure, in which a subjective narrative – the story of the individual – and a generational narrative – the story of the family – is symbolically established in conjunction with a historical narrative. In Tóibín's case this historical narrative can be conceptualised in national terms (the 'stories' of Argentina and Ireland) or, more usefully, in terms of historical currents: the transformation of sexual norms by late twentieth-century social movements; globalisation; the neoliberal transformation of societies, cultural norms and subjectivities.

In *The Story of the Night*, this narrative conjunction is directly evoked from the outset. Richard's first-person narration begins with his recollections of his late mother. His maternal grandfather came to Argentina from Britain and his mother's manic Anglophile obsession with 'the emblems of empire' intensified as she declined.[1] At first, the tone of this opening – retrospection, decline, melancholic nostalgia – appears out of synch with the affirmative current of the ensuing narrative. Richard achieves material success and attains sexual and emotional fulfilment with Pablo, after childhood isolation and poverty. At the same time, Argentina transitions from brutal repression under the Generals to democratic freedom during the 1980s. But in both instances this optimism is undermined. Richard and Pablo's happiness is disrupted traumatically by the sudden onset of illness and learning that they have acquired HIV. The promise of a democratic Argentina is replaced by Richard's gradual realisation that the emergent Argentinean democracy is effectively a stratagem of US power – embodied by his friends, Susan and Donald – and that the country has become an experiment in neoliberal 'shock therapy'.[2] The intimation of early death, after the news of Richard and Pablo's HIV infection, casts the foregoing narrative in grieving retrospection which makes clear the significance of the sombre opening mood. The novel ends with the two men standing by the sea near the house they share, but as it begins with Richard, addressing us in the present tense, alone at his late mother's apartment, we are left to assume that in the intervening time Pablo has died. And, in light of the contrapuntal rhythm – the play of optimism and pessimism – of the entwined biographical and historical narratives – Richard's recollections of his late mother's Anglophilia now take on a political as well as a familial significance. To what degree, the novel asks, is the emerging neoliberal, globalising order, in which Richard can apparently secure material and sexual freedom, merely a different phase in the same capitalist and imperialist world system; a different hegemon exercising a different style of power?

In *The Blackwater Lightship* Declan, a young gay man gravely ill with AIDS-related illnesses, travels from his hospital bed in Dublin to his grandmother's house in County Wexford for a final visit. There he is cared for by his grandmother, Dora, his mother, Lily, and his sister, Helen – along with his friends, Paul and Larry. Declan kept his illness, and that he is gay, from his mother and grandmother. While Helen knew that he was gay she knew nothing of his illness. One index of how little she knows of her brother's life is that she does not know Paul when he arrives at her house to tell her how ill Declan is.

Notably, Declan is not the narrator and his perspective and consciousness is registered very little in the third-person narration; his fear, anxiety, hope and despair are mainly reported by other characters rather than narrated. Instead, the narration is focalised around Helen. The prose style of the third-person narration is ostentatiously, and according to Tóibín deliberately, bland: tonally flat and syntactically simple descriptions of daily life.[3] Thus the dramatic and emotional focus is confined to the extended sections of dialogue and to extended sections of narration framed as Helen's childhood memories. Those memories pivot on what Helen now recognises as the originary trauma that has shaped her emotional life; her father's death, when she was 11 and Declan was 8, and their sense of abandonment because they were sent to their grandparents' house (the house to which Declan returns in the narrative present) while their mother went to stay in Dublin with their dying father. Young Helen's feeling of emotional neglect is exacerbated when their grieving mother returns, is seemingly indifferent to her children's grief and maintains, as the child perceives it, a chill distance from her daughter. From this the estrangement between mother and daughter deepened, leading to a final rupture when Helen, having trained as a schoolteacher in Dublin, refuses her mother and grandmother's injunction to return to Wexford and pursue her career there. This estrangement is most obviously indexed by the revelation that Lily has never met her son-in-law or two young grandchildren. The novel depicts Dora in a warmer, more appreciative light than her daughter, particularly through her lively, humorous dialogue flavoured with local turns of phrase – yet Helen, in conversation with Paul, recalls her carelessness towards the grandchildren left in her care and, most sharply, the summers of exploitative, unappreciated drudgery spent working in Dora's guesthouse during her student years.

In this way narrating modern Irish gay men's lives – complex relationships with their families; distinctively varied texture of their sexual and emotional relationships; HIV, and the devastation of AIDS, powerfully shaping erotic and emotional reality – is embedded within, and, as critics have noted, subordinated to, a family narrative.[4] This type of plot has been significantly favoured by Tóibín's generation of Irish novelists, a choice that has generally met with approval from readers, reviewers and academic critics. It provided the template for Tóibín's first two novels – *The South* (1990) and *The Heather Blazing* (1992) – and has featured prominently in the work of his notable contemporaries, such as Ann Enright, Sebastian Barry and Roddy Doyle. Arguably, these were also following a pattern laid down by distinguished predecessors in the previous generation, most notably Edna O'Brien and John McGahern (of whom Tóibín, as a young journalist, wrote appreciatively).[5] In this plot type family as such is emotionally problematic – a space of conflict, alienation and psychic wounds – but narratively productive. The reverberation of these conflicts and wounds across generational time – the emotional climate of the protagonist's present determined by their past – propels the plot. The web of familial relationships in these novels determines the narrative horizon, though the family plot is also expected to symbolically echo with the reverberation of the national historical narrative. Thus, through a story of suicide, childhood neglect, abuse, sibling love and estrangement in one family, Enright's *The Gathering* (2007) confronts the disclosures about child sexual abuse in Ireland since the 1990s. In *The Heather Blazing* Eamon Redmond is, like Helen, emotionally disabled by the early death of his mother and his father's subsequent distance. But he is a senior judge, in which role he adjudicates on politically fraught constitutional cases, including the state's regulation of sexual morality and private life, in the novel's present. Through the narration of his career the novel interrogates the conservative project of modernisation propelled most actively by Fianna Fáil from the 1960s. (And here we might note that Tóibín's family were heavily involved with that political party in Wexford.)

So far, we have identified one of Tóibín's responses to the aesthetic problem of depicting gay men's lives. That approach can be framed in terms of genre, story and character. By contrast, his alternative response to this aesthetic problem is primarily a matter of prose style, mood and tone. In an interview with Fintan O'Toole, Tóibín argues that 'in a plain statement you can bury emotion. You do not specify the emotion, it is not named but it's there ... it comes as plain statement containing emotion somehow in the rhythm, the cadence. The writer is managing emotion, but not declaring its presence.'[6] Elsewhere, in his collection of critical essays *Love in a Dark Time*, Tóibín develops a theory of literary sexual politics premised on this insight – emotions and feelings expressed most powerfully in writing that is rigorously 'managed'. His argument encompasses authors, such as James Baldwin and Thom Gunn, who openly identified as gay; of Gunn's poetic response to the AIDS pandemic in *The Man with Night Sweats* (1992) he praises 'the play between the wounded elegiac voice and the poems' formal, almost impersonal tone'.[7] However, he particularly associates this alchemy of repressed feeling into resonantly expressive literature as intrinsic to the artistic achievements of an earlier generation of novelists – Thomas Mann and Henry James – who were compelled by their historical conditions to supress their homosexual desires, and in the case of Mann to live a life of respectable and fertile heterosexuality. Thus, of Mann Tóibín writes: 'he saved his desire, his erotic energy, his secret sexuality for his work'.[8]

This paradox – the psychosocial condition that we now term 'closetedness' as simultaneously destructive and creative – is the central thematic concern of *The Master*. Focalised around the consciousness of Henry James, as speculatively reconstructed by Tóibín – a Jamesian novel about Henry James – the novel conjures the oppressive homophobia of Anglo-American culture in the late nineteenth century and the inhibiting psychic ramifications of that culture. An early chapter narrates Henry's intense fascination with Wilde's trial, suggesting that the terrifying example of the Irish playwright's spectacular shaming and punishment definitively solidifies the American novelist's deliberate repression of his homoerotic desires. In Tóibín's telling, Henry's consciousness is shaped by the dialectic of powerful passions incited by male bodies and an equally powerful control exercised over those passions. However, as the narration of his relationships with his women friends and relations (his sister Alice; Minny Temple; Constance Fennimore Wooton) repeatedly attest, this suppression of homoerotic desires exists on a spectrum of emotional repression, coldness, and betrayal. But, the novel insinuates, the costly maintenance of this emotional distance from those who love him, and need his love and care, appears to be essential for the creative exploitation of Henry's relationships and the transmutation of suppressed emotions into his fiction.[9]

Along with being a thematic concern in *The Master*, the creation of a prose style in which homoerotic desires are embedded is part of the texture of the novel. Moreover, we can also locate instances of this style within the more 'direct' narrative mode of the earlier novels in how Tóibín's writes about male bodies, sexual pleasure and physical suffering. *The Story of the Night* is Tóibín's most directly erotic novel and Richard's narration is punctuated with accounts of his sexual encounters. Near the beginning of the novel he recounts cruising the Buenos Aires streets as a student during the Generals' regime of the late 1970s and remembers one casual encounter 'not for the sex we had, but because of a sound that came into the room as we made love'.[10] The sound is of car engines repeatedly revving. From the window Richard's partner points to the police station, outside of which the cars are parked, and driverless, with wires attaching them to the building. He explains to Richard that 'they need extra power for the cattle prods'. Richard, in the narrative present, claims to still not know if what this man said was true and 'if we fondled each other and came to orgasm within moments of each other to the sound of the revving of cars which gave power to the instruments of torture'. Moreover, he admits that at the time he was indifferent to what his partner told him, remembering more vividly 'the pleasure ... of my hands running down his back'. But now he grasps this as one of the few times that he came close to knowing anything about what was happening politically in the city where he lived. And yet this moment of near clarity is obscured by his confusion about his partner's knowledge; 'I have often wondered how he knew or thought he knew, or if he imagined, what the revving of car engines meant in our city at that time.'

The thematic of knowledge telegraphed in Richard's response to his partner's explanation about torture is central to the depiction of sexuality and politics in the novel. On one hand, there are various scenes of Richard disclosing that he is gay and of Pablo hiding his relationships with other men from his parents. At the same time, this condition of simultaneously knowing and not knowing is shown to be the ethical and psychic cost of surviving under a dictatorship. Elsewhere Richard's claim to ignorance, or at least a lack of any substantial knowledge, about the disappearances under the Generals is directly challenged when a minor character, Francisco, recounts to a visiting International Monetary Fund (IMF) team the disappearance of his girlfriend who was also Richard's classmate at university: 'She disappeared. They murdered her. Ask him. He pointed at me. He knows about it ... I had no idea what he was talking about. I didn't understand, I said to him.'[11] We share Francisco's incredulity that somebody could live through the murder of between eight and nine thousand fellow citizens, and the detention of up to one hundred thousand, by agencies of the state and remain largely oblivious to what was unfolding.[12] However, in his account of the Argentinean 'dirty war' – based on his coverage of the later trials of the regime's leaders – Tóibín claimed that in Argentina during those years 'life continued as normal, as it did elsewhere in Europe under similar circumstances'.[13]

Richard's description of the pleasure of touching his lover's body recurs throughout the novel when he and Pablo are making love and Pablo's body is a site of intensely intimate pleasure for him. The style is strikingly 'plain' with simple, precise language and rigorously uncluttered syntax: 'he held me in his arms. Then after we had kissed for a while he quickly took his shoes off and pulled mine off as well. I could not believe how beautiful he was, how earnest and concentrated'; 'he put his hands under my arms and then gripped my shoulders until I began to relax, until his being inside me gave me pleasure and almost no pain'.[14] Arguably the effects of this style are not just literary – the expressive clarity of concrete description – they are also epistemological and political. By inscribing sex between men as a cluster of quotidian affects and sensations Tóibín's prose resists by dislodging – or simply ignoring – those cultural frames – theological; psychiatric; political; literary – through which modern society has stigmatised or sacramentalised erotic desires and needs. As Gayle Rubin observed in her influential essay 'Thinking Sex', 'sexual acts are burdened with an excess of significance. Modern Western societies appraise sex acts according to a hierarchical system of sexual value'.[15] By resisting figurative and symbolic language the prose resists signification – the demand that sex be 'meaningful' – and its attendant distribution of moral value.

Richard's recall of his early sexual encounter startlingly juxtaposes bodies in pleasure and in pain. Likewise, the precise prose style used to convey erotic pleasure recurs when the narrative presents vividly detailed accounts of men's bodies suddenly made vulnerable to the AIDS-related illnesses precipitated by HIV infection. These include: the description of Richard's pneumonia during his trip from New York, which leads to his diagnosis ('my skin was on fire and I had a terrible thirst ... I felt that I was choking. I walked away and lay down on a bench. I tried desperately to catch my breath, to breathe calmly'); the recollected account of Frank, Pablo's late lover, declining into dementia ('Frank had this terrible anger, I don't know where it came from, he had been such a calm placid guy. Now he was shouting all of the time, he was incontinent and almost blind and covered in Ks and yet he wouldn't die. He went on and on'); and the narration of Pablo's treatment for CMV.[16] We find the same linguistic sparseness and tonal austerity in *The Blackwater Lightship*, as Declan undergoes the terrifying physiological and psychic debilitation as well as the banal humiliations of dying: 'he's had a bit of an accident ... there's diarrhoea all over the bed and vomit as well'.[17]

This pellucid prose foregrounds the somatic experience of AIDS, thereby displacing those moralising discourses through which responsibility and blame are apportioned to those affected. As Paula

Treichler observes, 'AIDS is a nexus where multiple meanings, stories and discourses intersect and overlap, reinforce and subvert each other.' Along with being an epidemic of a transmittable disease it was also 'an epidemic of signification'.[18] Tóibín's narrative style also resists that expectation – powerful in popular narratives at the time, such as the Hollywood film *Philadelphia* (1993) – that the body afflicted by AIDS be a site of sentimental pleasure and potential redemption for readers and viewers.[19] Nevertheless, the somatic experience of AIDS was also determined politically, just as Richard's account of his sexual encounter juxtaposes the adjacent spaces of bedroom and barracks – the body as instrument of pleasure and political terror. In *The Story of the Night*, Tóibín's plot captures how the AIDS pandemic came about because a virus met with new opportunities for dissemination provided by a globalising world: those movements of people and capital taking Pablo, in search of possibilities for sexual freedom, to San Francisco, while bringing IMF bankers, CIA agents and investors in search of neocolonial domination and profit to Argentina.

The Master is patterned by Henry's recurring encounters with male bodies which compel profound responses within his consciousness.[20] Just two of these occur in the narrative present. At the beginning of the novel, during his visit to Dublin after the failure of his play in 1895, Henry is soothed by the calm presence of the 'extraordinarily handsome' Hammond, the Irish-born corporal assigned to be his servant by his hostess – the wife of the commander of the British army in Ireland.[21] Henry does not share the anti-imperialist and pro-Home Rule views of his siblings, Alice and William. But staying in this socially claustrophobic enclave of imperial rule in, as he observes from his carriage, a deeply impoverished, mismanaged colony rekindles his sense of foreignness from the British society in which he has lived and worked for most of his adult life. This alienation is emotionally and physically discomfiting. Lying in bed, after a dinner at which his family's Irish origins were mocked by a fellow guest from England, Henry 'was disturbed by the idea that he longed now more than ever, in this strange house in this strange country, for someone to hold him, not to speak or move even, but to embrace him, stay with him'. Just before he had gone to bed Hammond, noticing his agitation, had in fact suggested that 'I can look in during the night if you like, sir.'[22] Unsure of the exact meaning of this offer, but keenly aware of his 'susceptibility' to it, Henry politely declines. Tóibín orchestrates this episode to amplify its ambiguities. Is Hammond conforming to the colonial and class hierarchy – making himself available to his social superior – while also capitalising on this opportunity to profit from his desirability? After all, the following chapter narrates Henry's absorption in the Wilde trial which included luridly detailed evidence of such transactional cross-class encounters between 'gents' and their 'bit of rough'. Or is Hammond compelled to ease Henry's distress and comfort him – an access of empathy intensified by some shared connection as marginal or subaltern figures in British imperial society?

Towards the end of the novel Henry meets Hendrik Andersen at a social gathering in Rome in 1899. Later that year Andersen visits Henry at home in England. This friendship is an ambivalent admixture of admiration (of the aging novelist for the vitality and energy of the younger sculptor; of the younger man for the artistic achievements, social poise and detachment of the older man), condescension (Henry's, towards the young man's inflated self-belief but lack of discipline) and self-interest (Andersen suggests that Henry write an article promoting his work). Scattered throughout Henry's fine-grained observations and judgements on Hendrik's character and talent are precisely detailed references to his body: his 'blond and big-boned handsomeness'; the 'tears in eyes' (after hearing Henry speak); his 'strong white hand'; the 'wonderful open agility of his movements'. As he goes swimming at Rye he 'became a moving version of one of his own sculptures, his torso richly smooth and white, his arms and legs muscular'.[23] Like Hammond, Andersen responds spontaneously to comfort Henry. Standing at Constance Fennimore Woolson's grave in the English cemetery in Rome Henry weeps for his friend, and as he 'tries to regain control' he 'found that he was being held by the sculptor, his shoulders cupped against Andersen's chest and Andersen's hands reaching around to grasp his hands and hold them as firmly as he could'.[24]

While the novel is bookended with these episodes in the narrative present there is a particular cluster of such episodes in the sequences narrated as Henry's memories of the American Civil War. The first of these is induced by the visit of Oliver Wendell Holmes to Rye and begins with Henry's memories of the summer after the war when he, Holmes and John Gray – the latter both veterans of the conflict – visited Minny Temple and her family. This chapter is primarily concerned with Henry's memories of his youthful friendship with Minny, his later failure to respond to her subtle requests for help when she was dying and how, after her early death, he incorporated her personality into some of his heroines – most notably Isabel Archer. But the chapter begins with an extended description of a night in the summer of 1865 when Henry and Holmes are obliged, due to a misunderstanding about their accommodation, to share a bed in their lodgings.

Again, the narration focuses on Henry's gaze – 'Henry studied his strong legs and buttocks, the line of his spine, his delicate bronzed neck' – and his appraising eye is signalled by allusion to art: 'for a second, as his friend remained still, he could have been a statue of a young man, tall and muscular'.[25] This sculpture motif recurs later in this chapter. On the following day the war looms over the conversation between the Temple sisters and their visitors, not least because the Temple's cousin, Gus Barker, was killed. At the mention of his name, Henry is visited by a vivid memory of a day five years earlier. He arrived at the studio where William James was taking a life drawing class to find Gus modelling naked on a pedestal: 'his form was beautiful and manly, and Henry was surprised by his own need to watch him … he studied William's drawing closely so that he could then raise his eye and study at some length his naked cousin's perfect gymnastic figure, his strength, and his calm sensual aura'.[26]

In contrast with the other episodes of Henry encountering men's bodies that with Holmes is directly erotic:

> He wondered if he would ever again be so intensely alive. Every breath, every hint that Holmes might move, or even the idea that Holmes too was awake, burned in his mind … Henry longed to know if Holmes were as conscious as he was of their bodies touching, or if he lay there casually, unaware of the mass of coiled heat which lay up against him … he was not surprised then when Holmes turned and cupped him with his body and placed one hand against his back and the other on his shoulders. He knew not to turn or move … subtly he eased himself more comfortably into the shape of Holmes, closing his eyes and allowing his breath to come as freely as it would.[27]

It is worth noting here the obsessive, almost comical, discretion that is an effect of adhering to Jamesian style and perspective; under the conventions of realist narrative both the narrator and a protagonist through whom this narrative is being focalised are 'present' in this room, and yet we remain uncertain about what actually happens.

The vision of Gus Barker's vigour and erotic allure is sharply poignant because of his early and violent death between the encounter in the studio and Henry's recollection of it. Likewise, the narrative discretion, in the earlier bedroom episode, leaves open the possibility that it is Holmes's vulnerability, after the trauma of the war, which impels his need for Henry's body. This is underscored in the narrative present when Holmes surprises Henry with a stark admission of how emotionally damaged the war left him.[28] The second sequence of Henry's memories about the Civil War is set in motion by the arrival of a letter and photographs from William in 1898, describing the unveiling of a monument to the 54th Massachusetts Regiment in Boston. The first mixed-race regiment in the Union army was also the one in which their brother, Wilky, had served. The chapter is concerned with Henry's avoidance of military service – less through outright refusal than an unspoken conspiracy between him and his mother to exaggerate the debilitating effects of a back injury. However, the latter part recounts in some detail Wilky's service in the war and, most vividly, being brought back to the family home after suffering catastrophic injuries: 'The house lived on the ebb and flow of Wilky's pain ... [Henry] had no choice but to take in the scene in all its horror. Wilky's hair was matted and his body limp and sweaty. Wilky did not seem to sleep; he lay on his side, constantly moaning and as the pain intensified crying out suddenly. Sometimes the cries turned into shrieks and they filled the house.'[29]

We can distinguish two ways of reading these encounters. In one, our analytical interest is concentrated on the emotional responses and motivations of the characters – essentially, the style of analysis I have brought to bear above. Thus, we speculate about the traumatic effects of Holme's war experiences and how this might shape his needs, or the ambiguous combination of spontaneous affection and calculated self-interest in the gestures of Hammond and Andersen. Centrally, of course, our attention gathers around Henry's consciousness. We attend to the fusion of erotic excitement and anxiety, of confused uncertainty and cool appraisal, of disruptive desires and learned inhibition; Henry calculating that his erotic fascination with Gus's body must be masked as appreciation of William's drawing, for instance, or realising that what unfolded with Holmes 'belonged to the secret night'.³⁰ Above all, the novel foregrounds the complex layers of Henry's responses, in particular to Wilky's suffering, as a developing novelist. His anguished empathy, as he sits holding his brother's hand, is evidently sincere and moving. And yet within a few months this encounter with his brother's suffering became the raw material for a work of fiction. His sudden realisation of what he had done, without being consciously aware of it, shocks and disturbs him. At the same time, it affirms his belief in his emergent creative abilities: this 'raid on his own memories, this parading of an object so close to him' gives him a 'feeling of power'.³¹

One consequence of this mode of reading, with its focus on character as the location of depicted emotions, is that even while acknowledging the degree to which individual subjects might be shaped, impinged on or harmed by history the autonomy of that subject is nevertheless affirmed. An alternative mode of reading would attend to the cumulative effects of these descriptions of the male body in the text, rather than the narrative meaning of any specific instance; in short, our interpretive focus would not be on characters but on the type of literary effects that Rachel Greenwald Smith terms 'impersonal feelings'. In *Affect and American Literature in the Age of Neoliberalism*, Smith argues that there is a ubiquitous affective hypothesis – 'the belief that literature is at its most meaningful when it represents and transmits the emotional specificity of personal experience'– in contemporary literary culture and criticism.³² Her principal challenge to this phenomenon is that, even in literary criticism informed by trauma studies and queer studies with radical political commitments, the primacy of the individual is ultimately assumed and endorsed. Feelings are always anchored in an individual who does the feeling; the affective hypothesis 'casts feeling as necessarily owned and managed by individual authors, characters and readers'. This emphasis on feelings as the personal responsibility of an autonomous individual is in striking comportment with neoliberal culture and its 'emphasis on the necessity of personal initiative, along with its pathologising of structures of dependence'. That culture calls on subjects to 'see themselves as entrepreneurial actors in a competitive system'.³³ While challenging this consensus, Smith is still committed to the political value of thinking about affect and feeling in literary and cultural criticism. For that reason, she puts forward a distinction between 'personal feelings' and 'impersonal feelings' in literary texts. The first describes the representation of character's emotions; the second refers not to characters but to the formal aspects of texts and 'how works of art envision, enact, and transmit their specific effects'. As she acknowledges, her conception of 'impersonal feelings' merges the idea of effect – as in the distancing or alienation effect – in Brecht's political aesthetics with Raymond Williams's 'structure of feeling' formulation. Smith is specifically interested in literary effects which 'destabilise the connection between the emotional and the personal ... these feelings affect readers in ways not entirely recognisable as individually owned emotions'.[34]

Viewed from this perspective then, Tóibín's style of writing the male body generates nodes of tonal intensity within the circuit of texts otherwise notable for their tonal austerity. The artistic effects of this are multivalent. The cadences and rhythm of the prose are sensual and erotically vibrant, even when, as in *The Master*, the language is drawing our attention to renunciation and repression. The narrative context emphasises tragedy, and specifically the tragic reverberations of historical dynamics – dictatorships; political violence; pandemic; war – on individual lives. Yet this reiteration of that central ideological binary of capitalist modernity – 'personal' contra 'political'; 'private' contra 'public' – is undermined by the concrete precision of the language used to evoke bodily sensations. Our attention is drawn to the body not as an autonomous entity but an unbounded cluster of desires and needs, of pleasures and vulnerabilities, that exists only and always in relation to other bodies. A body that is always already social and political, since only through the political organisation of social relationships can those desires and needs be met.

What then are the various political resonances of these different literary styles in Tóibín's fiction? The political symbolism of the character-based narrative mode is relatively straightforward. The demand for recognition of lesbian and gay people by the state, as a definable minority with specific rights that ought to be vindicated, has been a foundational premise for the lesbian and gay political movement as it evolved since the 1970s. In the local Irish instance, the campaign for civil partnership and then marriage rights, culminating in the 2015 constitutional referendum, is a notable recent instance of this political strategy at its most effective. An earlier instance, at the time Tóibín was working on these novels, was the successful lobbying campaign to have sexual orientation included among the nine grounds on which discrimination was legally outlawed by the Irish state in 1997 and 1998; enforcing the legislation, along with developing policies promoting equality on these same grounds, was the remit of new statutory bodies established at the same time. (Wealth, it need hardly be noted, was not included among these nine grounds.)

Tóibín's artistic choices about style and form – and the imaginative effects these produce on the reader – are a literary correlative of this political strategy. He uses the techniques and conventions of literary realism (narrative perspective to convey interiority and psychological depth; concrete language, uncluttered syntax and dialogue to create verisimilitude) to construct complex, legible gay male characters. These characters become legible – visible; recognisable – in and through existing forms and genres. In an artistic strategy that is analogous with the pursuit of marriage equality in the political sphere – using an existing form, civil marriage, through which to attain legal and cultural recognition for same-sex relationships – Tóibín does not create a new type of novel to write about gay men but uses inherited forms.

Thematically, *The Blackwater Lightship* offers the most direct endorsement of this political position. Larry briefly refers to his attendance at an historical event – a meeting between President Mary Robinson and a group of lesbian and gay activists at Áras an Uachtaráin in 1993.[35] Thus the gay men in the novel are aligned with the advancement of progressive and pluralist politics in Ireland signalled by the Robinson presidency. Notably though, Larry incidentally mentions the presidential visit and his political activism within a story that is primarily about coming out to his parents. As is characteristic of the narrowed horizons of the family plot form, the political dynamics of social change – the role of feminist and lesbian/gay social movements, for instance – is displaced to the margins of narrative interest.

Nevertheless, the novel's generational plot structure lends itself to being read as an allegory of social change and modernisation in Ireland from the 1960s to the 1990s. The younger generation, particularly exemplified by Helen and Paul, are confidently assured, skilled and successful. An episode in chapter one narrates a meeting at the Department of Education and serves little apparent function other than registering that Helen is an unusually young school principal and highly regarded in her field. Paul's account of his relationship with François, including their unorthodox Catholic marriage, and the portrayal of Helen and Hugh's marriage, foregrounds that this generation is more capable of forming healthy, emotionally honest, sexually compatible relationships. But the older generation are no less adept at successfully negotiating the opportunities offered by the economic impact of globalisation on 1990s Ireland. Most indicatively, Lily's prosperity – indexed by an architecturally stylish new house – comes from digital technology, that most modern of industries.

Along with *The Heather Blazing*, *The Story of the Night* is Tóibín's most political novel, in the precise sense of a novel that manifestly depicts the operations of power and the institutional infrastructure of states and geopolitical strategy. The novel is concerned with the process of neoliberal state formation in 1980s Argentina, and specifically how countries like Argentina were the laboratory for the earliest experiments in the restructuring of the state and its resources in favour of local and global elites. These historical events are narrated for us by a Lukácsian 'mediocre' or 'typical' hero, whose perspective is that of somebody in close proximity to these events but with only a partial view of what is unfolding. For Lukács, this narrative characteristic was essential for capturing in fiction how history can be experienced as dynamic and plastic – and thus as alienating, but also transformable – by modern individuals.[36] As a translator and local fixer, Richard facilitates communication between local elites and the IMF, during the application of the 'structural adjustments' programme, and later with the representatives of US corporations as the Argentinian oil industry is privatised.

As the privatisation process unfolds with surprising ease, Richard realises that the lack of opposition is rooted in the trauma of the recent past and its relationship to a neocolonial world order: 'Argentina after the humiliation of the war and the disappearances would have done anything to please the outside world, and privatisation was the price the outside world required. Everything the country had that was valuable would be sold, and this would tie Argentina to outside interests so that it would never be able to behave badly again ... I became convinced that the privatisation of the oil industry would be bad for Argentina.'[37] In a curious echo of his consciousness under the dictatorship – the ambivalent combination of knowing and not knowing – this conviction makes no immediate impact on how Richard performs his role of reassuring foreign investors that the privatisation was important to Argentina, including resorting to racist neocolonial tropes: 'we had the discipline and the European background to put through the reforms'.[38]

However, twice in the novel Richard encounters survivors of, or foreign witnesses to, another historical event: the 1973 military coup against Chile's democratically elected socialist government and the regime of state terrorism that ensued. As a young tourist in Barcelona, he befriends a group of young Chilean political exiles and listens to their traumatised accounts of being tortured by Pinochet's regime. Later he listens to Susan's guilty account of being stationed as a US agent in Santiago during the coup but claiming that 'it was only afterwards we really knew what happened'.[39] As Naomi Klein and David Harvey have outlined, the earliest experiment in neoliberal state formation took place in Chile in the wake of the coup. The contradictions of this project were stark: the zeal of the 'Chicago Boys' – Chilean economists trained by Milton Friedman and his monetarist colleagues – for the freedom and democracy that only a deregulated market could truly guarantee; the brutally violent suppression of freedom by an undemocratic military state torturing and murdering its citizens that was the essential precondition for their economic 'reforms'.[40] Juxtaposing the Chilean and Argentinian historical experiences Tóibín's novel illustrates Harvey's argument that there has been no singular trajectory to neoliberalism's assent. A map of its progress globally since 1970, he observes, would feature 'turbulent currents of uneven geographical development ... to understand how local transformations relate to broader trends'.[41] A brutal military regime or the democratic overturning of a brutal military regime: each could equally well provide fertile conditions for the reconstruction of the state along neoliberal lines.

Richard is sympathetically moved by the Chilean exiles and left disturbed and uneasy by Susan's story, but otherwise the inclusion of the references to Chile seems to serve a limited narrative function. However, combined with the expression of Richard's developing unease about privatisation, the resonances of these references for the novel's political imagination are clear. In this way the novel registers a manifest critique of neoliberalism, where neoliberalism is defined as a constellation of economic policies, including deregulation, privatisation and financialisation, directed at remodelling the state in accord with free market principles. The pursuit of these policies has cast citizens to the mercy of the market and entrenched inequalities within and between nations. And, as Harvey argues, underlying the apparent historical novelty of these economic policies is a historically familiar political project of reconfiguring class politics and consolidating an empowered and enriched elite.[42]

But taken together, the political imagination of *The Story of the Night* and *The Blackwater Lightship* is in closer alignment with that other indispensable element of neoliberalism: the cultural project of securing consent for this reformation of the postwar social order – translating a relatively obscure cluster of ideas in political and economic theory into a 'common sense'.[43] While neoliberal state transformation was imposed violently and disruptively on Chile, Argentina and other victims of structural adjustment programmes, its ideological ascendency in Western liberal democracies has been more gradual, incremental and various. As Wendy Brown observes, 'neoliberalism governs as sophisticated common sense, a reality principle remaking institutions and human beings everywhere it settles, nestles, and gains affirmation'.[44] Critically revising Foucault's initial formulation, Brown conceptualises this aspect of neoliberalism as a form of political rationality – that is, the norms of subjectivity or selfhood valorised and prescribed in our contemporary culture. We must, Brown argues, comprehend neoliberalism's distinctive governmentality and the various regulatory mechanisms through which it 'normatively constructs and interpellates individuals as entrepreneurial actors in every sphere of life'.[45] Where liberalism drew distinctions (albeit unstable and contradictory) between different forums for human action (moral, associational, economic) the neoliberal order deconstructs such distinctions and subordinates all action to the entrepreneurial logic of the market and finance capital. This does not necessarily mean that all aspects of life are monetised, but that the logic of finance capital – investing one's human capital successfully; attracting investors – is instilled into the fabric of life. From employment and welfare to education and health the contemporary citizen is insistently encouraged to conceive of themselves as a 'free' subject, wholly responsible for their own self-care and rationally making choices to maximise the benefits accruing to them.

But this rationally calculating individual must also bear sole responsibility for the consequences of their choices, regardless of the actual structural constraints on their freedom to act and choose. In this way the effects of structural inequalities are translated into the failure to 'manage' one's life successfully, and this judgement of failure is cast in moral rather than political terms. This, as Brown argues, 'is a new mode of depoliticising social and economic powers [which] reduces political citizenship to an unprecedented degree of passivity and political complacency. The ideal neo-liberal citizen is one who strategises for her- or himself among various social, political and economic options, not one who strives with others to alter or organise those options.'[46]

Richard's role in the privatisation of Argentina's state industries and national resources, a self-employed translator and consultant, is a distinctively neoliberal form of labour. And while rationally he begins to apprehend the strategic logic of neoliberal restructuring this is not how he actually experiences it. Just as he welcomes outside investors coming to view Argentina as 'normal', he lives his historical moment as a time of freedom and opportunity – reaping the material, emotional and sexual rewards of managing his life and skills, under Susan and Donald's tutelage, with greater rigour and efficiency. His occupation of a new house by the marina indexes that success, while the description of the building as an architectural assertion of modernity – open-plan spaces and expanses of plate glass – is symbolically evocative of the openness and transparency promised by neoliberal reform.[47]

Like Richard, Paul and Larry exemplify the well-managed lives valorised by neoliberal ideology. Indeed, there is an interesting echo of the figurative function of the marina house since Larry is an architect, whose plans promise light and rational order for the wasteful, irrationally arranged space of Dora's house. In another echo, Paul is also a translator facilitating geopolitical negotiations; he lives in Brussels where he works for the European Commission. Unlike Richard's narration though, any description of his work is an incidental detail within the account of his life with François which he recounts to Helen. In his story 'Europe' does not signify political and economic institutions but a culture that is emotionally open and honest, in contrast with the emotional repression and disconnection obscured by 'banter' in Irish culture. Meeting François' parents for the first time he 'loved how straightforward they were', and of François he 'loved how clear he was, and how careful he was about everything he did and said'.[48]

While Paul is neither the narrator nor the principle focus of the narrative perspective his world view sets the tone, since it chimes with the novel's structure and style. The language and syntax deploy clarity and precision to oppose those forms of sexual repression that require silence and conformity. Likewise, the plot is shaped into a very orderly narrative composed of eight chapters, one for each of the days over which the story unfolds. In keeping with Paul's commitment to communicative honesty, the thematic of knowledge, secrecy and disclosure is prominent, and this is reflected structurally in the importance of storytelling and conversation in the narration; as Tóibín observes, 'the dialogue does all the work'.[49] However, the effects of this 'plain style' are ambiguous, generating a duality of tone, hope undercut by pessimism, similar to that in *The Story of the Night*. That Helen's assured poise is so fragile – the emotionally debilitating legacy of family trauma sweeping her back into its currents – is the defining motif of the novel and reiterates how the past cannot be that easily overcome. This is also registered in the plot structure, in which the current family trauma, precipitated by Declan's illness, oscillates with the recounting of that earlier trauma, their father's death, through Helen's reignited memories. The tension between optimism and melancholia is reinforced by the ending, where the tentative rapprochement between Helen and her mother is overshadowed by Declan's impending death.

As Sianne Ngai observes, 'so much of ideological communication is tonal' and turning our attention from characterisation to the tone of Tóibín's fiction we find less endorsement of the prevailing norms than resigned submission to their inevitability.[50] The effect of the precise but flattened austerity of the prose is a literary correlative of the condition which Mark Fisher defined as 'capitalist realism'. In Fisher's essay, this capitalist realism is less an aesthetic category or ideological position than a 'pervasive atmosphere, conditioning not only the production of culture but also the regulation of work and education, and acting as a kind of invisible barrier constraining thought and action'.[51] As Jeremy Gilbert notes, in his response to Fisher, one of the distinctive attributes of neoliberalism as a hegemonic formation is how few committed adherents it actually mobilises.

Politicians have not stood on a platform explicitly nominated as 'neoliberal' and the majority of people, in most Western societies, disagree with the dismantling of socialised protections and the privatisation of public resources. As Gilbert observes, 'perhaps the most commonplace relation to capitalist realism – or neoliberal ideology – in the contemporary world is an explicit rejection of its norms and claims accompanied by a resigned compliance with its demands'.[52] The characteristic neoliberal structure of feeling has individuals publicly assent (conforming with intensified bureaucratic regimes of self-monitoring in their workplace, for instance) while privately withholding their consent; conforming with the forms of regulation matters less once one does not 'really' believe in them.[53]

Interestingly, Tóibín made frequent use of 'realism' as a political category in his journalism during the 1980s, when he addressed the urgency of reform, modernisation and liberalisation in Ireland. Using a recurring trope, he argued that in Irish society, and Irish political discourse, during the twentieth century there had been a damaging disparity between reality, as it was lived in Ireland, and the perception of reality. Thus, for instance, he wrote in 1984 that, 'there is a war in Ireland ... between reality and the perception of reality; between de Valera's vision of Ireland and Patrick Kavanagh's *The Great Hunger*'.[54] As a diagnosis of conservative nationalist rhetoric this is persuasive; but as an analysis of political conflict, it projects an oddly empty conception of social change. There is no explicit commitment to any vision of what a changed society might actually be like once it becomes more 'realistic' in its perception of itself; that vision could just as easily come from the Right as from liberalism or the Left. This political commitment – or more accurately, perhaps, depoliticising commitment – to the value of developing a more 'realistic' perspective on one's conditions, rather than mobilising to transform them, finds an echo in the pervasive tone of the fiction, which projects a similarly 'realist' political imagination; unenthusiastic submission to the existing social order, and its prevailing political rationality, as the best we can hope for and at least better than what we had. As Matthew Ryan observes, 'while responding ambivalently to the prizes and pitfalls of a changing culture Tóibín's fiction never succumbs to a pure celebration or complacent description of present conditions'.[55] For Ryan, Tóibín's writing of landscape – more precisely, coastal landscape – as a space of disconcerting affects provides an important symbolic reservoir for the imaginative 'reterritorialisation of the self' in the face of the endemic alienation of post-nationalist globalisation.[56]

By contrast I have argued that Tóibín's writing of the body – more precisely, the male body in pleasure and pain – is the location of similarly discombobulating affects, but which reiterate the vulnerability and porousness of the self. The tone of Tóibín's fiction is a contrapuntal play between a major and minor chord. There is that pervasive 'realistic' tone, quietly affirming as inevitable the hegemonic norms, the reality principle, of neoliberal's diversified dominant. But that major chord is repeatedly counterposed by those depictions of the male body, and specifically by the type of literary effects – those intensities and that palette of 'impersonal feelings' – generated by Tóibín's style of homoerotic writing. Above all, those literary affects imaginatively dislodge the primacy and autonomy of the individual by foregrounding the desirable and vulnerable male body. Jeremy Gilbert points to 'the tendency of neoliberal ideology to potentiate individuals qua individuals while simultaneously inhibiting the emergence of all forms of potent collectivity'.[57] By reframing sexuality as erotic needs, vulnerabilities and, above all, relationality, Tóibín creates a style of writing about homoeroticism and the male body which gives us ways of imagining just such 'potent collectivity'.

Notes

1 Colm Tóibín, *The Story of the Night* (London: Picador, 1996), p. 1.
2 Naomi Klein coined the term 'shock doctrine' to explain how various forms of economic, political and ecological crises, including deliberately provoked crises, have provided the staple condition for the implementation of neoliberal economic policies since the 1970s. Argentina from the late 1970s to the early 1990s, the period in which Tóibín's novel is set, unusually illustrates how the shock doctrine can unfold under very different political regimes. The military junta unleashed a reign of terror on its own citizens from 1977 to 1983 and in these conditions it brutally repressed trade unions, undermined developmental and redistributive policies, and reinforced the economic hegemony of the landed and industrial elites. The democratically elected governments of the 1980s inherited an enormous national debt from the junta,

primarily used for military spending or embezzled by the generals. This led to a so-called debt crisis in 1989 and the imposition of a 'structural adjustment programme' at the behest of the IMF (International Monetary Fund). The result was wholesale privatisation of national enterprises and resources, such as oil, primarily for the benefit of foreign capital, along with widespread immiseration for the majority of Argentinean citizens. See Naomi Klein, *The Shock Doctrine: the rise of disaster capitalism* (London: Allen Lane, 2007), pp. 87–93 and 165–8.
3 Joseph Wisenfarth, 'An Interview with Colm Tóibín', *Contemporary Literature*, 50,1 (2009), 1–27, 17.
4 As Eibhear Walshe observes, 'Declan is represented in an oddly absent or distant way, existing only as a catalyst for these combative familial relationships.' See Eibhear Walshe, *A Different Story: the writings of Colm Tóibín* (Dublin: Irish Academic Press, 2013), p. 91. For a concise account of Walshe's critical assessment of the sexual politics of Tóibín's oeuvre, see also his essay '"This particular genie": the elusive gay male body in Tóibín's novels' in Paul Delaney (ed.), *Reading Colm Tóibín* (Dublin: The Liffey Press, 2008). Likewise, Terry Eagleton suggests that the novel could be read as 'side-lining gay sexuality, offering up Declan as a kind of blood sacrifice for re-cementing familial bonds'. See Terry Eagleton, 'Mothering', *London Review of Books* (14 October 1999), p. 8. In response to such arguments, Kathleen Costello-Sullivan counters that the novel 'belies both the mythology of the idealized Irish family and the refusal to presence homosexuality in Irish society at once, challenging two myths rather than opposing them to one another'. Pursuing this characteristically affirmative argument, she claims that the novel 'offers a more whole and complete portrait of both Declan's family and Irish society'. Kathleen Costello-Sullivan, *Mother/Country: politics of the personal in the fiction of Colm Tóibín* (Bern: Peter Lang, 2012), p. 154. Arguably, Tóibín has not always been well served by this type of criticism, which tends to read the novels quite narrowly within a critical and political hermeneutic (invisibility/visibility; mythology/reality; tradition/modernity; nation/individual) closely in step with his own, producing a rather airless circulation of ideas.
5 Colm Tóibín, 'Out of the Dark; a profile of John McGahern' in *The Trial of the Generals: selected journalism 1980–1990* (Dublin: Raven Arts Press, 1990), pp. 94–102.
6 Fintan O'Toole, 'An interview with Colm Tóibín' in Delaney (ed.), *Reading Colm Tóibín*, p. 187.
7 Colm Tóibín, *Love in a Dark Time: gay lives from Wilde to Almodovar* (London: Picador, 2001), p. 26.
8 Tóibín, *Love*, p. 115.

9 For a richly perceptive reading of the novel's intertextual engagements with James's fiction see Stephen Matterson, 'Dreaming about the dead: *The Master*' in Delaney (ed.), *Reading Colm Tóibín*, pp. 131–48.
10 Tóibín, *Story*, p. 8.
11 Tóibín, *Story*, p. 118.
12 Tóibín cites these as the official figures compiled by the National Commission on the Disappearance of Persons (CONADEP), the independent body established to investigate the disappearances and other human rights violations during the 'dirty war'. However, he notes that many observers believed that these figures were conservative. Tóibín, *Trial*, p. 19.
13 Tóibín, *Trial*, p. 26.
14 Tóibín, *Story*, pp. 190 and 204.
15 Gayle Rubin, 'Thinking sex: notes for a radical theory of the politics of sexuality' in Carol S. Vance (ed.), *Pleasure and Danger: exploring female sexuality* (London: Kegan Paul, 1984), p. 279.
16 Tóibín, *Story*, pp. 277 and 236. CMV is an eye infection which is usually minor but can cause more serious organ damage for those with compromised immune systems. The condition affected some people in the advanced stages of HIV infection before the introduction of antiretroviral therapies in the 1990s.
17 Colm Tóibín, *The Blackwater Lightship* (London: Picador, 1999), p. 221.
18 Paula A. Treichler, *How To Do Theory in an Epidemic: cultural chronicles of AIDS* (Durham, NC: Duke University Press, 1999), p. 19.
19 See Robert T. Corber, 'Nationalising the gay body: AIDS and sentimental pedagogy in *Philadelphia*', *American Literary History*, 15,1 (2003), 107–33. Douglas Crimp was the most astute radical critic of that nexus of homophobic, sentimentalising and moralising discourses framing AIDS in US culture; see Douglas Crimp, *Melancholia and Moralism: essays on AIDS and queer politics* (Cambridge, MA: MIT Press, 2002).
20 Eibhear Walshe has explored in some detail the thematic of homoeroticism in *The Master*, and how Tóibín explores its fertile contribution to James's writing. He locates the novel within a broader consideration of Tóibín's position on sexuality and creativity, and in particular Tóibín's ambivalent response to what Walshe terms the 'post-gay moment'. In essence, while Tóibín is politically committed to, and welcomes, the progressive evolution of a contemporary culture that is more open and welcoming to gay men, he is emotionally and artistically more engaged by the psychic effects of repressive cultures, where homosexual desire is inhibited and repressed. Using the genre of historical fiction in *The Master*, Tóibín 'can explore his sense that an "out" gay life is, for fictive

purposes, a less interesting life because of the absence of conflict and tension'. Walshe, *A Different Story*, p. 102.
21 Colm Tóibín, *The Master* (London: Picador, 2004), p. 47.
22 Tóibín, *Master*, pp. 39–40.
23 Tóibín, *Master*, pp. 281–308.
24 Tóibín, *Master*, p. 286.
25 Tóibín, *Master*, p. 97.
26 Tóibín, *Master*, p. 105.
27 Tóibín, *Master*, pp. 98–100.
28 Tóibín, *Master*, p. 117.
29 Tóibín, *Master*, p. 188.
30 Tóibín, *Master*, p. 100.
31 Tóibín, *Master*, p. 195.
32 Rachel Greenwald Smith, *Affect and American Literature in the Age of Neoliberalism* (Cambridge: Cambridge University Press, 2015), p. 1.
33 Greenwald Smith, *Affect and American Literature*, p. 2.
34 Greenwald Smith, *Affect and American Literature*, p. 11.
35 Tóibín, *Blackwater*, p. 144.
36 Georg Lukács, *The Historical Novel*, trans. Hannah and Stanley Mitchell (Lincoln, NE: University of Nebraska Press, 1983 [1937]), pp. 35–9.
37 Tóibín, *Story*, pp. 259–60.
38 Tóibín, *Story*, p. 260.
39 Tóibín, *Story*, p. 157.
40 Klein, *Shock Doctrine*, pp. 75–87. David Harvey, *A Brief History of Neoliberalism* (Oxford: Oxford University Press, 2005), pp. 7–9.
41 Harvey, *Neoliberalism*, p. 87.
42 Harvey, *Neoliberalism*, pp. 16 and 31–6.
43 In developing his concept of hegemony Gramsci opposed 'common sense' – knowledge widely held to be obvious, natural or the way things are or ought to be – with the 'good sense' sparked by critical and dissenting engagement. Antonio Gramsci, *Selections from the Prison Notebooks*, trans. Quintin Hoare and Geoffrey Nowell Smith (London: Lawrence and Wishart, 1971), pp. 321–43.
44 Wendy Brown, *Undoing the Demos: neoliberalism's stealth revolution* (New York: Zone Books, 2015), p. 35.
45 Wendy Brown, *Edgework: critical essays on knowledge and politics* (Princeton, NJ: Princeton University Press, 2005), p. 42.
46 Brown, *Edgework*, p. 43.
47 Tóibín, *Story*, p. 220.
48 Tóibín, *Blackwater*, p. 166.
49 Wisenfarth, 'An interview with Colm Tóibín', p. 17.

50 Sianne Ngai, *Ugly Feelings* (Cambridge, MA: Harvard University Press, 2005), p. 46.
51 Mark Fisher, *Capitalist Realism: is there no alternative?* (Hants: Zero Books, 2009), p. 16.
52 Jeremy Gilbert, 'What kind of thing is "neoliberalism"?', *new formations*, 80/81 (2013), 7–22, 13.
53 Fisher offers a dispiriting, though alarmingly familiar, account of his first encounter with this dynamic while working in further education in Britain in the late 1990s. Mark Fisher and Jeremy Gilbert, 'Capitalist realism and neoliberal hegemony: a dialogue', *new formations*, 80/81 (2013), 89–101.
54 Tóibín, *Trial*, p. 93.
55 Matthew Ryan, 'Abstract homes: deterritorialisation and reterritorialisation in the work of Colm Tóibín', *Irish Studies Review*, 16,1 (2008), 19–32, 30.
56 For an alternative, more critical reading of the politics of Tóibín's landscape writing see Conor McCarthy, 'Geographies of liberalism: the politics of space in Colm Tóibín's *Bad Blood: a walk along the Irish border* and *The Heather Blazing*' in Glenn Hooper (ed.), *Landscape and Empire 1720–2000* (Aldershot: Ashgate, 2005), pp. 220–35.
57 Gilbert, 'What kind of thing is "neoliberalism"?', 21.

4

Time and politics in Irish gay male fiction

In *Diverse Communities: the evolution of lesbian and gay politics in Ireland* (1994) Kieran Rose charts the development of the movement for lesbian and gay rights in Ireland, from the founding of the Irish Gay Rights Movement in 1974 to the decriminalisation of sex between consenting adult men in 1993. Rose provides a precisely detailed but lively account of the lobbying campaign in the late 1980s and early 1990s directed towards securing decriminalisation. This account is intimately informed by his prominent role in that campaign. At the same time, he is keen to situate the achievement of decriminalisation as just one, albeit significant, strand in the concerns, objectives and achievements of the Irish lesbian and gay movement. His account has a double orientation: towards the past to understand the gradual formation of a political consciousness and mobilisation of energies leading to 1993; towards the future, identifying pressing needs and political goals demanding continuing effort. The future goals he identifies include: HIV services; ending discrimination in the workplace and in society at large; securing rights for same-sex families; solidarity with human rights activists internationally.

Rose's account situates 1993 as a pivotal moment between the past and the future. In addition, Rose's analysis synthesises political currents in two other significant ways. Firstly, he argues for a distinctive evolution of the Irish lesbian and gay movement, which took its coordinates from metropolitan developments and models while at the same time articulating with radical anti-imperialist and socialist republican traditions within Irish history. For Rose, decriminalisation was a belated act of decolonisation. The laws annulled in 1993, dating from 1861 and 1885, had been passed in the Westminster parliament and retained on the statute books after 1922. As Rose reiterates, the retention of the laws was symptomatic of the counter-revolutionary tenor dominant in the two new states on the partitioned island. More speculatively, Rose argues that institutionalised homophobia was a colonial implant in Ireland, and other British colonies, and alludes to the Brehon Laws and other evidence that Gaelic Ireland was more tolerant of same-sex relationships.[1]

In the twenty years before decriminalisation it became possible, Rose argues, to 'construct a new identity which meant that it is possible to be Irish *and* lesbian *and* gay'.[2] He is keen to challenge the notion that decriminalisation was enforced or imposed on the country by Europe, which, he argues, was a narrative peddled by right-wing activists. The finding of the European Court of Human Rights in 1988, in favour of David Norris's case against the constitutionality of the law, compelled the Irish state to act. But Rose is keen to stress that the 1993 law reform was far more extensive, progressive and egalitarian than the similar law reform in Britain in 1967. This outcome, he demonstrates, had less to do with the court judgment than with fertile conditions in Irish politics. These included strategic opportunities for alliance building (the support of trade unions and the Irish Council for Civil Liberties), support from key institutions, such as the Law Reform Commission, and key figures in political parties. Above all, Rose claims, this egalitarian and progressive reform was possible because of 'positive traditional Irish values arising from the anticolonial struggle reinvigorated and amplified by the new social, cultural and economic influences of the 1960s onwards'.[3]

To support this position, Rose situates right-wing activist organisations, such as the Knights of Columbanus or Family Solidarity, as strategically powerful but essentially minority groupings atypical of Irish political culture. By contrast, he draws attention to sympathetic and progressive figures in conservative institutions and parties: the dissenting Supreme Court judges who ruled in Norris's favour in 1983; Fianna Fáil politicians such as Márie Geoghegan-Quinn, the minister responsible for the 1993 legislation. In keeping with his socialist commitments then, Rose offers a variegated historical narrative, avoiding the simplistic binary of modernity and tradition favoured by liberals, and he maps a complex political terrain where the 'modern' – progressive and even revolutionary potentialities – emerge dialectically from within 'tradition'.[4]

Rose's second synthesis is between the divergent political philosophies that have animated the modern lesbian and gay political movement as it emerged in the latter half of the twentieth century, and most actively in the early 1970s.[5] Rose's analysis of the oppression of lesbian and gay people is manifestly informed by socialist and anticapitalist commitments, foregrounding the necessity of transforming society structurally to achieve sexual liberation for all. Likewise, his historical account of Irish gay and lesbian activism in the 1970s and 1980s particularly highlights the Cork and Dublin Gay Collectives and Gays Against Imperialism, small but vibrant leftist, left-republican, and gay liberation groupings.[6]

But at the same time, Rose's account is primarily taken up with describing the political activities of the Gay and Lesbian Equality Network (GLEN). As Rose puts it, GLEN 'evolved' from the movement of the 1970s and 1980s and in 1988 was 'given the remit to campaign for equality'.[7] As the vagueness of this passive locution suggests – who exactly did the 'giving'? – the *modus operandi* was no longer collective mobilisation but a small, highly focused group speaking *for* a community and mediating between that community and the wider society. The chosen political terrain was the nexus of media, academia, non-governmental organisations, state bodies and party politics where policy is formulated, public opinion nudged in required directions and politicians and civil servants lobbied through multiple forums of varying transparency. The central objective was now 'equality' within the existing social and economic structures.

In this way Rose's account of the Irish lesbian and gay movement captures at a local level the central tension between two political currents in the metropolitan lesbian and gay (latterly LGBT) movement as it emerged post-Stonewall. One is a universalising, liberationist and utopian political imaginary that took its coordinates from the writings of Marcuse and variants of Marxism, feminism, anticolonialism and the New Left. From this gay liberation and lesbian feminist perspective, the struggle against the oppressive stigmatisation of homosexuality is necessarily inseparable from the struggle for a revolution in which social institutions – notably marriage and the family – and all social relations – gender, race, class – would be radically transformed. Paradoxically, since this revolution aimed to undermine wholesale the modern sex-gender system, it would of necessity bring about 'the end of the homosexual', as Denis Altman predicted in his pioneering manifesto of the 'gay lib' position.[8] The other strand is a reformist or assimilative liberal/social democratic project seeking recognition, protection and civil rights for a lesbian and gay minority. This is predicated on a formative connection between erotic desire and identity, the notion that each of us 'has' a 'sexuality', as well as the relative autonomy of sexuality from other social relations. It assumes the continued existence of a fundamental hetero–homo binary, albeit one more tolerantly mediated by cultural norms and, where that fails, actively policed by the state to ensure parity. In short, freedom from oppression for lesbians and gay men can, in this view, be secured within the existing social order; indeed, it can only really be secured within the dominant liberal democratic and capitalist order.[9]

When GLEN was remaking the Irish lesbian and gay movement along reformist lines from 1988, it was also adapting to the chief political mode of contemporary Irish politics. The pluralist and consensual politics exemplified by the achievement of decriminalisation, and the subsequent creation of the Equality Authority in 1999, was also the ideological basis for what was known as social partnership which took shape at almost exactly the same time as GLEN's emergence. The Programme for National Recovery was agreed between the government, the trade unions and employer organisations in 1987. This was the first of six triannual agreements through which Irish governments gained consent from the sectoral groups for government policy on public spending, pay and labour relations. During the 1990s and 2000s social partnership was ritually celebrated by mainstream economists and centrist political commentators for providing the 'stability' deemed essential for economic prosperity. However, analysis from Marxist, word systems and other critical perspectives convincingly debunked this myth. For one thing, rather than social partnership generating economic growth its primary function was to create the conditions – low taxation; low public spending; pliant, 'flexible' labour force – for the integration of Ireland into a globalising world economy. In other words, the achievement was not a dynamic economy – as its cheerleaders claimed – but a dependent economy, in which democratic control was thoroughly subordinated to the priorities and demands of global capital.

Moreover, under the comforting illusion of consensus the corporatist structures of social partnership undermined representative democracy since control over significant elements of social policy shifted from the political realm into more opaque bureaucratic processes. Social partnership, as Peadar Kirby argued in 2001, 'marks an emasculation of politics as power is more concentrated in the hands of small elites and it is these who decide who gets a seat at the decision-making table'.[10] Crucially, through controlling wages in an era of accelerated expansion of profits, the agreements effectively facilitated the redistribution of wealth, on a very significant scale, from the majority of Irish citizens to local and global elites.[11]

There are two points of note here. One is the degree to which social partnership exemplified the central characteristics of neoliberal governance. Recasting the Irish state as a neoliberal rather than a democratic state – that is, a state whose primary goal is to sustain and protect the market rather than any democratic notion of the public good – was never a political objective for which politicians campaigned or citizens voted, and nor was it forced on those citizens. Instead, the majority consented – literally in the case of workers, though their trade unions – to this diminution of their rights as citizens because such consent *felt* like either a positive affirmation (moving beyond outmoded class antagonism to 'partnership' and 'solidarity') or an unavoidable submission to 'common sense' – or some combination of these. Moreover, the cultural discourses constructing this 'common sense' signified political dynamics in individualised and moralised terms; thus, demanding higher pay was cast as 'selfishness'.[12] Secondly, the affinity between the institutional apparatus and discourses of social partnership and the mode of minoritarian politics pursued by GLEN points to a significant contradiction; the mainstream of lesbian and gay politics was successfully pursuing the goal of equality within Irish society just as inequality was being systematically re-entrenched in that society. Was this merely coincidence? Or was the concept of equality subtending lesbian and gay politics actually compatible with – useful for the purposes of – the ideology producing inequality?[13]

In literary critical terms, my starting point for this chapter is to approach the fiction analysed here as the literary form of that political formation outlined by Rose; that is, to approach the fiction as giving narrative and literary expression to the forms of consciousness underpinning and endorsed by that politics. Engaging with the fiction from this perspective, there are three principal questions to ask of it. The first concerns how these novels give imaginative expression to the dialectic of liberation and reformism. As Les Brookes argues, it is not that radicalism/liberation and reformism/assimilation constitute two internally coherent but mutually exclusive positions within the LGBT political movement; rather, we can envisage a dynamic oscillation *between* radicalism and assimilationism as the defining ideological struggle within that politics.[14] Indeed Rose's historical narrative, propelled by the synthesis of his commitment to both positions, exemplifies this. Brookes argues that fiction, and specifically a category he defines as 'gay male fiction since Stonewall', is one cultural terrain where the tension between these political impulses is richly productive. This unresolved conflict is the key faultline, in Alan Sinfield's formulation of that concept, animating this fiction.[15]

Coincidently – a helpful quirk of publication history – the earliest novel under analysis here was published in 1993 (a year before the term 'Celtic Tiger' was first coined) and the latest in 2008; in other words, these novels coincide historically with Ireland's millennial economic boom and its dramatic and disastrous bust. Thus, the second question concerns the relationship of these novels to the hegemonic values governing Irish politics and society during that time. Conventionally, literary critics have taken for granted that this fiction is dissenting from, and challenging to, the dominant values of Irish society. Sometimes, in the critic's account, this dissent takes a rather weaker form of 'visibility' – to make visible 'gay lives' or 'gay bodies' that were heretofore 'invisible' is sufficient to be considered dissident.[16] Such readings are susceptible to an odd temporal lag. They presuppose that the dominant ideology which needed to be challenged by such literature was conservative nationalism and Catholicism. There is very little sense that by the time this fiction was appearing those ideological formations were rapidly becoming residual rather than dominant; arguably those ideological formations becoming residual was one of the conditions of possibility for this fiction to be produced.

By contrast, my approach here differs from such readings by shifting the critical focus from representation to aesthetics; moving from discussing the social world depicted in this fiction to analysing the discourses, ideas, political perspectives and forms of historical consciousness sedimented in the style and aesthetic texture of this fiction, and in the structures of feeling and affects generated through that style. My approach will also differ by working from the assumption that if we want to understand the political imagination of this fiction, and its relationship to the hegemonic values of its contemporary Ireland, we must grasp those hegemonic values as a form of neoliberalism. Moreover, we cannot take for granted that the fiction's relationship to the hegemonic values will be dissident, but will in fact exhibit a complex, volatile combination of dissent and assent.

As we will see, the manifest political perspectives in this fiction are often critical and sometimes socialist in their sympathies. But, beneath these manifest commitments, the aesthetic form and texture of the fiction – plot; narrative and prose style; tone – generates forms of historical and political consciousness. The principal objective of submitting these novels to literary critical scrutiny is to map the variegated political valences of those forms of consciousness. In other words, the political imagination of these novels may be radical, disruptive and utopian, or it may be in comfortable alignment with the hegemonic neoliberal conception of the individual and of social relations in 'boom-time' Ireland – and most likely it may exhibit some volatile combination of these.

The third question concerns the discursive figure of the gay man projected in this fiction, and the novels' literary engagement with the hermeneutic of identity which undergirds contemporary lesbian and gay/LGBT politics. To think critically about that relationship between fictional narratives and politicised identity, it might be useful to begin with a philosophical critique of that hermeneutic.

In *States of Injury* Wendy Brown addresses what she terms the 'problematic of politicised identity'.[17] Her particular focus was on the United States in the 1990s, while also mapping deeper discursive and historical currents underpinning this political dynamic in late capitalism. Brown alerts us to a central paradox here: a political discourse underpinning various movements for progressive social change in the late twentieth-century (anti-imperialism; anti-racism; liberal feminism; LGBT rights) invariably reinforces the existing ideological and social structures of capitalist liberal democracy. This paradox stems from the political grammar and the type of demands formulated in the name of politicalised identity. In their most essential form those demands centre on recognition and inclusion. But, and here is a second paradox, while ostensibly securing redress and justice the demand for recognition – 'a recognition predicated on injury, now righteously revalued' – institutionalises and entrenches the same discursive, social and psychic processes of subjection and injury through which stigmatised identities are formed.[18] Rather than freedom what is achieved is a permutation or recalibration within the existing forms of regulation and reification.

These demands for recognition and inclusion are propelled by a conception of identity predicated on injury. Politicised identity, as Brown observes, 'enunciates itself, makes claims for itself, only by entrenching, restating, dramatizing, and inscribing its pain in politics; it can hold out no future – for itself or others – that triumphs over this pain'.[19] In this way, Brown argues, politicised identity must be understood as symptomatic of – as 'product of and reaction to' – the pervasive *ressentiment* – the fusion of powerlessness, abjection and anger, which Nietzsche identified as intrinsic to modernity. As Brown outlines: 'it is … the prior presumption of the self-reliant and self-made capacities of liberal subjects, conjoined with their unavowed dependence on and construction by a variety of social relations and forces, that makes all liberal subjects, and not only markedly disenfranchised ones, vulnerable to *ressentiment*'.[20]

This generalised incitement to *ressentiment* has been notably intensified by the conditions of late capitalism and the ascendency of neoliberal political rationality: the emergence of a society 'in which individuals are buffeted and controlled by global configurations of disciplinary and capitalist power of extraordinary proportions, and are at the same time nakedly individuated, stripped of reprieve from relentless exposure and accountability for themselves'.[21] On one side, a capitalist world system where our lives are determined by deterritorialised and potentially cataclysmic processes that are difficult to apprehend, let alone bring under democratic control: financialisation; outsourced production; ecological destruction and climate change. On the other, that relentless expectation – amplified in almost all facets of life, from education and employment to well-being and leisure – that we exercise rigorous control over our fate while we construct well-managed lives as model entrepreneurial subjects.

In a third paradox, politicised identity is a formation generated in reaction to the oppressive and alienating conditions of capitalism, which at the same time supresses the possibilities of anticapitalist critique and politics – or, more precisely, as Brown puts it, 'what we have come to call identity politics is partly dependent upon the demise of a critique of capitalism and of bourgeois cultural and economic values'.[22] Those 'differences' which are an effect of the exploitative structural relations inherent within capitalism are neutralised as attributes inhering in individuals. Any injustice suffered because of these 'differences' can be resolved by individuals aggregating into groups whose specific 'interests' can be adjudicated on, and protected by, a supposedly neutral liberal state which is autonomous from capitalism. Irish politics in the 1990s provides an obvious example of this in the discourses and regulatory framework of 'equality' underpinning the passing of the Equal Status and Employment Equality Acts, and the creation of the statutory infrastructure to enforce these.

Likewise, politicised identity rescripts capitalism's endemic alienation as a question of inclusion and exclusion. Thus, identity politics finds itself committed to the perpetuation of exclusion, since its political demands are so thoroughly structured by this distinction. For identity politics to seek to move beyond the discursive economy of inclusion and exclusion would subvert the basis of its own claims; the identity being politicised is dependent on exclusion for its identity. By definition then, the political demand must be for a more just realignment or adjudication of inclusion/exclusion, rather than an end to that dynamic as such. A useful illustrative example is a political objective the success of which Brown may not have been able to predict when writing in 1996 – securing same-sex marriage rights in Western countries (including Ireland) since the turn of the millennium. 'Marriage equality', the commonly adopted term for this political demand, is in fact ironic. The institution of marriage is by definition rigorously discriminatory since it establishes a rigid distinction between the legal rights and benefits of the married (i.e. those *included* within its ambit) and the unmarried (i.e. those who are *excluded*). If this inequality and exclusion was not constitutively generated by marriage laws there would have been no point in actively seeking access to the institution.

Moreover, as Brown argues, the discourse of inclusion/exclusion presupposes something from which one is excluded that one values and desires since one is seeking inclusion within it. In other words, through its commitment to the discourse of inclusion/exclusion politicised identity discloses an unacknowledged investment in a 'universal' subjectivity – a valorised subjectivity that is, in fact, not universal at all but indicatively white, middle class, heterosexual and masculinist. Thus, as Brown asks, in contrast with the 'Marxist critique of a social whole and a Marxist vision of total transformation' to what extent 'do identity politics require a standard internal to existing society against which to pitch their claims, a standard that not only preserves capitalism from critique, but sustains the invisibility and inarticulateness of class – not accidently, but endemically?'[23]

Needless to say, Brown clearly distinguishes her critique of politicised identity from the reactionary rejection of identity politics by the political Right, which is essentially a vehicle for rearticulating racist, misogynistic, homophobic or transphobic prejudices. Crucially, the logic of politicised identity analysed by Brown is not confined to liberal, progressive or radical movements. Notwithstanding its rejection of 'identity politics', right-wing politics is in fact discursively organised around various formulations of national, ethnic, religious and gendered identity and impelled by deep reservoirs of *ressentiment*. Indeed, as I write, over two decades after Brown was writing, politics almost everywhere is even more unrelentingly and violently dominated by reactionary, right-wing forms of politicised identity: religious fundamentalism; ethnonationalism; white supremacy; 'inceldom'.

By contrast, Brown develops an immanent critique motivated by solidarity with, and affective identification with, forms of progressive politics mobilised around identity, such as the modern LGBT movement. At the same time, this solidarity is tempered by an impatient desire that the political consciousness and strategic energies mobilised by such movements impel more ambitious and transformative political aims; be at once more mundanely materialist – rigorously attentive to the exploitative and destructive effects of neoliberalism – and more ambitiously utopian. By this stage it might come as little surprise to the reader that this standpoint, which I ascribe to Brown, is also my own.

Rather than repudiating identity politics Brown suggests moving beyond the impasse of 'bartering political freedom for legal protection' by redirecting the needs, desires and affects contained within such politics and reformulating the grammar of its demands.[24] 'What if', Brown proposes, 'we sought to supplant the language of "I am" – with its defensive closure on identity, its insistence on the fixity of position, its equation of social with moral positioning – with the language of "I want this for us"?'[25] Since the claim here is for a collective and political good we have moved away from the liberal expression of self-interest. The shift from 'being' to 'wanting' resignifies the political demands from identity to need, from recognition to redistribution and from inclusion to insurrection. Moreover, moving from the fixed, historically determined position sedimented in 'I am' to the mobile, active, open-ended position implied by 'I want' moves our historical orientation from redressing past injury to imagining a radically transformed future.

For Brown, the paradoxes of politicised identity are symptomatic of the form of historical consciousness – 'the loss of historical direction, and thus the loss of futurity' – that characterises late capitalism.[26] In light of this, it is notable that temporality is the common compositional principle in the Irish gay male fiction addressed in this chapter. These novels are plotted around either biographical or historical time. In other words, they can be divided into two genres: the coming-out romance and the historical romance.

In *When Love Comes to Town* (1993) and *Crazy Love* (1999) Tom Lennon created two versions of the coming-out romance. The belief that self-disclosure – coming out – is simultaneously personally liberating and politically transformative has been a core principle of the lesbian and gay social movement since the 1970s; in this concept the 'personal' imbricates most powerfully with the 'political'. In tandem with this political principle, Lennon's plots hinge on the value of subjective coherence and authenticity, and what, in a different context, Eve Sedgwick describes as 'people's sense of the potency, magnetism, and promise of gay self-disclosure'.[27]

Published in the year of decriminalisation and set three years before, *When Love Comes to Town* begins as Neil is preparing for his upcoming Leaving Cert exams and about to celebrate his eighteenth birthday. It concludes a few months later when he is about to begin college. With its teenage protagonist on the cusp of adulthood and its familiar thematic (educational and moral formation; vocation; navigation of the social world) Lennon's first novel hews closely to the conventions of the *bildungsroman*. What is unusual is the compression of the generic narrative arc – crisis compelling the attainment of maturity – into such a short time frame. The pace is hectic as, in just a few weeks, Neil: completes his exams and argues with his parents about his choice of college course; begins socialising on the gay scene; is befriended by a number of older gay men, including two married cross-dressers; visits another of his new friends who is dying of AIDS; is left unconscious for three days after being gay-bashed; comes out to his friends and family; attempts suicide; has his first relationship; begins a second relationship – and gives an emotional interview to the late Marian Finucane on national radio.

One reason for this narrative compression is that the plot is compelled by a crisis of revelation rather than formation. Underpinning both of Lennon's narratives is the certainty that an authentic gay identity lies beneath the artificiality of his protagonists' dissembling performance of heterosexuality. Thus, Neil comes to the reader fully formed as it were. He experiences considerable anxiety and even moments of self-disgust about being gay, but no confusion or uncertainty. The romantic ending affirms this idea; Neil is overjoyed to learn that Ian, the angelically beautiful blond schoolfellow he has secretly adored since he was 14, feels the same way. The aura of innocence underpinning this authenticity, romance unsullied by adult sexuality, is left firmly intact since we never actually see how this relationship might unfold.

A second reason for the hectic pace is a compulsion to address 'issues' and an anthropological impetus to 'explain' gay subculture to the dominant culture. The novel's depiction of that subculture is ambivalent. On the gay scene Neil finds kindness, understanding and fun. Nevertheless, the narrative perspective and tone does little to ironise, or distance itself, from Neil's unease at the seediness and desperation he perceives everywhere in the gay social world – not to mention his moralising revulsion at those over 30 being in any way sexual. Moreover, Dublin's gay subculture, as depicted in the novel, is entirely confined to the commercial scene – one pub, to be precise – without any other form of activism or organising being registered. Neil and his mother see 'Daphne', Neil's camp friend from the scene, collecting for an HIV charity, but the point of the episode is Neil's anxiety about being recognised and his subsequent relief and self-recrimination. Moreover, the meaning of Daphne's impending death from HIV is entirely confined within the domestic sphere, when Neil and Shane go to visit him in his family home, and within the affective sphere of pleasurable sentimentality, focused specifically around his loving and grieving mother, without having any possible historical or political meaning. Within Neil's coming-out narrative his gay identity is in no way registered as a form of political consciousness. At most it might be considered a form of moral consciousness, as he is more acutely alert to the hypocrisy, deceit and self-delusion everywhere in his bourgeois social world – though recalling Holden Caulfield's disgust at the 'phonies' this motif is hardly new or specific to the coming-out novel.

But depicting this depoliticised form of gay identity is, of course, entirely political. The novel's anthropological mode suggests a pressure not just to represent gay life but to be representative, and thereby to stake a claim for recognition from the majority culture for this minority identity. Politically, the terms on which recognition is being sought remain firmly within the ambit of liberal pluralism and individualism; hence the emphasis on Neil's developing moral consciousness emptied of any political potential. Moreover, the claim for recognition relies entirely on the affective potential of the narrative rather than any conception of justice. The primary affect which the narrative relies on to achieve this recognition of the gay protagonist's 'humanity' from the reader – pity; sympathy – installs suffering and injury at the definitional core of their identity. Paradoxically then, the cost of being recognised as 'human' requires a diminution of human potentiality – sacrificing agency for abjection, and gambling on the greater affective potential of the latter. This political standpoint is instilled in the structure and tone – a fusion of comedy and pathos – of both novels.

While Lennon's first novel pivots on teenage self-exploration and formation, *Crazy Love* draws primarily on the conventions of the popular romance rather than the *bildungsroman*. In the opening chapters, we see Paul at his workplace and his home, and we learn that he is 28, married to the younger, patiently devoted Anne, father of a small child and a very successful executive on the cusp of a lucrative promotion. Then, in the midst of describing the stress of driving home through busy traffic, Paul is sexually aroused by a handsome cyclist he sees at traffic lights. Thereafter he briefly and impressionistically reconstructs for us the delusions (assuming his attraction to men was a phase), conformity to social conventions, omissions and failure of nerve that led to his marriage. But soon, in the narrative present, his precarious closeted life collapses when

Paul begins a passionate affair with Johnny, a younger male colleague. Balancing two lives precipitates a nervous breakdown for Paul, but out of this crisis we reach, relatively smoothly, a happy ending – an amicable break-up with Anne, which means he can still be a father, and a new (equally comfortable) domestic life with Johnny.

When Love is narrated in the third person, but extensively focalised around Neil. There are also recurring passages where the narration slips into an odd conjunction of first and second person in an inner monologue framed as Neil addressing the figure of Jesus. This adoption of prayer is humorously colloquial and ironic, but also earnest. While institutional religion is easily sloughed off as irrelevant by Neil and his contemporaries, the novel seems keen to retain some notion of religious faith as valuable – not least through the wholly sympathetic, rather idealised, figure of Neil's teacher, Father Donnelly. When Neil finds himself distressed and spiralling towards suicide the symbolism of the prayer motif – particularly Neil's identification with Jesus as a son – manifests itself as the religious concept of martyrdom, reiterating again how abject yet purposeful suffering, and the sympathy this evokes, is such a defining structure of feeling in the novel's political imagination. *Crazy Love* is narrated by Paul, but in the second person. This emphasis on interiority, and on the struggle to bring the inner self into alignment with the social self, foregrounds the conjunction of sexual desire, self-knowledge and attainment of a coherent identity that is central to the novel's vision. Again, the recurring use of emotional crises as pivotal plot devices reiterates the urgency of attaining such an identity as the only viable route to psychic well-being. While Paul's use of the second person might suggest an unstable process of attaining the wholeness of identity, the narration is not a stream of consciousness; the prose has the rhythm and cadences of speech – short declarative sentences; colloquialisms; plain 'unliterary' language – but conforms to grammatical and linguistic convention and therefore solidifies around a coherent perspective. In other words, the central problematic animating the narrative is not so much identity as authenticity.

Neil and Paul inhabit a remarkably circumscribed social world: south Dublin; prosperous professional middle class; privately educated. The limited scope of Lennon's canvas is not of itself problematic. It is, for instance, typical of the *bildungsroman*, which is so often steeped in the material of the author's biography. To take just one example from Irish writing, the rigorously circumscribed social world depicted in McGahern's novels was no impediment to creating richly complex fiction. That the now deceased Lennon wrote under a pseudonym – a publisher's website tells us that this was because he was then teaching in a fee-paying secondary school – illustrates how the drama of self-disclosure narrated in the coming-out novel can be profoundly informed by personal history.[28]

For critical purposes, the fiction's political perspective on class relations is more interesting than merely focusing on the social world it describes. There is a striking shift in tone between the two novels. In *When Love*, Neil's visit to Daphne's home in a working-class estate is cast in the same anthropological mode as his visits to the gay bar. The twist, of course, is that underneath the threatening aggression palpable in the neighbourhood – indexed by some homophobic graffiti – Daphne's family and neighbours are open-minded, tolerant and accepting – 'Don't worry, we don't give a fuck if yer gay', as Daphne's sister puts it.[29] This tokenistic, sentimental and cliché-heavy celebration of the Dublin working class – there is, of course, a generous-hearted 'mammy' – feels rather forced. So it is unsurprising that a darker reactionary tone emerges in *Crazy Love*. This is particularly encapsulated in one episode. Having dinner with Anne and their friends in a Chinese restaurant, Paul witnesses two gay men being harassed by a group of working-class men; naturally they are also aggressively racist towards the staff. However, to the relief of the embarrassed middle-class customers, the intruders are defeated by the courageous verbal wit of one of the gay men – his condescending verbal dexterity in marked contrast to their monosyllabic stupidity – and the imposing physical presence of a Chinese chef. Paul notices that one of these men has a tricolour tattoo on his arm and observes that 'the ugly leer contorting his face leaves the two lads in no doubt that they don't exactly fit into his vision of Ireland'.[30] Trading in lazy stereotypes and caricatures the episode is a burlesque of the neurosis and paranoid *ressentiment* lurking just beneath the pluralist veneer of Irish liberalism. And while Lennon's novel satirises so much about middle-class life, irony and satire are banished in this episode – that paranoid structure of feeling is earnestly endorsed by the novel.

Ultimately, Lennon's novels demand a peculiarly narrow form of pluralism and inclusion: the right of a young middle-class man to be gay, without losing any of the patriarchal dividend and inherited class power to which he is entitled by birth and gender. The narrative perspective and tone of the novels – the irony and satire directed at middle-class suburban values – can distract us from the conservativism of this animating investment in a bourgeois, individualist and masculine ideal. In *Crazy Love* especially the acquisitive, competitive and, the novel suggests, spiritually hollow consumerism of Paul's 'Celtic Tiger' generation is heavily satirised. But rather than serving a political purpose, Lennon's satire supplants political critique with moral and ethical critique. Thus, in *Crazy Love*, for instance, it is not the structures of the modern corporate workplace that are in question but that *some* people in such workplaces are devious or unpleasant.

From the governing perspective of these novels, the pressing question is not wealth distribution or the structure of social relations which reproduces that distribution of wealth, or the ideology underpinning this system. The fundamental problem is that well-off people in this society are inauthentic. And here the figure of the gay man, far from challenging that society, is redemptive and affirmative. The bad faith of the closeted gay protagonist, a necessary survival strategy, is eventually redeemed by their coming out. Thus, this figure offers an example to the dominant society of how it too could overcome the bad faith of its endemic hypocrisy and double standards by embracing openness and pluralism. At the same time, while challenging liberal capitalism's bad faith – its failure to live up to its promises – the gay man affirms that system's values through his abiding desire to successfully embody the masculine ideal – now recalibrated to encompass gay male identity – of liberal individualism underpinning those values.

By adapting the conventional comic ending of the romance genre to create a satisfying resolution for his readers, Lennon's plotting reinforces this affirmative but conservative effect. While challenging Irish society to progressively change the values and ideas governing its sexual morality the novels simultaneously endorse the sacramentalism underpinning those values – while things should change, they should also stay the same. The domesticated monogamous couple is the most reassuring guarantee that a healthy identity has been achieved. And to reiterate this point, the novels casually stigmatise other forms of sex between men (casual encounters; anonymous cruising) as a distressing sign of dysfunction and merely symptomatic of underdeveloped or stalled identity formation. That these stigmatised sexual styles are invariably associated with older men affirms the developmental narrative; hopefully, the novels imply, such residues of the unhappy past will gradually disappear. Moreover, the endings affirm that a satisfying resolution can be achieved in the present. As we have seen, it is striking how little actually needs to change in the protagonists' lives for this resolution to be reached – as the style of narration reiterates the crucial change is emotional and physic, not political. The endings are open – the promise of new relationships – and yet also closed; there is no need to imagine the future since it will be a continuation of the present.

As Alan Sinfield argues, a central thematic of lesbian and gay fiction and cinema since the 1970s is that the ideal gay and lesbian relationship is inherently egalitarian, free from hierarchies of gender, age or class. That this idea must be so anxiously reiterated reveals the degree to which such hierarchies persist. But, as Sinfield asserts, the 'prevailing sex/gender system [...] is geared to the production of hierarchy and, as part of that, to the production of anxious, unhappy, and violent people. It produces us and our psychic lives – straights and gays – and it is not going to leave us alone.'[31] The hierarchal power relations of the capitalist social order structure what we believe to be most intimate and private: our sexual desires, fantasies, and pleasures. To believe otherwise is, as Sinfield puts it, 'a liberal-bourgeois delusion'. This perspective, in Sinfield's view, ignores the reality that, ultimately, 'all power is about command over the means of life'. Therefore, the 'intense commitments that we call "love" may, ultimately, be intricately mediated versions of a will to survive, ontologically as well as materially. This may lead us into interpersonal opportunities which seem to afford a reassuring exercise of our own power. Equally, it may draw us into the orbit of people who appear powerful and may protect us.'[32]

Jarlath Gregory's *Snapshots* (2001) and *G.A.A.Y: one hundred ways to love a beautiful loser* (2005) imaginatively confront the paradoxical erotics of power – power as sexy, because contemporary society leaves us fearless and vulnerable – while ultimately shying away from the radical implications towards which this confrontation leads. In contrast with Lennon's fiction, these novels subvert and ironise the conventions of the coming-out romance, thereby conveying a more paradoxical and qualified affirmation of gay male identity.

Firstly, Gregory's plots complicate the coming-out narrative since coming out does not necessarily bring catharsis and resolution through the fulfilment of a more authentic selfhood. This is because being closeted about one's sexuality is not the only, or even central, problem confronting the young protagonists. Set in the Catholic nationalist community of Crossmaglen, beneath the comic surface of *Snapshots* there is a darker undertow: a war held at bay by a brittle ceasefire and a legacy of violence, loss and bitterness. The crisis in Oisin's life – overwhelmed by depression and inertia – is not precipitated by disguising or revealing his sexuality but by reverberations of a familial and political tragedy. His brother, Sean, was killed accidently some years before while transporting explosives for the IRA. However, a chapter narrated by Sean suggests it may have been suicide as he had grown disillusioned.[33]

G.A.A.Y. is narrated by Anto, a young gay man living with his family in a council flat in Dublin. Since 22-year-old Anto is ostentatiously open about his sexual identity, and has been since he was 15, the generic crisis of dissimulation and revelation focuses on his two ostensibly straight potential lovers: Khalid, a British Asian man working in Dublin, and Cathal, a neighbour whose sporting prowess gives the novel its punning title. However, the narrative is equally concerned with Anto's energetic commitment to pursuing glamour and success – through, he hopes, the boy band he and his friends have formed – while negotiating the dreary reality of working life – in his case, the highly regulated, emotionally exhausting tedium of a call centre.

This thematic dislodgment of the coming-out crisis as fulcrum of the plot is reinforced by Gregory's style of narration. *Snapshots* alternates between the first-person perspectives of Oisin and Jude, interspersed with brief third-person 'snapshots'. These shifting perspectives (rotating between characters – including the dead – and also temporally) along with the episodic, picaresque plotting of both novels – sequences of conversations, social gatherings and sexual encounters – disperses the narrative consciousness and decentralises the developmental biographical narrative. In *G.A.A.Y.* this narrative dislodgment is reinforced by Gregory playing with the conventions of realist narrative. This relatively short novel is divided into one hundred titled sections ('Anto sets the tower blocks alight'; 'I am a gay cliché') of varying length, though none more than four pages. Conversations by SMS and email, and even the list of contacts from a mobile phone, are incorporated into the novel's heteroglossia. In both novels, the prose is energetically mannered: staccato sentences; speech rhythms; extensive use of dialect and slang.

In *G.A.A.Y.* Anto is cynically alert to the superficiality of his popstar ambitions – desiring the glamour and wealth rather than any fulfilment from performing. At the same time, he is conscious of the actual yearnings underpinning such ambition; the longing for freedom from the alienation, humiliation and dispiriting grind of contemporary working life – indexed by his descriptions of that distinctively neoliberal workplace, the call centre. Thus, in one of those brief lyrical passages which punctuate the narrative, Anto's characteristic irony recedes as he conveys not just what the boy band means to him but what its performance style will offer to its audience – an experience cynically manufactured and yet actually responsive to real human needs: 'the lyrics are easy. It's all about you, me, a sunny day and a climbing killer chorus that kids can sing the first time. What you can't fake is us: when we smile, we mean it; when we laugh, we feel it; when we tell you we love, we need you, it's true. We want you to buy us, and learn how to always be happy too.'[34]

Here, and throughout, Anto's tone is paradoxically camp – an unrelentingly ironic and provocatively superficial performance that strategically camouflages while enacting an earnestly held commitment to a romantic, utopian longing for the world to be different. It is a precarious performance of strength propelled by alienation and vulnerability. As Fabio Cleto puts it, 'camp does not make fun of things grave, momentous and solemn: it makes fun *out* of them, cherishing them as it transcends their solemnity into irony'. Camp is 'a dressed-up transfiguration of stigma, the aesthetic displacement of marginality into metaphorical splendour and the laughing off of history's material urgency'.[35] This camp tone and structure of feeling is central to the political imagination of Gregory's novels. Potentially this camp tone is much more generative of radical insight into contemporary ideology and consciousness than mere sociological verisimilitude – Anto's astute observations about housing, working and consumption in late-Celtic Tiger Dublin, for instance – or Lennon's moral-satiric mode.

Inevitably, this camp paradoxical tone encompasses the novel's perspectives on the sexual, emotional and social drama of coming out. In various ways Gregory's novels ironise the minoritising conception of gay identity narrated in the coming-out romance. Gregory eschews the crisis and the developmental plot type, with its incitement to pathos and its installation of injury as essential to identity. Likewise, he eschews those styles of narration which foreground individual psychic wholeness; hence the dispersed consciousness of *Snapshots* and Anto's camp voice, along with the formal playfulness, in *G.A.A.Y.* Thus, for instance, Section 75 of *G.A.A.Y.* is 'Anto's guide to coming out (for Khalid)'.[36] Given the novel's prevailing tone, the reader might expect a parody of self-help culture ironically undermining that conception of subjective authenticity underpinning the idea of coming out: a spontaneous revelation of the real self, underpinned by faith in subjective coherence and integrity, that is also – rather like the boy band – a performance to be managed, staged and negotiated. His 'guide' is replete with Anto's typical jokes and just such a knowing sense of coming out as performance and performative. Nevertheless, the content of his guide would not be out of place in an actual workshop, booklet or online resource directed at LGBT youth. Again, we note the camp paradox of ironic detachment and earnest attachment.

Arguably, Gregory's novels are less concerned with destabilising politicised identities than with establishing hierarchies between them. One hierarchy is between those protagonists who are relatively unambiguously gay – Oisin, Jude, Anto – and those men who identify as straight while being sexually attracted to other men and are in various states of denial or repression about this. Thus, while the hesitant and awkward progression of a romantic relationship between Oisin and Jude winds circuitously through the plot of *Snapshots*, their sexual encounters are not with each other but with 'straight' men from among their acquaintances. Characteristically *G.A.A.Y.* presents a comic burlesque of closetedness, with Anto recounting a sequence of such encounters – mainly with a series of his sister's boyfriends. Then his friend Cathy, in humorous yet also serious denial about being lesbian, has an affair with Anto's heretofore straight mother which he discovers in suitably farcical circumstances.[37]

This comedy might suggest the novel is moving towards a radical perspective on the minoritising and sacramentalising framework of discrete sexual identities. To be legitimate and authentic – redeemed from mere sinful pleasure – must sex always be 'meaningful' and deliver some truth about ourselves? But, once again, the camp dialectic of irony and sincerity short-circuits the emergence of any such critique. Anto jokingly wonders if he has 'backed two losers in the coming-out race', and the ultimate trajectory of the plot is towards the protagonists finding the courage to overcome the obstacles towards attaining a coherent and authentic identity.[38]

The second hierarchy is between those types of politicised identity (national; religious) which are fundamentally negative (insular; aggressive; psychotic), and those other types of politicised identity, indicatively gay identity, which offer a route to freedom. In *Snapshots*, nationalist and republican politics is depicted as little more than instinctual prejudice; it is most associated with father figures, who are invariably the least well-drawn characters, caricatures of hostile indifference, in Gregory's fiction. The episodic, impressionistic chapter narrated by Sean about his involvement with paramilitaries begins with his and Oisin's upbringing and foregrounds the differences between them. The implication is that unthinking conformity to gender norms is also unthinking conformity to inherited prejudices, leading to tragedy and waste, whereas flouting such conventions – even at the cost of being different, unhappy and bullied – gives you critical distance on your world and freedom from history. Likewise, in *G.A.A.Y.*, Khalid and Cathal's stories imply that some cultures – here, British Asian Muslim and Irish Catholic – place particularly difficult barriers across the route to subjective coherence. Thus, the biographical narrative of courage needed to attain psychic coherence is overlaid with a cultural and historical narrative; the trajectory of the self towards authenticity is complicated by the trajectory of the culture towards modernity – where modernity is coterminous with the consumer capitalism ambiguously endorsed through the narrative's libidinal investment in contemporary media culture.

Evidently then, Gregory's fiction simultaneously confronts and evades the implications of that determinative connection between sexuality and power. Contradictory impulses coexist within its political imagination: affirming the liberal pluralist ethos of lesbian and gay identity politics while also yearning for a more radical reimagining of freedom and human potentialities. The thematic and narrative trajectory of coming out affirms the hermeneutic of politicised identity, while the simultaneous concern with the thematic of success and failure – indexed through the figure of the 'beautiful loser' – undermines that hermeneutic. Or, more precisely, that thematic of success and failure, again we recall the boy band, potentially undermines the model of the autonomous, entrepreneurial self that is endorsed through liberal discourses of gay identity.

Arguably, the animating figure of Gregory's fiction is not the gay male subject but the male body in various states of attraction and abjection. As their homophonous names suggest, perhaps Khalid and Cathal are not to be read as literary characters – figures embodying a 'closeted' subjectivity – but as interchangeable avatars, emblems of a masculinity which is politically troubling (violent, competitive, emotionally repressed) but erotically irresistible. Gregory's novel reiterates that erotic enthrallment to embodiments of patriarchal masculinity is not necessarily a fetish of gay men but symptomatic of neoliberal culture as such. It is, after all, one of the contradictions of the hegemonic ideology that the aggressive competitiveness characteristic of conventional masculinity (in our dominant gender ideology) is highly prized as an attribute of the entrepreneurial self – that neoliberal ideal of what it is to be human – even while the misogyny, homophobia and racism that is equally constitutive of conventional masculinity is abjured in the name of liberal pluralism. Moreover, living under a cultural dominant that constitutively engenders anxiety and precariousness, as we all do, must invariably lead us to form strong libidinal investments in symbols of strength and invulnerability. In contemporary media culture, the finely honed – and heavily commodified through advertising and branding – body of the male sport star functions as just such an object of cathexis.

The paratext of Gregory's second novel has fun with this: the punning title along with the cover image of a young man photographed from behind, a Dublin GAA (Gaelic Athletic Association) jersey and jeans framing his pert body for our gaze. But within the texts of both novels that invulnerable sporting male body skilfully at play, exerting control over its environment, is overshadowed by recurring descriptions of the male body as dishevelled, damaged and debilitated – vulnerable to assault and alcohol. Shifting the site of pain from the psyche to the body, the novels imaginatively replace injury with vulnerability, symbolically dislodging that impetus to minoritising identification with an alternative potential source of collective mobilisation against the depredations of capitalism. *Snapshots* ends with Oisin and Jude sharing a beer at Sean's grave. Jude plucks petals from a wreath and throws them at Oisin, who wryly describes them as 'confetti'.[39] Juxtaposing that futurity promised by a romance sacramentalised in marriage with the persistent nullity of death and war Gregory's ending scrambles the temporality of the coming-out narrative – the trajectory towards maturity and authenticity – as well as the political temporality central to liberal sexual politics. As the image of Sean's destroyed body lying in its grave viscerally reminds us, the instability, conflict and violence endemic to capitalism cannot be so easily transmuted into 'differences' to be gradually reconciled through the chimera of neoliberal 'equality'.

Jamie O'Neill's *At Swim, Two Boys* (2001) and Denis Kehoe's *Nights Beneath the Nation* (2008) are historical romances which use fiction to unearth, and imaginatively recreate, an archaeology of same-sex passions between men in pre-1970s Ireland. These tragic romances speak powerfully to a yearning to make the silences of history speak. Both novels are propelled by a belief that fiction can work some alchemy on the past that is inaccessible through other modes of history writing. They are motivated by the belief that, as Scott Bravmann puts it, 'lesbian and gay historical self-representation – queer fictions of the past – help construct, maintain and contest identities – queer fictions of the present'.[40] The difficulty with which they must contend is to create a style of narration which can imaginatively encounter, without condescending to, the alterity of the past. The real political risk of failing to encounter that alterity is not actually to the past but to our ways of imagining the present and to the future – the risk of imaginative encounters with the past which, as Sedgwick observes, '*re*naturalise' the present.[41]

Kehoe confronts this challenge by arranging his narrative into a series of alternating chapters, set in Dublin in 1997–98 and in 1950–51. In the narrative present Daniel, the first-person narrator, is visiting from New York after over forty years away from Ireland. In the alternate chapters he recounts moving from a small town to Dublin as a young man to become a civil servant, and his friendship with Maeve, an older woman who introduces him to the city's bohemian artistic circles and casts him in an amateur production of Lorca's *Blood Wedding*. At the centre of this story is Daniel's account of his passionate love affair with Anthony. The tragic ending of their relationship, we learn, precipitated his flight to New York. In the novel's present, Daniel befriends Gerard, a young man who is writing a novel about bohemian, theatrical, and homosexual subcultures in 1950s Dublin.

Through this temporally bifurcated structure, along with the deliberate incorporation of a character resembling the author but distinct from the narrator, the novel self-consciously foregrounds the act of storytelling – the conscious and dynamic activity of narratively reconstructing the past. Unfortunately, this formal self-awareness is inconsistently applied. Daniel tells his story with the fluent assurance of an omniscient narrator and a scholar's attention to historical detail, so that the complex problematic of human memory, its creative dynamism and fragility, is never broached. Moreover, some grammatical slipperiness confuses the perspective of Daniel's narration of the past, and so he ascribes to his younger consciousness ways of thinking about his circumstances that are more plausibly those of a historian or novelist in the 1990s. Thus, attending church with his family 'I could feel the fear in the air, the fear and misguided devotion. I could see how people were being strangled, suffocated slowly; how their minds, their desires and their bodies were being taken away from them bit by bit.'[42] Likewise, Kehoe diligently describes the geography of the 1950s cityscape and attempts to evoke the spaces and atmosphere of its bohemian demimonde. But factual accuracy is less vital in historical fiction than storytelling which vividly animates the sensuous, intellectual and emotional experience of living in another time. The challenge to the historical imagination is to capture the essential difference of the past and avoid reducing it to a simulacrum, or a cluster of caricatures, shaped by our present preoccupations. What matters in the historical novel, as Lukács argues, is 'the poetic awakening of the people ... that we should re-experience the social and human motives which led people to think, feel and act just as they did in historical reality'.[43]

As he is reminded when he goes to the National Library to read the newspaper archives, Daniel's past has been grossly misrepresented – Anthony's suicide covered up and the case reported on with a hypocritical mixture of sensation and moral outrage. But in Kehoe's narrative this acknowledgement that historical interpretation might be volatile and contested does not precipitate an encounter with the fluidity and openness of history – history as a dynamic struggle for the future as much as for the past. Instead, the narrative solidifies history into a series of schematic binaries. Just as the reader is reassuringly secure epistemologically (our suspenseful confusion about the events surrounding Anthony's death is satisfyingly resolved through Daniel's account) we are likewise encouraged to feel secure politically. Throughout, the reader is reassured that they would never have been complicit with that irredeemably hypocritical and oppressive majority – the 'nation' – and would inevitably have been in sympathetic conformity with the glamorous and politically virtuous minority 'beneath' it. Kehoe is surprisingly anxious to reinforce this point didactically through the rather clunky insertion of references to historical events. Thus, Daniel is explicitly outraged about Irish clerical support for Franco during the Spanish Civil War, about de Valera visiting the German legation in Dublin after Hitler's suicide, about opposition to the Mother and Child Scheme in 1951, and so on. Paradoxically then, as the novel incorporates detailed 'facts' of history its story becomes less historical, since the competing ideological perspectives and conflicts of history are translated into an ahistorical and reassuring moral binary.

The tone reinforces this historical and moral schema. Daniel is cynical, world-weary and casually offensive – recurring dismissive references to 'fags', for instance – but the effect of this is to heighten the pathos suffusing the novel. His cynicism, we must conclude, is less conviction than a symptom of injury – a reaction incited by pain, guilt and grief. It is essential to the novel's world view that he and Anthony are uncomplicated victims. In particular, Anthony's victimhood is melodramatically overdetermined by the deployment of Gothic tropes: scheming, villainous parents; enforced confinement in an asylum; an arranged marriage; dying in a 'fountain of blood' having slit his throat.[44] The novel sets out to answer affirmatively Gerard's question to Daniel; 'if love, true love, was possible between men at that time'.[45] But the novel's historical imagination is much more powerfully compelled by suffering than by love. To narrate the joy and pleasure of Daniel and Anthony's relationship Kehoe's prose struggles to escape the overwrought but deadening effects of adapting narrative tropes from popular romance and pornography: 'I moved my body to the rhythm of him hard inside me. And soon we were flying, flying off somewhere beyond ourselves ... and it was magic, unbearable, exquisite, unbelievable magic and we kept our eyes closed, flying away until there was no end to it but that violent release.'[46] To reiterate the tragedy of their love being destroyed by history, that love must be idealised into banality.

There are some striking and dispiriting paradoxes here. As the recurring references to the Spanish Civil War foreground, albeit in a rather forced way, the novel's overt political sympathies are critical and broadly socialist. Yet the commitment to a moral hermeneutic of injury is much more deeply embedded aesthetically: in plot, tone and mood. Love, hope and a sense of history as dynamically open – those indispensable conditions for the radical political imagination – are subordinated to the pleasures of injury, the consolations of morality and the reassurances of history as progress. Rather than enriching our perspectives on the past, such fiction may in fact reinforce our complacent sense that present arrangements, of political economy as much as of sexual identity and freedom, may not be ideal but are the best we can achieve. And, thus, in the most painful irony for a novel with critical and socialist sympathies, while striving to ensure its readers are morally attuned to oppressive ideologies in the past, the novel's historical perspective affirms oppressive ideologies in the present. Unwittingly, the novel's historicism endorsed the hegemonic neoliberal conception of 'Celtic Tiger' Ireland as being committed to tolerance and pluralism, on one hand, and to a financialised global economy, with all its attendant exploitations and inequalities, on the other.

In *At Swim, Two Boys* O'Neill confronts that problem of the historical imagination – how to encounter the past as discomfortingly other – more successfully. He uses two formal strategies – intertextuality and characterisation – to convey the political and intellectual ferment of the past and the creative activity of engaging with this. As Joseph Valente points out, O'Neill's gay reworking of the *bildungsroman* explicitly acknowledges its debt to Irish antecedents of the period when the novel is set, notably *The Picture of Dorian Gray* (1891), *The Last September* (1929) and, most obviously, *A Portrait of the Artist as a Young Man* (1916).[47] The titular nod to Flann O'Brien is rather misleading, since it finds no echo beyond the front cover and O'Neill's style in many respects hews rather respectfully to the conventions of classic realism. By contrast, the novel bears its debt to Joyce more heavily, especially in the deliberately Joycean fashion that O'Neill uses free indirect discourse throughout the narration. Thus, the opening chapter, in which the kindly but socially self-conscious Mr Mack walks through the morning streets of Glasthule, the seaside village in Dublin's southern suburbs where the novel is set in the year leading up to the 1916 Rising, is none too subtle in its stylistic echoes of the second chapter of *Ulysses*: 'In delicate clutch an *Irish Times* he held. A thruppenny piece, waiting to pay, rolled in his fingers. Every so often his hand queried his elbow – Parcel safe? Under me arm, his hand-pat assured him.'[48] Likewise, those sections of the novel narrated from Anthony MacMurrough's perspective includes imagined comic dialogues between the allegorical figures of 'Dick', 'the chaplain' and 'Nanny', echoing, in less hallucinatory mode, the dialogue in the 'Circe' chapter. MacMurrough also has recurring 'conversations' in his mind with his now dead friend Scrotes, and these include a conversation narrated in a pastiche of the 'Ithaca' chapter's parody of the Catechism's interrogatory format. However, Joyce is only the most prominent source of these intertextual allusions. The novel's fabric is a densely woven palimpsest of direct quotations and indirect allusions. The former include quotations from sources as diverse as St Augustine, Irish rebel ballads, Douglas Hyde's poetry and Wilde's epigrams. Likewise, the referents for O'Neill's indirect allusions range just as widely, from the history of Irish agrarian militancy – 'MacMurrough woke at the peep of day' – to the fiction of E.M. Forster – 'are you telling me you are an unspeakable of the Oscar Wilde sort?'[49]

While O'Neill's novel is playfully explicit about its relationship to *Ulysses*, there is no direct acknowledgement of its close formal affinities with James Plunkett's *Strumpet City* (1969). But in fact, O'Neill's novel is much closer in form, style and tone to the latter than it is to *Ulysses*. These are two historical novels written in the latter half of the twentieth century, with each adapting the form and narrative techniques of nineteenth-century European realism – filtered lightly through, though not fundamentally altered by, Joycean Modernism – to engage imaginatively with political events in early twentieth-century Dublin (the 1913 Lockout and the 1916 Rising, respectively).

Most strikingly, O'Neill follows Plunkett in making use of characters and characterisation to imaginatively capture the volatile structure of the city's multilayered class relations and the historical dialectic of conflicting political perspectives. The narrative is finely tuned to the gradations, injustices and petty snobberies underscoring the cultural valuation of respectability. As importantly, O'Neill's cast of characters maps the class geography of Glasthule: from young Doyler (living in abject dehumanising poverty with his family in the back lanes of the village; literally shovelling the shit of the better-off for his wages) to Mr Mack and his son, Jim (living behind their grocer's shop; grasping the promise of mobility offered by Jim's scholarship; anxious of the fine line separating them from descent into the realm of the desperately poor) to MacMurrough and his aunt Eveline (scions of Catholic gentry; grandson and daughter of a Parnellite MP; living in the stately grandeur of Ballygihen House).

Likewise, the novel has historical figures representing diverse, allied and opposed positions in Irish politics (Kettle; Casement; Pearse; Connolly; Carson) crossing paths with its fictional characters – the political and social prominence of the MacMurroughs is a useful plot device for facilitating this. More crucially, the fictional characters engage with, articulate and commit themselves to various positions within a spectrum of Irish nationalism: Mr Mack's pro-empire Irish patriotism (veteran of the Boer War; his son, Gordie – named for Gordon of Khartoum – now in Gallipoli); the bourgeois politics of securing Home Rule that is Eveline's family legacy; the militant separatism towards which – like Casement, with whom, we are told, she was in love – she has moved (including running guns for the Volunteers in preparation for the Rising); Fr Taylor's reactionary nativism and clericalism; the socialist anti-imperialism of Doyler, a militant 'Larkinite' who joins the Citizen's Army.

This sense of national history in a period of acute flux – heterogeneous visions of the Irish future – runs parallel with a sense of the history of male sexual identities in similar flux. Again, various historical and fictional characters embody the diverse discourses and stereotypes that were, in the decades just before and after Wilde's death, circulating in European culture and beginning to cohere into the, to us, recognisable figure of the homosexual – and his later politicised successor, the gay man. Centrally, MacMurrough, who was raised in England, has come to live with Eveline after serving two years hard labour for gross indecency; the war meant he could not, like Wilde after his time in prison, go to continental Europe. In prison, he was befriended by Scrotes, an elderly Oxford classicist imprisoned for the same offence who died serving his sentence. Thus, their fate foregrounds that pathologising and criminalising apparatus that merged old ideas with contemporary anxieties – about social disorder and imperial decline – in late nineteenth-century Britain, fusing medical science, law and morality, and mediated to the public as moral panic through the emergent popular press. MacMurrough also pays younger working-class men like Doyler for sex, invoking that other figure – the upper-class 'gent' and his 'bit of rough' – that had gained popular currency through the sensationalist media coverage of Wilde's trial.

O'Neill uses the device of imagined conversations between MacMurrough and Scrotes to allow a dialogic evolution in how MacMurrough understands his experience. Specifically, we see his consciousness move from the stigmatised abjection of injury to grasping the structural and ideological determinants of his imprisonment. In this way, the novel imagines how the tragedy and pain of history can be transmuted into solidarity rather than congealing into a form of subjectivity. Moreover, the figures of MacMurrough and Scrotes equally foreground those counter-discourses that, in this same period, artists and intellectuals were developing to legitimise, and even valorise, same-sex passion between men. As his recurring invocation of Wilde's epigrams suggest, MacMurrough adopts the ironic, insouciant style of the dandy. The figure of Scrotes invokes historical figures, such as Benjamin Jowett, Walter Pater and John Addington Symonds, and their application of the prestige accruing to classical and Renaissance scholarship, and in a particular way to Hellenism, to advance intellectual arguments for an idealised – ethically and spiritually purposive – conception of male friendship and passion. But Scrotes, we are told by MacMurrough, also knew Edward Carpenter who advocated a less elitist ideal of comradely love between men infused with his socialist politics. The novel's overt commitment to this latter, radically democratic, politicisation of the homoerotic is indexed by the prefatory epigrammatic use of Whitman.[50]

Mobilising politically around national identity and mobilising politically around sexual identity – more precisely, a proto-gay male identity – are expressly analogised in the novel. Typically, the novel demonstrates this use of the past – specifically the literary and poetic residues of the past – to mobilise around an imagined future through a playful allusion to the Irish political ballad tradition. Doyler and Jim are members of a pipe band, which MacMurrough is persuaded by his aunt to teach, and there they learn to play 'A Nation Once Again'. The imagined Scrotes explains to MacMurrough, and thereby to the reader, the allusions to classical history in Thomas Davis's lines: 'When boyhood's fire was in my blood, / I read of ancient freemen, /For Greece and Rome who stood / Three hundred men and three men.' MacMurrough later explains this to Doyler, specifically the reference to the Battle of Thermopylae and the tradition of Spartan warriors encouraged to be lovers to promote solidarity and devotion in their ranks. Doyler, in turn, recounts it to Jim.

Drawing our attention to this similarity between the deployment of Hellenism in two otherwise apparently distinct counter-hegemonic nineteenth-century discourses – cultural nationalist and homophile – is not, of course, unproblematic. This literary strategy resonates with an uneasy anxiety: the urge to validate same-sex passion through incorporating it into a national tradition – it was always there and is not a 'foreign' or 'modern' import – as well as into a model of masculinity defined through military violence – it is a manly passion, free from the stigma of effeminacy. Yet, despite, or perhaps because of, the earnestly naive tone through which these connections are explained to us, the novel's conjunction of these historical currents is rhetorically and affectively compelling. The dialogue of Scrotes – or more precisely the apparition called up by MacMurrough's mind – is deployed to make directly explicit, and persuasive, what the novel imagines as the political potential of this conjunction.

Referring to Doyler and Jim, the imagined Scrotes urges MacMurrough to:

> Help them make a nation, if not once again, then once for all ... a nation of the heart. Look about you. See Irish Ireland find out its past. Only with a past can it claim a future ... The struggle for Irish Ireland is not for truth against untruth. It is not for the good against the bad, for the beautiful against the unbeautiful. These things will take care of themselves. The struggle is for the heart, for its claim to stand in the light and cast a shadow its own in the sun. Help these boys build a nation their own. Ransack the histories for clues to their

past. Plunder the literatures for words they can speak ... and you shall name the unspeakable names of your kind, and in the naming, in each such telling, they will falter a step to the light. For only with pride may a man prosper.[51]

Critics of the novel, notably Valente, Jodie Medd and Patrick Mullen, affirm the radical potential of what Valente terms the 'narrative parallelism' between the boys' *bildungsroman* and that of the Irish nation.[52] Specifically, these critics believe the novel powerfully queers, in a deconstructionist rather than erotic sense, the national narrative. Thus, Valente celebrates the novel's 'articulation of an Irish nationalism that, far from reifying some ethnically proper spirit, orientation, or form of life, would fulfil the queer mandate of instituting ... "resistance to the very idea of the norm as such"'.[53] But it is not entirely clear how well this poststructuralist and revisionist perspective imputed to the novel chimes with the socialist republicanism, articulated historically by James Connolly and endorsed in the novel's political imagination. Most obviously, Doyler is passionately committed to this standpoint, and it is, after all, towards the young lovers, Doyler and Jim, that our political as well as our emotional sympathies are so strongly directed. In short, there is a curiously limiting, if depressingly familiar, calculus at work in Valente's 'queer' reading; affirming the novel's radicalism requires sublimating and abstracting the novel's actual socialist politics into something more politely amenable to contemporary neoliberal sensibilities.

Such readings assume that the traffic in ideological influence runs one way: that anticolonial, socialist and republican politics are being 'queered' – altered and radicalised – through being brought into narrative conjunction with sexual politics. But, arguably, this requires tuning out the novel's actual frequencies, in which the political scope of gay identity is radically expanded through imaginative conjunction with anti-imperial and anticapitalist politics. Most obviously, in the novel's political imaginary the politics of gay identity is distinctly insurrectionary. Doyler and Jim become revolutionary comrades as well as lovers; the narrative insistently interweaves the formation of their emotional and erotic consciousness with the formation of their political consciousness. Here O'Neill's attention to perspective through the use of focalisation and free indirect discourse, echoing Plunkett's style, is crucial. So, the passion of their desire for each other's bodies is not merely analogous to but constituted from the same psychic fabric as their desire for a socialist republic.

Again, this plot destination is foreshadowed through the rhythmic recurrence of an obscure historical allusion. Doyler's regular greeting to Jim is 'Are we straight so?', to which he encourages Jim to reply, 'Straight as a rush'. Eventually Doyler explains to Jim the historical origins of this in a formulaic exchange used when inducting members to the United Irishmen.[54] O'Neill is clearly having fun here, though not without serious intent. He is winking at his contemporary readers, who will inevitably but anachronistically tune into the colloquialism for heterosexuality.[55] At the same time, the boys' bourgeoning romance is brought into playful but politically suggestive conjunction with the history of insurrectionary republican politics, especially by reiterating how a style of coded communication was historically equally essential for same-sex romance and radical anticolonial and anticapitalist politics. Moreover, laying claim to the various other meanings of straight – not deviating; honesty – paradoxically asserts how political and sexual perversity hews closer than the political and sexual normal to what is actually most purposive.

The novel's palimpsest of intertextual allusions can be wearingly insistent, and the pastiche of writing styles sometimes laboured. But through analogising sexual identity with mobilisation around a nationalist politics that is anti-imperialist and anticapitalist, O'Neill's novel imagines a sexual politics that is historically dynamic and actively creative. We might note, for instance, Scrotes's declarative rhetoric and the abundance of verbs – 'see'; 'ransack'; 'plunder'. The energy of the prose reflects the energy with which the novel is itself performatively responding to Scrotes's injunction. The tumult of historical references and the vibrant patchwork of quotations is doing precisely the intellectual and political work that he advocates. As Scrotes reiterates, and as the novel instantiates textually, the political possibilities of imaginative literature are most powerfully a matter of style. O'Neill's novel is ever conscious – the comparison with Kehoe's novel is instructive here – that its primary goal is not to recover the experiences of earlier generations of gay men in Ireland but to elaborate a poetics of sexual politics for the present and the future. The novel's language, tone and rhythm are animated by this striving after a heightened, vibrant poetic style which might incite

Time and politics in Irish gay male fiction   149

our historical imagination to grasp the openness and potentialities of the future rather than the inevitability and injuries of the past.

Notes

1 Kieran Rose, *Diverse Communities: the evolution of lesbian and gay politics in Ireland* (Cork: Cork University Press, 1993), p. 8.
2 Rose, *Diverse Communities*, p. 2.
3 Rose, *Diverse Communities*, p. 3. Rose has been reprimanded for his anti-imperialist historical interpretation by cultural critics such as Kathryn Conrad. In conformity with the dominant liberal doxa of Irish cultural studies, Conrad asserts the primacy of globalisation as the motor of progressive changes in late twentieth-century Irish sexual norms and regulations. Kathryn Conrad, *Locked in the Family Cell: gender, sexuality and political agency in Irish national discourse* (Madison, WI: University of Wisconsin Press, 2004), pp. 21–4 and 47–52. For an interesting perspective on these divergent interpretations see Susannah Boyer, 'Queer patriots', *Cultural Studies*, 24,6 (2010), 801–20.
4 Here we might contrast Rose's dialectical perspective on social change with the schematic perspective, determined by rigid adherence to modernisation theory, favoured by Ivana Bacik in *Kicking and Screaming: dragging Ireland into the twenty-first century* (Dublin: O'Brien Press, 2004). As her crudely sensationalist title indicates, Bacik adopts an elitist model of historical change in which an embattled liberal vanguard struggles selflessly to redeem the masses. For a critique of such perspectives, see my 'What we talk about when we talk about sex: modernization and sexuality in contemporary Irish scholarship', *boundary 2*, 45,1 (2018), 231–52.
5 On the historical development of lesbian and gay political mobilisation in Ireland see Paul Ryan, 'Coming out of the dark: a decade of gay mobilisation in Ireland, 1970–80' in L. Connolly and N. Hourigan (eds), *Social Movements in Ireland* (Manchester: Manchester University Press, 2007), pp. 86–105. See also Paul Ryan, 'The pursuit of gay and lesbian sexual citizenship rights, 1980–2011' in E. Kiely and M. Leane (eds), *Sexualities and Irish Society: a reader* (Dublin: Orpen Press, 2014), pp. 101–26.
6 Rose, *Diverse Communities*, pp. 15–18. The Dublin Lesbian and Gay Collective (DLGC) was one of several radical Irish lesbian and gay political organisations, with small overlapping memberships, active in the first half of the 1980s. Other groupings included similar collectives in Cork and Galway, along with the Gay Defence Committee, Gays Against

the Amendment and Gays Against Imperialism. Patrick McDonagh and Maurice Casey have recovered and re-evaluated this previously occluded moment in the history of Irish queer activism. See Patrick McDonagh, '"Homosexuals are Revolting": gay and lesbian activism in the Republic of Ireland 1970s–1990s', *Studi irelandesi: a journal of Irish Studies*, 7 (2017), 65–91 and Maurice Casey, 'Radical politics and gay activism in the Republic of Ireland, 1974–1990', *Irish Studies Review*, 26,2 (2018), 217–36. Their work is highly original in its critical sympathy with the radical perspectives they are encountering, along with the innovative use of archives and oral history. Casey usefully situates the debates and currents of the Irish movement within broader political historical developments nationally and internationally, while also highlighting how the AIDS crisis diverted radical political energies towards more immediately pressing objectives. As he rightly notes, 'the history of gay activism in Ireland cannot properly be understood without accounting for the impression made upon the movement by those whose politics stood at the intersection of sexual liberation, socialism, feminism and republicanism' (230).

7 Rose, *Diverse Communities*, p. 3.
8 Dennis Altman, *Homosexual: oppression and liberation* (London: Serpent's Tail, 1971), p. 241.
9 Steven Epstein, 'Gay politics, ethnic identity: the limits of social constructionism' in Edward Stein (ed.), *Forms of Desire* (London: Routledge, 1990), pp. 239–93. Rosemary Hennessy, *Profit and Pleasure: sexual identities in late capitalism* (London: Routledge, 2000), pp. 42–9.
10 Peadar Kirby, 'Contested pedigrees of the Celtic Tiger' in Peadar Kirby et al. (eds), *Reinventing Ireland: culture, society and the global economy* (London: Pluto, 2001), p. 32. See also the essays by Colin Coulter, Denis O'Hearn and Kieran Allen in Colin Coulter and Steve Coleman (eds), *The End of Irish History?: critical approaches to the 'Celtic Tiger'* (Manchester: Manchester University Press, 2001).
11 For a detailed analysis of the operation, scale and destination of this wealth redistribution see Kieran Allen, *The Celtic Tiger: the myth of social partnership in Ireland* (Manchester: Manchester University Press, 2000), pp. 59–77.
12 Allen, *The Celtic Tiger*, p. 35.
13 The most searching critique of the subsequent trajectory of Irish lesbian and gay politics in the twenty-first century is developed by Ann Mulhall in '"Deviant" filiation and the (un)holy family' in L. Downing and R. Gillett (eds), *Queer in Europe* (Farnham: Ashgate, 2011), pp. 122–35. See also Michael Barron, 'Advocating for LGBT youth: seeking social

justice in a culture of individual rights', *Irish University Review*, 43,1 (2013), 23–30.
14 Les Brookes, *Gay Male Fiction since Stonewall: ideology, conflict, and aesthetics* (London: Routledge, 2009), pp. 12–40.
15 Alan Sinfield, *Faultlines: cultural materialism and the politics of dissident reading* (Oxford: Oxford University Press, 1992), pp. 38–47.
16 Key works addressing the emergence of Irish gay and lesbian fiction in the 1990s in this mode include: Jennifer M. Jeffers, *The Irish Novel at the End of the Twentieth Century: gender, bodies, and power* (London: Palgrave, 2002); Linden Peach, *The Contemporary Irish Novel* (London: Palgrave, 2004); Gerry Smyth, *The Novel and the Nation: studies in the new Irish fiction* (London: Pluto Press, 1997); Eibhear Walshe, 'The vanishing homoerotic: Colm Tóibín's gay fictions', *New Hibernia Review*, 10,4 (2006), 122–36.
17 Wendy Brown, *States of Injury: power and freedom in late modernity* (Princeton, NJ: Princeton University Press, 1996), p. 54.
18 Brown, *States of Injury*, p. 70.
19 Brown, *States of Injury*, p. 74.
20 Brown, *States of Injury*, p. 67.
21 Brown, *States of Injury*, p. 69.
22 Brown, *States of Injury*, p. 59.
23 Brown, *States of Injury*, p. 61.
24 Brown, *States of Injury*, p. 28.
25 Brown, *States of Injury*, p. 75.
26 Brown, *States of Injury*, p. 74.
27 Eve Kosofsky Sedgwick, *The Epistemology of the Closet* (London: Penguin, 1990), p. 67.
28 www.albertwhitman.com/author/tom-lennon/. Accessed 29 July 2021.
29 Tom Lennon, *When Love Comes to Town* (Dublin: O'Brien Press, 1993), p. 147.
30 Tom Lennon, *Crazy Love* (Dublin: O'Brien Press, 1998), p. 51.
31 Alan Sinfield, *On Sexuality and Power* (New York: Columbia University Press, 2004), p. 82.
32 Sinfield, *On Sexuality*, p. 143.
33 Jarlath Gregory, *Snapshots* (Dublin: Sitric Books, 2001), p. 159.
34 Jarlath Gregory, *G.A.A.Y.: one hundred ways to love a beautiful loser* (Dublin: Sitric Press, 2005), p. 35.
35 Fabio Cleto, 'The spectacles of camp' in Andrew Bolton *et al.* (eds), *Camp: notes on fashion* (New York and New Haven, CT: Metropolitan Museum of Art and Yale University Press, 2019), pp. 10 and 15.
36 Gregory, *G.A.A.Y.*, pp. 162–7.
37 Gregory, *G.A.A.Y.*, p. 200.

38 Gregory, *G.A.A.Y.*, p. 203.
39 Gregory, *Snapshots*, p. 197.
40 Scott Bravmann, *Queer Fictions of the Past: history, culture and difference* (Cambridge: Cambridge University Press, 1997), p. 4.
41 Sedgwick, *Epistemology of the Closet*, p. 45.
42 Denis Kehoe, *Nights Beneath the Nation* (London: Serpent's Tail, 2005), p. 175.
43 Georg Lukács, *The Historical Novel*, trans. Hannah and Stanley Mitchell (Lincoln, NE: University of Nebraska Press, 1983 [1937]), p. 42.
44 Kehoe, *Nights*, p. 238.
45 Kehoe, *Nights*, p. 121.
46 Kehoe, *Nights*, p. 86.
47 Joseph Valente, 'Race/sex/shame: the queer nationalism of *At Swim, Two Boys*', *Eire-Ireland*, 40,3&4 (2005), 63–5.
48 Jamie O'Neill, *At Swim, Two Boys* (London: Scribner, 2001), p. 7.
49 O'Neill, *At Swim*, pp. 177 and 309.
50 David Halperin, *One Hundred Years of Homosexuality* (London: Routledge, 1990), pp. 15–40. Linda Dowling, *Hellenism and Homosexuality in Victorian Oxford* (Ithaca, NY: Cornell University Press, 1994). Alan Sinfield, *The Wilde Century* (London: Casell, 1994). Sheila Rowbotham, *Edward Carpenter: a life of liberty and love* (London: Verso, 2009).
51 O'Neill, *At Swim*, pp. 328–9.
52 Valente, 'Race/sex/shame', p. 58.
53 Valente, 'Race/sex/shame', p. 60. Valente is citing here the work of David Halperin and Tim Dean. For similar arguments on the novel's queer radicalism see: Jodie Medd, '"Patterns of the possible": national imagining and queer historical (meta)fictions in Jamie O'Neill's *At Swim, Two Boys*', *GLQ: a journal of lesbian and gay studies* 13,1 (2007), 1–31; Patrick Mullen, *The Poor Bugger's Tool: Irish modernism, queer labour and postcolonial history* (Oxford: Oxford University Press, 2012), pp. 147–79; Matthew Schultz, *Haunted Historiographies: the rhetoric of ideology in postcolonial Irish fiction* (Manchester: Manchester University Press, 2014), pp. 97–128. The most imaginatively sympathetic, and perceptively critical, reading of the novel is offered in David Halperin's *LRB* review; David Halperin, 'Pal o' me heart', *London Review of Books* (22 May 2003).
54 O'Neill, *At Swim*, p. 225.
55 The *OED* cites a text from 1941 as the earliest such usage of 'straight'.

5

Homoerotic and hopeful spaces in 'Celtic Tiger' fiction

If temporality (biographical and historical time) was the governing topos of the 'Irish gay male fiction' in the previous chapter, here we turn to a group of Irish novels in which space is the defining compositional principle. It is not, of course, that the setting of those novels we examined was aesthetically and politically insignificant. On the contrary, that *Snapshots* was set in Crossmaglen cannot, as we saw, be considered incidental but is integral to the novel's mood, tone and political imagination. Likewise, comparing the novels of 'Tom Lennon' and Jamie O'Neill it is clear that different styles of writing about the geography of Dublin encode sharply divergent – conservative and socialist-republican – political perspectives on class relations. But in Keith Ridgway's *The Long Falling* (1998) and *The Parts* (2003), Micheál Ó Conghaile's *Sna Fir* (1999) and Barry McCrea's *The First Verse* (2005) it is not just that setting can be symbolically resonant, but space – more precisely, the circulation of bodies through space – is integral to the architecture of the plot. These novels exemplify chronotopic writing, in which time sediments and condenses in represented space and ways of narrating social space are a powerful vehicle for articulating perspectives on history. In the chronotope, as Mikhail Bakhtin defined it, 'spatial and temporal indicators are fused into one carefully thought-out, concrete whole. Time, as it were, thickens out, takes on flesh, becomes artistically visible; likewise space becomes charged and responsive to the movements of time, plot and history.'[1]

Specifically, two chronotopes are notably expressive in these novels: the city and the gay sauna. In these chronotopes the novelists contend imaginatively and dialectically with a central paradox of late-capitalist sexual freedom. Achieving new sexual rights and challenging patriarchal domination and compulsory heterosexuality has, over the last fifty years, proceeded simultaneously with the deepening penetration of consumerism into every facet of our emotional and sexual lives, making potential new freedoms inextricable from new forms of regulation. Paradoxically then, these novels in which the plot is structured spatially offer, I argue, a more complex and dialectical perspective on history. They are rich in what Walter Benjamin described as 'dialectical images'.[2] Their political significance, as novels from Ireland in the midst of an economic boom, goes beyond merely 'reflecting' that historical moment. Theirs is a more fundamental, and potentially revolutionary, purpose of allowing us to grasp imaginatively the neoliberal condition sensuously and dialectically. Primarily, they achieve that in two distinct but related ways. One is the construction of plots which sharpen our apprehension of social space as a mode of temporal reasoning; comprehending the contingent, dynamic, contradictory and revolutionary historical tempo of capitalist domination, and allowing us to understand that 'the "state of emergency" in which we live is not the exception but the rule' while simultaneously 'fanning the spark of hope in the past'.[3] The other is the creation of aesthetic affects that weaken our assent to neoliberal forms of consciousness – that ideologically dominant conception of a starkly autonomous subjectivity. Those aesthetic affects cluster most powerfully in this fiction around the human body. The sensual needs, vulnerabilities, pleasures and beauty of the human body – its waywardness and excesses – is the primary and visceral site of capitalist domination, and also of resistance to it.

In his pioneering elaboration of the concept of social space, Henri Lefebvre argued that the purpose of thinking about how we apprehend space is to uncover the social relationships embedded in it. The social relations of production, he argued, have a social existence to the extent that they have a spatial existence. Social relations 'project themselves into a space, becoming inscribed there, and in the process producing the space itself'.[4] Lefebvre contrasts this dialectical conception of social space with the ideologically dominant tendency to think of space as a passive receptacle being occupied. By contrast with this abstract 'spatiality', we need a dynamic conception of space, concentrating our attention on the production of space and the social relationships inherent in it. Those social relationships 'introduce specific contradictions into production, so echoing the contradiction between the private ownership of the means of production and the social character of the productive forces'.[5]

Lefebvre identifies two key elements for grasping space dynamically and, to use David Harvey's term, relationally.[6] One is the distinction between dominated and appropriated space. The former describes a space that is transformed, and mediated, by technology; dominated space, as Lefebvre observes, is 'closed, sterilised, emptied out'.[7] By contrast, appropriated space is 'modified in order to serve the needs and possibilities of a group' and so 'appropriative activity is creative rather than dominating'. The history of capitalist development, according to Lefebvre, has been a history of mutual antagonism between these forms of occupying space and 'the winner in this context has been domination'.[8] The second indispensable element for apprehending social space is the restoration of the human body to our spatial imaginary. It is, as Lefebvre argues, 'by means of the body that space is perceived, lived – and produced'.[9] Again, rather than the conventional conception of bodies passively inhabiting a space Lefebvre envisages a dynamic, creative relationship: 'each living body *is* space and *has* its space: it produces itself in space and it also produces that space ... the body with its energies at its disposal, the living body, creates or produces its own space; conversely, the laws of space ... also govern the living body and the deployment of its energies'.[10]

Lefebvre draws an analogy between dominated space and the condition of the human body forced to submit to capitalism's performance principle. His description of this condition now feels suggestive for thinking about the sexual body subject to the repressive incitements of late capitalism. The body is 'dominated by overpowering forces, including a variety of brutal techniques and an extreme emphasis on visualisation'. Thus, the body 'fragments, abdicates responsibility for itself – in a word, disappropriates itself'.[11] However, he reiterates that this is not to be grasped in totalising, homogenising or despairing terms. On the contrary, the 'fleshly (spatiotemporal) body is already in revolt'.[12] Primarily, this revolt is against those ideological forms – notably Platonic and Judeo-Christian – which instituted in Western culture a hierarchy sundering mind from body, along with the depredations of capitalism which extends the division of labour into the very bodies of workers so that the body becomes a 'mere collection of unconnected parts'.[13] To counteract this emphasis on the reified, objectified body as productive instrument, Lefebvre looks to a philosophical tradition in which 'waste, play, struggle, Art, festival – in short, Eros' is recognised as a necessity and endorsed as a virtue. In contrast to the 'mechanistic' tradition and principle of bodily economy represented by Freud, this tradition – in which Lefebvre surprisingly includes Marx, 'who detested asceticism', alongside Nietzsche – endorses excess and superfluity.[14]

Of these novels, Ridgway's *The Long Falling* appears to be most typically an Irish novel of the late twentieth-century. As in Tóibín's *The Blackwater Lightship*, the novel embeds stories of contemporary Irish gay men's lives within the established conventions of the family or generational narrative, and specifically a generational narrative structured around trauma. The first chapter is focalised around the perspective of Grace Quinn, on the night that she deliberately drives into her drunken husband on a road in rural Monaghan making his death look like a hit-and-run road accident. Woven through the narration of this night are episodes from Grace's memories. From these we gather that: Grace was born in England, to Irish immigrants, where she met her immigrant husband and returned with him to his family farm; her son, Sean, drowned as a small child while in her care; her adult son, Martin, went to Dublin after a fight with his father when he was 19 and has not been home since; some years before Michael Quinn killed a young woman while driving drunk – Grace kills him at the same site.[15] We also learn that Grace was subjected to unrelenting emotional and physically violent abuse from her husband. The rest of the narrative takes place in Dublin over the course of several weeks; after her husband's funeral, Grace is visiting Martin for the first time. The unnumbered chapters are nominated with the name of the character around whom the narration is focalised. These mainly alternate between Grace and Martin, with some chapters narrated from the perspective of Sean, Martin's friend who is a political journalist, and Ida Talbot, owner of the guest house to which Grace flees when her crime becomes known.

The time frame of the novel's present coincides with the historical events known as the 'X case' in February 1992. The parents of a 14-year-old rape victim, pregnant as a result of the assault, informed the investigating Gardaí that the victim would be having a termination in England. They did this to ensure that any DNA retrieved in the procedure could be of use when prosecuting the rapist. Subsequently the Attorney General sought an injunction to prevent the girl and her parents from travelling abroad, citing the Eighth Amendment to the Constitution passed in 1983, and this injunction was granted in the High Court. Amidst much public anger at the State's actions and sympathy for the young woman, the family appealed the injunction in the Supreme Court where it was overturned; the Court ruled that a termination was legal in Ireland where there was a 'real and substantial risk to the life' of a pregnant woman.[16] Ridgway weaves these historical events into his narrative in various ways: Grace walking on the quays outside the Four Courts sees opposed groups of protestors; conversations between characters; characters engaging with media; Grace imaginatively identifying with the girl as a fellow 'criminal' and, most obviously, through Sean, whose work gives him knowledge of what is unfolding before it becomes publicly known. Most significantly, the novel concludes with a historical event as the characters participate in the demonstration held in support of the young rape victim attended by several thousand people in Dublin on Saturday, 22 February 1992. Finally, the novel includes a paratextual note outlining these historical details.

Thus, as in *The Blackwater Lightship*, the novel interweaves biographical and generational time with the time of national history. And, as in Tóibín's novel, we can discern a broadly optimistic narrative of historical change in which modernisation is affectively aligned with the progressive tempo of generational succession, and within that historical narrative a younger generation of gay men occupy a symbolic role as emblems of the liberalising present. Thus, Sean works in the media and Henry, Martin's boyfriend, speaks fluent French and works in Paris; in political discourse the 'media' and 'Europe' were conventionally credited with propelling liberalisation in late twentieth-century Ireland. However, by contrast with Tóibín, Ridgway's artistic choice to end the novel with a vibrant account of a mass demonstration signifies a dynamic, democratic concept of social transformation propelled by the mobilisation of citizens rather than determined by institutions. This progressive temporality appears to be reinforced spatially by the novel. Rural Ireland is a space of hypocrisy, repression and trauma – death, tragedy and violence – from which first Martin, after coming out to his parents, and then Grace must flee. The city is a space of freedom, where Martin finds a subculture (he and his friends take

Grace to a gay bar) offering support and friendship along with the possibility of a fulfilling relationship with Henry, and where two men can live together as lovers. Moreover, the price of urban modernity and freedom is not, as expected, alienation; on the contrary, it is in the city that Grace finds compassion and friendship from Martin's friend, Philip, and from Ida.

In a richly perceptive reading of five symbolic spaces in the novel – rural roadway; urban street; grave; gay subcultural spaces; public and monumental spaces (particularly Dublin's GPO) – Ed Madden argues that Ridgway offered a searching critique of discourses of citizenship and national, gender and sexual identity in Celtic Tiger Ireland. The objects of that critique extended from the rigidities of conservative Catholic-nationalist positions to the unacknowledged lacunae and limitations of the liberal narrative of modernisation. Centrally, Madden argues, the novel provoked questions about the exclusionary and gendered model of citizenship on offer to minorities seeking recognition for their identity in liberalising Ireland. Thus, for instance, Ridgway's decision to set the novel in 1992 during the X case – and not the following year when decriminalisation was achieved – and to have his plot pivot dramatically and emotionally around a gay man betraying a woman to the 'machinery' of the state, symbolically challenged 'any easy correlation of gay and feminist politics'.[17] This is a compelling analysis of the novel's historical significance. However, I argue, the novel's challenge to progressive politics is also more searching, and troubling, and reaches beyond its historical moment, since it undermines the security of the foundational premise – the liberal subject – of that politics. That challenge is principally encoded in the novel's style.

As in *The Blackwater Lightship*, historical optimism about modernisation is tempered by a fearful respect for the persistent power of the past; reverberations from its traumas continually threaten to undermine the apparent stability of the present. Martin's paranoid, self-destructive insecurity about his relationship with Henry can be read as the inescapable legacy of his upbringing in a homophobic culture, and an effect of profound ambivalence in his feelings towards his father. By contrast, if Martin's insecurities and moral failings – his hostile, unforgiving lack of understanding for Grace after he discovers the truth – are a legacy of the bleak past, those of Sean – eager to exploit the X case and betray Grace to further his career

– might be seen as thoroughly modern, symptoms of the cynicism and alienation of competitive individualism. In addition, Ridgway's novel eschews that affective investment in symbols of imagined reconciliation between past and present we find in Tóibín (the idealised Catholic wedding of Paul and François, for instance, and the tentative rapprochement between Helen and Lily). By contrast, in Ridgway's novel personal relationships become the emotional terrain for more discombobulating affects, in which the promises of the future dissolve into the threats of the past. Thus, from Martin's perspective, as he considers his mother staying in their house while Henry is away: 'Henry and his mother. As if they were a pair, a balance of faces, a small conspiracy. He felt flung backwards, toppled off his feet by the absence of one and the presence of the other. His life in reverse.'[18]

As this passage suggests, Ridgway's novel subverts the naturalist aesthetic that, at first glance, it appears to exemplify. His prose style sets out, as it were, with the intention of diligently reporting the world as it is with clarity and precision. The frequent use of short declarative sentences, suggesting rigour and purpose, appears to confirm this intent. But that pursuit of clarity is eventually hindered rather than aided by the paratactic rhythm; rather than providing the reader with a smooth path towards understanding the surface of the text becomes jagged, and treacherously uneven. This effect is reiterated by abrupt, puzzling transitions from concrete to figurative language.

Thus, in the opening pages we have what is ostensibly part of a description of the Monaghan landscape:

> There is a church in Cootehill, just outside the town, on the road to Shercock. A tall and grey and silent place, dark against the dark sky. It is a building with eyes, the kind of building that looms, casting shadows across the graveyard that sits snug at its side, the gravestones looking like they might have fallen from the building itself, sticking into the soil like blunt knives, rupturing the wet ground in irregular rows of names and dates. It looks bigger than it is – the power of suggestion. Murders and stormy nights. Mad priests and fallen statues. Faces in the stained glass, whispers from beneath the stones. It never moves, but the sky moves behind it and changes it, making it solid and making it soft, depending.[19]

This is a very familiar style in Irish fiction: a lyrical passage, descriptive and functional – 'setting the scene' – while providing sensuous pleasure. The first sentence effectively situates us with topographical precision. But then we confront a series of imprecise locutions (a *building* might be 'tall and grey and silent', but a 'place'?), confusing figures of speech (in what way does a building have eyes? – unlike the gravestones *like* blunt knives, this is not formulated as a simile but is, apparently, just a description of what 'is') and a tumbling sequence of clauses (ostensibly defining the scene more precisely but actually confusing with its odd similes and metaphors). Finally we have those declarative sentences and their hallucinatory sequence of disassociated images. Within one paragraph we have moved very far from topographical verisimilitude. The narrative becomes so determinedly insistent on assigning symbolic meanings to this landscape, and does so with such a baroque rhythm and tone, that we find our epistemological hold slipping from us. Is this a poetic-realist description of a specific place, to which we can attach a set of symbolic and historical-political meanings (about rural societies, or rural Ireland; about the past, or Irish history; about the past and the present, tradition and modernity)? Or is it a simulacrum of such writing, in which the signifier – the Monaghan landscape – is no more 'real' than the signified, those 'ideas' being attached to it? There is no definitive answer here, which, arguably, is precisely the aesthetic and political affect Ridgway aimed for.

This epistemological uncertainty is compounded by the recurring shift in emphasis from verisimilitude to mood, as the quest for descriptive clarity invariably gives way to the creation of intensely sombre feelings. This mood is 'dark' in both the emotional sense, and in the sense of opacity and obscurity. As we can see in the passage above, that mood is reinforced – and the novel's realism further eroded – by the incorporation of Gothic elements. Thus, this ostensibly realist description of the graveyard is haunted by the presence of the dead, and the fragile membrane separating their world from that inhabited by the living. There are recurring descriptions of this graveyard throughout the novel. Again, these descriptions are a function of the novel's realism – Michael Quinn and his young son are buried here – but their rhythmic recurrence simultaneously creates a cluster of affects that go beyond any such plot function. In the same way, giving Martin's adult friend the same forename as his dead infant brother is entirely plausible in a realist novel set in 1990s Ireland; it is a particularly common name. At the same time, it was a deliberate artistic choice and evokes the Gothic trope of the doppelganger. Adult Sean is at once a character – and, as we have seen, one symbolically embodying a set of contradictory perspectives on modern Irish society – and a revenant, living a future that was extinguished when young Sean drowned.

Ridgway's plot has a linear structure, moving from Grace killing her husband to her arrest some weeks later. But the flow of the narration is non-linear. To summarise the first chapter above, for instance, I was obliged to impose an order on the elements of the story which does not reflect the fragmented, recursive – analeptic and proleptic – pattern in which these elements actually unfold. Moreover, unlike in Tóibín's novel, where the past is clearly demarcated in distinct sections of narration identifiable as memories or stories, here fragments of the past are scattered and embedded in the present narrative. In short, the narrative emphasis is on juxtaposition rather than sequence.

For instance, one of the longer 'Martin' chapters juxtaposes two events. One is a Sunday morning – by the end of the chapter we know, by recalling a fragment of detail from one hundred and seventy pages earlier, that it is five years before the narrative present. Martin goes to mass with his father where he has a brief, rushed conversation with a neighbour. This young man is now clearly fearful and ashamed about their recent sexual encounter (we learn very little more about this relationship) and becomes aggressive and insulting towards Martin. Later that day Martin comes out to his parents. The sparse, descriptive prose leaves opaque any connection between the events of the morning and this 'decision', if that is what we can call it: 'Martin lay on his bed and thought about Pat Bolton and about his father.' On hearing this, Michael Quinn reacts very violently towards Martin and Grace, and Martin leaves for Dublin. As we already know, he never returned. The other is a Sunday morning in the present. Grace did not return to Martin's house the night before and Sean arrives to tell Martin what she confessed to him – or more precisely, what Sean trapped her into confessing while secretly recording her. The chapter ends with Martin having a phone conversation with Henry later that day, telling him what has happened and being secretly glad that Henry is now flying back earlier than planned.[20]

These are evidently two of the most significant incidents in the plot, and especially in the story from Martin's perspective. But they are just placed alongside each other in two distinct sections – first the Sunday five years before; then the Sunday 'now'– and both begin abruptly: 'His father looked at him from the doorway'; 'What scared him most was that he had not thought of it.'[21] If there is a reason for placing them together and some connection between them it is up to the reader to make it. However, the obvious connection is confounded by the unfolding of the plot. Having such vivid detail from the history of Martin's relationship with his father, and his direct knowledge of how Grace was abused, we might very reasonably expect understanding and compassion from him. On the contrary, Martin is unreasonably unforgiving, even surprising the investigating policemen, and alienates his friends and lover – terminally damaging his relationship with Henry – by insisting on alerting the police to Grace's whereabouts and watching her being arrested.

Evidently, we could read Martin's conduct through a psychological lens; a consciousness so traumatically brutalised by the physical violence inflicted by his actual father and the psychic violence imposed in the name of his symbolic Father (before whom he has knelt in church that first Sunday morning), that it self-destructively identifies with the 'masculine' aggressor rather than its 'feminine' victim. However, such a reading presupposes an epistemological position, and a moral and political standpoint, from which to reach such a judgement. But, as we have seen, the aesthetic and affective force of the novel is predicated on destabilising any such secure position. Certainly, we can identify that some people behave well (Philip; Ida; Henry) and some behave badly (Sean; Martin) towards Grace; but the novel insists on obscurity, ambivalence and confusion around the motives impelling their behaviour.

These destabilising affects are reiterated stylistically through the use of focalisation and the shifting multiple perspectives militating against any secure point of view. These affects are further amplified through two recurring tropes: bodies and spaces. Martin and Grace's bodies are wayward and anarchic, refusing to align with emotional and social propriety. In particular, the urge towards inappropriate laughter is a recurring motif. Thus, telling Henry what he has learnt about Grace's role in his father's death, 'Martin had to put his hand over the mouthpiece. He was afraid that he would laugh. He clenched his eyes shut and bit his cheek and it passed ... he began to snigger. He started to rock back and forth. He held the phone away from him but it did not work. "Oh shit, Martin, don't cry. Please." Martin hunched over, doubled up, his mouth stretched, his eyes puckered closed, a riot beginning in his guts.'[22] The tonal intensity and contrariness is disorientating: the dark comedy of inappropriate laughter mistaken for appropriate weeping, and even as Henry is distressed we consider how much more distressing it would be for him to realise what is actually happening. The bluntly visceral language conveys the violent contortions of trying to bring Martin's body physically under control, while creating imagery that simultaneously suggests the gestural repertoire of vaudeville or silent film comedy and the hallucinatory primal expression of human pain in a Francis Bacon painting.

Similarly disparate affects cluster around the narration of Martin masturbating. The bodily experience of erotic excitement and pleasure is narrated through figurative language mobilising imagery of visual media technology: 'he shuffled through memories with a speed that astounded him ... he sorted on, his mind throwing random pictures at him that he could not predict ... seeing an open space filled with pictures, not memories, pictures, tiny pictures, living, breathing'. The sensation of orgasm is figured as panoptical vision – 'as if he lay at great height, a dizzy height, afraid to look down, afraid to look' – and then through imagery evoking drowning: 'slipping, stumbling, gone, and him falling, as if through water, as if the very skin of his body was the world entire, and all of it falling, collapsing, dropping through water like a stone in a pool'.[23] As is characteristic of Ridgway's style, the emphasis on sexual sensation as the apotheosis of what it is to inhabit a reified consciousness is suggestive, but so lyrically overdetermined that it becomes difficult to know how to respond: alienated mind as projector and camera, as technological instrument of repressive incitement; sexual pleasure figured as the domination of space; bodily rhythm corresponding to the accelerated tempo of capitalist space-time. But the rhythm of bodily sensations – 'the very skin of his body was the world entire' – also disrupts that temporality. The sensation of the body floating through space is simultaneously a sensation of floating through time since the recursive pattern of imagery – panoptical perspective (as we noted on the opening page, for instance); water – has the punctual moment of sexual pleasure enfold past and future within it, juxtaposing the vulnerable bodies of the two brothers; the anguished, traumatised adult and the drowning child.

Just as the analeptic and proleptic tempo of the narration distorts the linearity of the plot, movement through the city is depicted as simultaneously purposeful and dilatory: moving to a destination through a recognisable cityscape registered through named landmarks and buildings; distractions, impediments and a variety of alternative routes to the same destination. For Grace specifically the city is an overwhelming sensory experience, and her spatial confusion and her distracted, circular walking can be read as a metaphor for the emotional and moral muddle of her son. Furthermore, since it is characteristic of Ridgway's style to overwhelm concrete description with the evocation of mood – and to underscore this through incorporating elements from genre fiction, notably Gothic and crime fiction – Dublin is at once a recognisable space and an atmosphere. Thus, for instance, the recurring motif of characters having disturbing encounters with angry, distressed figures suffering from impaired mental health. Again, these episodes are narratively functionless in the plot yet form a pattern. And, as with the contortions of controlling the wayward body, the textual affects are confusing and unsettling: sudden, random, and impossible to control – these figures are beyond the reach of persuasive, rational communication; a sense of constant proximity to violence; the protagonists' ambiguous responses acutely reflecting those of the liberal reader in similar real-life situations – concern, care and pity merging with anger, disgust and repulsion.

As with the masturbating male body, these affects are amplified around the narration of Martin and Sean moving through the distinctively homoerotic and homosocial space of the gay sauna. As we might expect, Ridgway's novel offers a plurality of frames through which to interpret the significance of this. The most straightforward is Sean's neatly functional view: 'he came to the sauna to relax, to rest in the warmth, to wander through a gentle maze of possibilities. He slept well afterwards.'[24] This is not the gay sauna as site of perversion, or socially subterranean gulag to which the stigmatised are banished. On the contrary, this is the gay sauna fully integrated into capitalism, fulfilling the restorative function of 'free time' to buttress, not threaten, the performance principle. But from Martin's anguished, guilt-ridden, drunken perspective the sauna presents an 'asylum scene' – as he looks through a doorway framing slumped figures gazing stupefied at porn – and a hallucinogenic encounter with fragmented body parts and disconcerting, memory-evoking sensations: 'brushing slightly against the warm walls, stared at by an elderly man with hair like his father's. He rubbed his eyes and saw parts of Henry spin around in front of him like branches broken off in a storm … inside there were grey bodies piled in a corner and the smell of poppers was like a gas leak, and almost immediately his cock was in somebody's hand.'[25] While Martin appraises the sexiness of different bodies as he wanders, their eyes are identical: 'They looked like men given some terrible task. They wanted it over with.'

This joyless vista of despairing automatons appears ripe for moralising and psychologising modes of interpretation. We can easily imagine differences in emphasis and political intent between homophobic and anti-homophobic versions of this framework; this squalid dysfunction is symptomatic *of* being gay, or symptomatic of being stigmatised *for* being gay. Alarmingly though, beneath the political divergence there is an epistemological and interpretive similarity – the culturally ingrained habit of granting meaning to human sexual acts according to the parameters of sacramentalism. And given that *The Long Falling* is both historical – a post-decriminalisation novel about the time just before decriminalisation – and, at this stage, an historical artefact from almost two decades before marriage equality, such modes of reading might now be amplified by an unimaginative historicism and the emergent ubiquity of homosacramentalism.

Characteristically, Ridgway's novel does not rebuke or contradict such moralising and psychologising frames; indeed, the tone and mood appear to illicit them. But it does destabilise and ironize such standpoints. The sauna episode is spread over two chapters, and so narrated from the quite different perspectives of Martin and Sean. In addition, the second chapter is largely narrated as dialogue thereby amplifying the sense of discordant and competing points of view. Thus, in response to Martin's self-disgusted denunciation – 'and the smell and the eyes, rotten in some way, rotting, as if we're thrown here, dead' – Sean replies, 'it's the sauna, Martin, not Dante's fucking Inferno'.[26] Likewise Martin's perspective is comically undermined or burlesqued by the prose – for instance, the allusions to the Nazi extermination camps ('grey bodies piled in a corner'; 'gas') – underscoring the misplaced, overwrought absurdity to which moralising perspectives are susceptible.

Ridgway subsequently orchestrated similar literary techniques to create the formal and tonal complexity of *The Parts*, and to experiment more exuberantly, and with more obviously comic intent, with the conventions of realism. To foreground the polyphonic narration, for instance, the novel is divided into sections rather than chapters. Each section is narrated in the third or second person but focalised around one of six characters. Ridgway uses typographical devices to indicate which character is the focus of a section. He uses an ideogram with a stylised image for five characters: house/Delly; cutlery/Kitty; car/George; radio/Joe; male figure/Barry. To indicate where the narration is focalised around the sixth protagonist, Kez, he uses a different font. These sections are of widely varying length and their sequencing lacks any discernible pattern. Indeed 'Kez' narration occasionally disrupts other sections mid-sentence. Just some of the novel's other playfully Joycean tricks include: incorporating a work conversation in memo form between Joe and Barry (on 'stationery' with the logo of the radio station where they work); incorporating a newspaper review of Kitty's novel; incorporating online conversations that Kitty now spends her time conducting, under various fabricated identities, in internet chatrooms when she is supposedly 'working' on her long delayed second novel; 'newspaper articles' summarising the fictional history of The Pony Bar, involving gangsters and property developers with political connections.

Furthermore, plot types and tropes from genre fiction are transparently incorporated into the framework of a literary novel. It is difficult, for instance, to read George Addison-Blake as a conventional realist character, since he is such a Romantic-Gothic assemblage. He is: a foundling of unknown origins adopted by a wealthy benefactor – for uncertain motives; a cuckoo intent on destroying his adopted family; a doctor not using his scientific knowledge for good but to surreptitiously experiment on human bodies (including those he kidnaps and murders) in pursuit of the nefarious and fantastically outlandish goal of controlling human memory; a figure devoid of empathy or psychological complexity – a motiveless force of evil. Even his name, we are told, was assembled from non-human and human parts: Addison-Blake, the Alabama hospital where he was abandoned as a baby; George, the janitor who found him. George now lives in a modernist mansion in the Dublin mountains with Delly, his elderly adopted mother and widow of Daniel Gilmore. Gilmore's pharmaceutical company made him enormously wealthy. They share this house with Kitty, Delly's friend, carer and lover. Though ostentatiously modern, the house is replete with elements of the 'Big House' from Gothic and Irish fiction: a doomed family; old letters disclosing dangerous secrets from the past; a warren of hidden chambers, holding the corpse of one young man and the imprisoned, tortured body of another; a dying woman, Delly, who, it transpires, is not actually dying but another victim of George's experiment. To further his strange plan – bringing to fruition Gilmore's experiments with a drug for erasing human memory – George collaborates with a network of organised criminals and so the novel also draws on conventions from crime fiction: violence; debts; loyalties; betrayals.

The novel also incorporates more recognisably realist techniques and storylines. For all the experimentalism, its characters still move through a precisely delineated, historically specific and recognisable social world. There is a high level of verisimilitude created through layers of exacting detail. Joe and Kitty are comically grotesque in their abjection. The first a radio presenter paid to be fatuous, spiralling drunkenly, and deeply unpleasantly, through a crisis of self-hatred, bereavement and marital breakdown. The second a once promising novelist, now overeating, overweight and fatally mired in luxury by her unexpected proximity to enormous wealth. Yet there is an undertone of sincerity in their characterisation and just about enough emotional texture to elicit more variegated responses of understanding and sympathy from us. Barry and Delly are more reassuringly and sympathetically human. Their stories merge the quotidian (Barry negotiating the trials of 20-something middle-class life in Celtic Tiger Dublin: greedy, unscrupulous landlords; unfulfilling work and a demanding employer; desultory pleasures of the gay scene) with the romantic (Delly grieving for her lover, who died – or was deliberately killed – with her husband in a helicopter crash years before; worldly, cynical Barry unexpectedly falling in love with Kez).

By contrast, Kez is, as a character, closer to George, while morally occupying the opposite pole in the narrative. Where one is too villainous to function as a realist character the other is too idealised.

Around Kez the tone of the novel shifts; irony and satire drop away in favour of a speculative, dreamy lyricism. The novel's naturalist style is just about sufficient for us to begin reading Kez in the sociological and moral modes that the stereotypical figure of the sex worker in modern literature and culture invariably elicits: disempowered victim of an alienated society where human bodies, desires and pleasures are thoroughly reified and commodified; humane and authentic – 'tart with a heart' – precisely because of their routine proximity to the hypocrisy and moral degradation pullulating beneath bourgeois respectability. But that style of reading is unsettled by paradoxes. Kez's thoughts include memories of concrete incidents (comic or grimly violent) from the precarious life of a sex worker. But the narrative emphasis is on his feelings about these incidents as parables of the unfathomable power of the 'Fates' over his destiny. Kez's family, including his pimp/brother, profitably exploit him. Yet the narration of his visit home is enveloped in easy affection, tenderness and love. The money he can freely spend and give to his brother and mother suggests a canny ability to survive and succeed in a dangerous world. Yet the tone of the 'Kez' narration suggests an alert and sensitive but essentially unworldly, childlike observer. Barry observes the extraordinary effect which this unusually handsome young man has on strangers, yet Kez is almost ethereally unselfconscious about this beauty – even while so profitably monetising it.[27]

Inevitably, in a novel depicting Dublin during the Celtic Tiger boom there is satire. This clusters particularly around Barry's story: negotiating with his landlord and listening to his father advising about buying property, for instance, or the listed brand labels on clothes, shoes and fragrance as he grooms and dresses for a date.[28] More subversive than the comedy of affluence though is the burlesque of a pervasive style of liberal-left commentary on the boom, which was preoccupied with culture and 'values' rather than economics. Thus, Barry speculates about which night Kez might be free to go for a drink:

> What would be the busy nights in male prostitution in Dublin at the beginning of the century, in a time of widespread affluence, during a good summer? … Are rich men hornier than poor men? Perhaps in times of recession there was more for your average rent boy to be busy with – his busyness corresponding maybe with that of the St Vincent de Paul Society or the Simon Community or Age Concern.

> The spirit of the times would come into it too. The nation's sense of its spiritual self, and its place in history. The peace process and the fall of the Church. The exposure of Haughey and the retirement of Gay Byrne. Would men panic at the passing of old certainties and seek solace in a shag from the small ads? A blow job at the side of the road? He thought that there might have been an end of millennium rush, a hedonistic panic, and maybe things were quieter now. Or would that work the other way around? A general purity as the clock turned over, followed by a general lusting after young flesh as the perception grew that we had gotten away with it? He wasn't sure. And in any case, either of these peaks or troughs would have levelled out by now.[29]

As this suggests, the novel is aware of the limitations of both naturalist exposure and satire – even as it delights in the latter's comic pleasures – when imaginatively confronting the material reality, the psychic and social effects, of capitalism's 'peaks and troughs'. Like the psychological/culturalist mode of liberal political analysis, the naturalist and satiric literary modes invariably struggle to move beyond a moral critique of conduct, and so their critical perspectives can be easily assimilated to conservative ends.[30] This became most obviously apparent in the years after the publication of Ridgway's novel and the 2008 financial crash. The subsequent political project to restore the dominance of finance capital, reconfigure class politics and consolidate an empowered and enriched elite was euphemistically termed 'austerity' in the Anglophone world – a lexical manoeuvre disguising a political project in moral terms and depending for its common-sense force on the secular afterlife of religious ideas about human susceptibility to sinful hedonism; after all, 'we all partied' and so a period of self-denial could only be restorative.[31]

Playing with the conventions of narration and presentation, Ridgway displaces the unique individual perspective from the centre of the novel. In contrast with *The Long Falling* he also dislodges the family as the basic plot unit, and unsettles the primacy of the 'Irish family', and its idiosyncratic dysfunction, as the most pressing theme for contemporary Irish fiction. In place of the diachronic time of generations the novel is shaped around the synchronic time of social space. Dublin – or, as the narrator comically insists on listing, a multiplicity of coexisting 'Dublins' – provides the fulcrum on which the plot turns.[32] When the omniscient narrator occasionally intervenes it is to create a panoptical vision of the city: imagined as seen by a dreaming Kitty flying over the city at the beginning; seen from the perspective of Kez (rescued from George's experiments) being flown to safety in a helicopter in the closing pages.

Moving between diverse cityscapes and planes of experience the novel gives imaginative shape to the fractured, stratified yet interconnected social spaces of the modern city. Our view shifts dramatically from Delly's mansion in the Dublin mountains to the inner-city quayside workplace of Kez and his fellow sex workers; from The Front Lounge, city-centre meeting place of well-heeled gay men, to The Pony Bar, inner-city meeting place of ruthless gangsters; from the fashionable city-centre road where Barry pays a fortune to live in cramped conditions, to the recently gentrified inner suburb of Inchicore, where Joe lives, and from there to the outer suburbs and the working-class estate to which Kez travels to visit his family. Furthermore, transnational circuits of wealth and people embed this imagined Dublin in the geography of global capitalism. On one side, structures of corporate and finance capitalism, and leisured mobility, connect Delly in Dublin with Paris, London, Zurich and New York. The systemic obverse of this are those structures of poverty, labour and migration which brought Joe's Nigerian neighbour to work in Dublin. As Katherine O'Donnell observes, the novel presciently captured the economic boom as 'transitory noise' by establishing the perspective of an omniscient narrator whose 'gaze incessantly ranges over a multiplicity of synchronous realities'.[33] In late capitalism so many of the processes shaping our lives – financialisation; outsourced production; ecological destruction and climate change – routinely overflow territorial boundaries and defy the human capacity to grasp them systemically. Ridgway's novel responds to the literary challenge of rendering visible and concrete those abstract and occluded webs of interconnectedness spun by the expanding capitalist world economy; to tackle 'capitalism's innate tendency to abstract in order to extract', as Rob Nixon describes it in a different context.[34] But the novel does this not by attempting to depict the effects of those processes, but by creating a style in which their spatial-temporal rhythm is embedded. Thus, the intricate geography of the city's class relations is woven into the plotting of the novel as an affective sensation of motion. The novel's percussive tempo echoes the pulsating rhythm of capitalist space-time: what Harvey describes as the 'circulation, the perpetual motion' of exchange which 'perpetually reshapes the coordinates within which we live our daily lives'.[35]

With their first-person student narrators, *Sna Fir* and *The First Verse* seem formally closer to the coming-out romances discussed in the previous chapter. Ó Conghaile's title captures this fusion of the *bildungsroman's* claim to universality with the particularity of the coming-out narrative of identity and sexuality. It can be translated as 'Amongst Men', foregrounding, for the English-language reader, the homoerotic desires and pleasures impelling John Paul's burgeoning identity. This title captures a central aspect of the plot, since John Paul is regularly 'amongst men' in spaces that are homosocial (his family's pub, for instance) or homosocial and homoerotic (outdoor cruising areas in Dublin, for instance, and the gay sauna). At the same time, for the Irish-speaking reader, the idiomatic expression of maturity and coming of age – an equivalent to 'becoming a man' in English – may be more apparent. Thus, his grandfather says to John Paul: 'Tá tú fásta suas. Tá tú sna fir.' ('You are grown up. You are a man now.').[36]

Deaideo (Grandad) also observes: 'is leatsa dul as stúir féin anois, a mhac' ('it is up to you to steer yourself now, my son'). Here again the various resonances of the title phrase merge, since these assertions of John Paul's maturity and autonomy are part of Deaideo's affirmative response when John Paul tells him that he is gay. Placed at the end of the novel, this conversation between grandfather and grandson gives shape to the coming-out romance plot. The narrative takes place over a year in 19-year-old John Paul's life, during which he finds romance in his first relationship, but also encounters tragedy when he later learns that his former boyfriend, Donal, has committed suicide. Spontaneously coming out to his grandfather is precipitated by their conversation about a song, 'Dónall Óg' – a young woman's lament for the lover who has abandoned her – which had been sung at the funeral of their friend and neighbour, Johnny Rua, earlier that day. In a further resonance of the song's opening line – 'A Dhónaill Óig, má théir thar farraige...'/ 'O Dónal Óg, if you cross the ocean...' – grandfather and grandson have their conversation walking on the Atlantic seashore near the Connemara village where John Paul's family live.[37]

Ó Conghaile orchestrates a cluster of tropes and affects which subtly complicate the conventional emotional and political significance of the coming-out narrative. Of course, Deaideo's insouciant reception of John Paul's confidence – 'Tá Deaideo san aois nach gcuireann mórán rudaí iontas air' ('Granda is old enough now not to be surprised by much'), as he puts it – might be considered implausible for one of his background and generation, and the type of fantasy resolution we saw in Tóibín's *The Blackwater Lightship*. But judging a novel on its documentary accuracy is less useful than thinking about the affective and political resonances of *how* the fantasy is narrated. Here what is of most interest is the stress not on the grandfather adapting to what is new, but rather assimilating it to what exists. Rather than a confession about his difference – formulated in terms of abjection or pride – situated as the culminating point in an individual quest for identity – the type of crisis narrated in Lennon's novels, for instance – John Paul's coming-out event emphasises the solidarity of shared needs and emotions. Deaideo and John Paul are *equally* 'croíbhriste' ('heartbroken') after the shared loss of their friend, as John Paul is after his lover's suicide. Thus, the emotional tone is less that of a confession than an encounter, a shared moment of communication facilitated by collective rituals and cultural artefacts – such as the funeral rites and the song.

This dialectic of individual and collective is reiterated in the narrative style, and specifically the interplay of first-person narration with the heteroglossia of voices, social registers and languages. As here with Deaideo, a considerable portion of the narration is composed of dialogue between John Paul and another character. Along with these conversations there are multiple, overlapping conversations among the locals which John Paul observes while working in the family's pub. We get varied and clashing perspectives here – what John Paul says to the customers, and what he actually thinks of them, for instance – but we also get different languages. John Paul and his neighbours move between Irish and English (and even a version of French, when a neighbour mockingly imagines Johnny Rua participating in the Eurovision Song Contest – 'Johnny Rua *dou point*. Johnny Rua *sanc point*'), in a vibrant linguistic hybridity: 'Ca bhfuil an *remote control*? Ardaigh suas an *volume sky high* ... *dive*áil se isteach. Nach bhfaca tú é.'[38] As Sorcha de

Brún observes, Ó Conghaile's style resembles that of Mairtín Ó Cadhain in being 'propelled by the central position given to talk and gossip'.[39] Moreover, as de Brún argues, the novel thematically affirms the political perspective instantiated in the prose style and its critique of any absolutist conception of a linguistically – and therefore socially and politically – 'pure' Gaelic culture which must be idealised and protected from modernity. Thus, for instance, John Paul's ironical and incredulous response to a gay Irish-speaking group in Dublin; in his view, their politely 'correct' language indexes their aspiration after a confected authenticity.[40]

John Paul's scepticism about this project – premised on merging two reified identities – is echoed in the novel's unsettling of identity as a narrative, epistemological and political category. In place of the linearity of the coming-out narrative – and its symbolic affirmation of a progressive (biographical as well as historical) temporality – in this novel time is discombobulating and fluid. Thus, Deaideo's stress on John Paul's maturity and coming of age – condensed in the image of him steering his life into the future – reiterates a sense of futurity and potentiality. At the same time this open futurity is anchored in, takes its coordinates from, one's cultural inheritance; the past is not so much past as a continuing resource for orientating oneself towards the future. That structure of feeling is indexed in John Paul's emotional connection with the older generation (his grandfather and Johnny Rua), but perhaps it is most powerfully exhibited in his emotional response to 'Dónall Óg' as a medium for grieving his male lover. Here the 'traditional' cultural text has the plasticity to accrue a further 'modern' layer of affective meaning. It is also worth noting that John Paul's relationship with this cultural inheritance is never pious or insistent on the static meaning of that inheritance. Hence, for instance, his parody of a seanfhocal or proverb as a source of euphemistic comedy when narrating one of his sexual encounters – 'Mol an óige agus tiochaidh sí' ('Praise youth and it will come along').[41]

The novel begins and ends in Connemara, but the narrative is mostly concerned with John Paul travelling to Galway, where he attends college, and, during his holidays, to Dublin and London. Specifically, his experiences in the cruising grounds and commercial gay scene of Dublin, and to a lesser extent London, form a very significant proportion of the narrative. As with *The Long Falling*, the potential symbolism of the novel's geography initially seems very familiar in Irish literary and political discourse. John Paul's movement across space from the *Gemeinschaft* of the rural Irish-speaking 'West' to the *Gesellschaft* of the urban Anglophone 'East' is simultaneously a movement across time. Moreover, this symbolic geography takes on a further significance within the conventions of the coming-out romance: we expect this movement in space to precipitate an emotional crisis in which John Paul, as a gay *gaeilgeoir*, negotiates competing cultural and sexual identities projected onto different social geographies.

However, the novel subverts the generic conventions of the *bildungsroman* and the coming-out romance by disrupting the linear biographical narrative (a year in the life) through an episodic rhythm. As we've noted, the narration emphasises dialogue and conversation as the plot is constructed around John Paul being 'amongst men' in various (homo)social spaces: listening to the conversations in the pub; talking to his sexual partners and older men that he meets while cruising; listening to Johnny Rua's folklore for a college project. Likewise, mobility is a central compositional principle: John Paul travelling across the country; John Paul walking around Dublin and London. With this emphasis on talk and movement over story, the novel is primarily a picaresque tale about going 'ag crúsál' which situates John Paul in what Bakhtin terms 'adventure time' rather than the biographical time of the modern novel.[42] Hence the generic crisis of identity – our expectation that a conflict between homoerotic desire and culture must be resolved comically or tragically – is undermined.

The significance of social space is reiterated in the novel's closing episode of the conversation between grandfather and grandson. Deaideo's use of maritime imagery for John Paul's maturity – echoed in the lines from the song – draws our attention to their setting during this encounter. The ocean functions here as a repository of dialectical images: open expansiveness and futurity, but also a mode of human orientation dependent on the accumulation of collective knowledge. The sea as appropriated space, indexing a set of cooperative and creative relationships within the community and between the community and its ecological habitat; but also the sea as a space of danger and tragedy – a constant reminder of the vulnerability and (inter)dependence of the human community.

McCrea's *The First Verse* begins with Niall leaving his home in the wealthy South Dublin suburbs to begin his first year at Trinity College. A scholarship allows him to live on campus, so that college opens new intellectual, social and emotional horizons while also giving Niall the opportunity to furtively make his first forays into the Dublin gay scene, have his first sexual encounters and to tentatively begin his first relationship with Chris. The opening two chapters set our expectations for a relatively conventional realist novel. There is much finely detailed description of student social life in Dublin in a precisely delineated historical time frame – references to the statutory ban on smoking in public places and the newly opened tram system, for instance, so we know the novel takes place during 2003 and 2004. Niall's social antennae are unusually well-tuned to the markers, gradations and absurdities of class – especially the political semiotics of accent – in contemporary Dublin, so we can expect some comedy of social manners. We also have a loving, proud family from whom Niall keeps his sexual identity secret, so we can anticipate a drama of revelation. Niall is our anthropological guide through a vibrant commercial gay scene, while he also meets with homophobic violence on the street – so a 'social problem' novel alerting us to Ireland's incomplete liberalisation. And, of course, his relationship with Chris incites the usual narrative curiosity of a romance plot: can they overcome the emotional and social obstacles – Niall's closetedness; the gap in age and social background – to attain a happy ending?

But already in these opening chapters the prose style alerts us that our readerly expectations are to be dashed. The depth of sociological, topographical and even meteorological verisimilitude is achieved without the linguistic and tonal austerity characteristic of contemporary Irish naturalism. On the contrary, the prose is decadent, luxurious, exulting in its own extravagant virtuosity, self-consciously mannered and wilfully, even perhaps adolescently, archaic. Cruising the reader, the prose recklessly confronts the risk that its seductive overtures might be met with laughter. Thus, this Proustian and Joycean burlesque on the opening page:

> For a long time I used to lie and say that words had 'always' been my 'trade', while in fact mine is just the rude tongue of my homeland, the bourgeois suburbs on Dublin's southern side, a Levantine country reaching from the tree-hushed redbrick of Ranelagh, Rathmines, and

Donnybrook, on the edge of the city centre, stately places of canals, cornices and quiet burghers, extending east and southbound along a glittering Mediterranean coast.[43]

This tonal unsteadiness is reiterated by disconcerting shifts in mood. At one moment Niall is archly camp. Recalling waiting for a phone call from Ian, the school friend on whom he had a crush, Niall likens himself to 'Bernadette in a rainswept Lourdes waiting uselessly for a divine apparition to burst with a ring from the silent phone'.[44] But abruptly the mood is sombre and flecked with Gothic traces. In autumnal gloom, Niall unpacks in his room on a still deserted campus until interrupted by a man calling up to him and reciting lines from the Cockney rhyme ('Oranges and Lemons, say the bells of St Clements') used as a recurring motif in Orwell's *Nineteen Eighty-Four* (1949). Though unknown to Niall, this handsome man knows Niall's name and introduces himself as Pablo Virgamore before disappearing into the night – with the advice that Niall should 'send me a song' if he needs Pablo's help.[45]

This is our first overt indication that the novel's central drama lies elsewhere, and the plot will proceed along parallel tracks. Just as Niall conducts parts of his life, as a young gay man, secretly, he also comes to lead another secret life in a cult-like activity with Sarah and John, whom he first encounters as odd, unfriendly acquaintances in his new social circle. Gradually he discovers that they practice a form of divination with books, or bibliomancy, which entails interpreting randomly chosen lines of text to answer questions. We later learn from Sorcha that versions of this practice can be found in various ancient cultures, but the best known is the Roman *sortes virgilanae* – *sortes* from the Latin for drawing lots, and originally practiced by consulting the *Aeneid*. She also explains that the term synchronicity, adapted from the Jungian concept, can be used interchangeably with *sortes* to describe the practice.[46]

Initially this seems to be merely an intellectual parlour game; indeed it is first demonstrated to Niall on the morning after a house party. But Niall is fascinated and realises that for Sarah and John it is much more serious and that their lives are almost entirely directed by consulting books in this way. Niall discovers that he can locate the pair in their nightly progression around the city centre by practicing synchronicities with his books; when Sarah and John realise he is doing this they very grudgingly accommodate him into their group. They then induct him into a more advanced form of *sortes* in which they ritualistically read and reread a selection of randomly chosen passages to induce a hallucinogenic state. Moreover, Sarah is taking email instructions on how to develop their practice from a man called Luis, whom she claims to have met while studying in Germany. He is her only contact with an organisation called PMV (Pour Mieux Vivre), which is dedicated to researching esoteric reading practices as part of a quest for more holistic forms of consciousness; 'its whole thing is unifying art and life, expanding the mind', as John explains, while admitting how little he actually knows of them.[47] Soon Niall's life consists entirely of nights spent with John and Sarah at these occult rituals, and days spent wandering the city – guided, when he wishes to be guided, by doing *sortes*.

As Daniel Soar observes, one of the novel's strengths is the absence of any definitive revelation about the *sortes* and the PMV.[48] We are given no 'rational' explanation for the *sortes* and the visions they induce, and no confirmation either way if the PMV even exists let alone whether they have attained access to some higher truth or are merely charlatans. The novel ends with Niall abruptly, unexpectedly, and without explaining to the reader, parting ways with Sarah and John in Paris. He returns to Dublin, while they make plans to travel to Rome to further their all-consuming quest. Niall's precipitous change in direction is all the more disconcerting because of the tremendous effort and sacrifice – and pain to others – he had just made to rejoin the pair.

How then are we to interpret this strange story, in which the narrator moves around Celtic Tiger Dublin hearing Latin verses and seeing neoclassical statues come alive? Various possibilities present themselves. One is that this palimpsest of quotations is a work of metafiction in the modernist and postmodernist tradition – a Borgesian novel in which the referent is not reality but other literary texts, and in which the primary aesthetic and intellectual objective is not depicting the world but investigating the epistemological and ontological claims of literature as such. With their male undergraduate narrators wandering the streets of Dublin, the novel's obvious Irish antecedent is Flann O'Brien's *At Swim-Two-Birds* (1939). And sure enough, O'Brien's unnamed narrator's description of alcoholic intoxication – 'despite the painful and blinding fits of vomiting which a plurality of bottles has often induced in me' – forms an intertextual refrain in McCrea's novel. [49] Indeed the phrase is central to the plot. On hearing Niall jokingly quote this several times John feels reluctantly obliged to tell him more about the *sortes*, since it is a synchronicity – his own use of the phrase had led to his induction – which he cannot ignore. Furthermore, since McCrea is also an accomplished literary critic it is entirely plausible to read the novel's recurring descriptions of a protagonist ingeniously wresting meaning from a text as a parody of, and a mediation on the ethics of, literary interpretation. However, the novel's aesthetic sets clear limitations to this style of reading. In *At Swim-Two-Birds* the student narrator's 'biographical reminiscences' cannot be read as the base level of reality, as it were, against which the other, increasingly surreal, narrative strands – framed as a working draft of the narrator's novel – can be situated as fantasy. For one thing, his narrative is woefully underdeveloped and lacking any semblance of plot. For another, while his 'fictional' characters are loquacious Dubliners, whose vernacular speech conveys a sense of social reality, the narrator's own prose is, as Joseph Brooker describes it, 'purposely cold', 'meticulously drained of abbreviation and colloquialism' and alienating – 'the world is made unfamiliar'.[50] By contrast, McCrea's novel has the detailed verisimilitude, well-wrought plot and emotional heft we expect of classic realism. And, unlike O'Brien's narrator, Niall Lenihan has a name.[51]

Another style of reading McCrea's novel that presents itself is to view it as an allegory of closetedness. Niall's increasingly absorbing participation in the *sortes* requires ever more elaborate levels of subterfuge, as he is forced to fabricate plausible lies to explain his lengthening absence from ordinary life and neglect of his social and intimate relationships. Over time he becomes well-practiced at this routine dishonesty, and rather than feeling guilty he sees this as essential to protect his more authentic but necessarily secret life. Of course, the obvious problem with this reading is that an allegory of closetedness is entirely superfluous running parallel to a story directly narrating a young man's sexual attraction to men, along with his conscious, not notably anguished, reflections on how and when to tell his friends and family that he is gay. As one might expect, the novel self-consciously transforms this allegorical possibility into a source of comic irony. After suffering a physical and emotional breakdown precipitated by his gruelling life dedicated to the *sortes*, Niall attends a counsellor. But to avoid disclosing the real cause of his breakdown, Niall deliberately crafts a story about feeling anxious and guilty about his sexuality. Indeed, he begins to derive pleasure from this creative activity. As detoxification from the *sortes* he is avoiding reading, so this fiction of himself as a conflicted young gay man with 'baggage' becomes a surrogate text to occupy his attention. His pleasure is intensified by the counsellor's transparent susceptibility. For Niall, it is almost too easy to prompt Deirdre's self-satisfied belief that she is encouraging Niall towards confronting the 'truth', when she is actually responding predictably to the well-managed performance of a familiar script.[52] If anything then, the novel can be read less as an allegory of closetedness than a parody of neoliberal discourses of sexual expression and well-being which translate the rich complexity of our lives as social beings into reifying, rigidly individualist narratives of injury, authenticity and truth-telling.

More conventionally, perhaps, the novel can be read as a critical commentary on life in Ireland during the economic boom. This is the style of reading suggested by Colm Tóibín's endorsement on the front cover of the 2008 edition: 'set in the new Dublin, brash and venal' McCrea's novel passionately dramatises 'the knotty sad subject of how the young can be led astray'. This neatly illustrates the mobilisation of cultural/moral discourse so characteristic of liberal political commentary in Ireland. Class distinction – how exactly might we distinguish 'brash' from 'non-brash' wealth? And was the 'brashness' of the wealth really the problem? –is combined with a rigidly narrow focus on individual conduct that is at once archaic and neoliberal; characterised as susceptibility to sin, 'venal', or as failure of entrepreneurial discipline, the central problem is self-control. Moreover, if we were moved to forward a more purposively materialist analysis of 'the new Dublin' which it depicts, the novel, in this reading, offers a clear warning against the dangers of travelling down that route. It is not to be supposed that Tóibín believed esoteric cult movements so common in contemporary Ireland that a novel warning young people against them was necessary. Therefore, we must assume that he reads this fictional depiction of a bibliomancy cult allegorically, as a parable warning 'the young' against radical, 'extreme' (or 'populist', to use the more recent term favoured by centrists), political perspectives. In this interpretation then, conformity to a realist aesthetic – when Niall reports his visions we are to read this as rationally explicable hallucination, for instance – supports and endorses a realist epistemological and political perspective (in other words, conformity to the hegemonic norms).

However, it is not entirely clear how well the novel actually supports this reading either. For one thing, in so far as the novel depicts Dublin during the economic boom it is more attuned to contradiction and class politics than Tóibín's 'brash and venal' characterisation would allow. After a night at their *sortes* rituals, Niall watches John dress for work noting his transition from 'wild adept of a mystic reading system' into a 'smooth young Celtic Tiger banker'.[53] As we know from their web of mutual acquaintances, John and Niall share a background: prosperous middle-class South Dublin families and privately educated. In short, the novel suggests, prior to his absorption in the *sortes* John's trajectory in life was not fundamentally altered by the economic boom. Global financialisation, and Dublin's role within this, may provide different opportunities for accumulating wealth, but the boom reinforced, rather than recreated, an existing structure of class domination – attending to the superficially 'new' Dublin diverted attention from this.

More crucially though, this style of sociological interpretation sits oddly with the novel's aesthetic and affective characteristics. McCrea's distinctive prose style features recurring descriptions of Niall wandering through Dublin and Paris. This listing of place names and landmark buildings is lyrical, rhythmic and incantatory. Thus, 'she left me to get her bus to a party in Foxrock and left me alone to Trinity on the Feast of the Immaculate Conception, people disappearing into the frosty streets of Dublin and thence to Busáras, Parnell Square, Heuston, Connolly and the buses and trains which would carry them away from here to Stranorlar, Castlecomer, Carrickmines, and Nenagh, places like these'.[54] This reaches a crescendo in an extended description of Niall and John searching for Sarah in Paris: 'and so we pushed on through the city, which became ever less Paris and more a palimpsest of Paris and Dublin. At the end of the Roman rue Saint-Jacques, instead of the Tour Saint-Jacques, the O'Connell Street Spire rose up before us ... the Dublin postal sorting codes overlayed themselves without apology on top of the arrondissements: out in the fifteenth where we should have found the church of Notre Dame de l'Arche de l'Alliance, we stumbled on the church of Saint Thomas the Apostle of Carpenterstown, Dublin 15'. In Niall's imagination, a series of people from his life in Dublin appear in Paris: 'I saw Chris dive, naked and muscular as a swan, from one of the turrets of the Pont Neuf.' [55] As with John Paul's encounters in the Phoenix Park and Soho in *Sna Fir*, mobility in *The First Verse* is melancholic and erotic. At the mercy of random events, coincidences and synchronicities, the cruising gay man balances vertiginously between freedom and alienation.

In this style of writing we do not merely observe Niall moving through the city but inhabit, as part of the reading experience, the *flâneur*'s ambiguous perspective on modernity – caught between the soothing reassurance of place names, with their promise of solidity and permanence, and the discombobulating affects of movement and ceaseless flux. The perception of Dublin folding into Paris is less a spatial than a temporal affect, as McCrea's style of writing social space distorts the illusion of linear developmental time. Hence the rhythmic eruption of the archaic into this contemporary, 'new Dublin', narrative. This is registered through the rhythmic recurrence of religious allusions: noting the date of an event according to a religious rather than secular calendar; the prominence of religious sites in his descriptions of modern urban space; the Latin verses Niall regularly hears when he is absorbed in the *sortes*.[56] And the *sortes* too is a practice merging contemporary materials (novels, that paradigmatically modern literary form) with an ancient belief system.

As we have noted, this disruption of linear developmental time is accentuated by the rhythm of McCrea's plot, a characteristic it shares with the other novels. Hence the description of Niall walking through Paris incorporates characters and incidents from other episodes in the story to become a fragmented achronological *precis* of the plot. Likewise, the novel begins with a 'Preface' proleptically narrating a central episode from the tenth chapter, and the novel ends with Niall on board a bus travelling south to his family home in Sandycove – a reversal of the journey with which the novel began. Thus, in both *Sna Fir* and *The First Verse* that developmental narrative of self-formation, for which the singular 'voice' of first-person narration and the trajectory of the *bildung* plot serve as symbolic guarantors, is dissolved by the echoing heteroglossia, the ostinato rhythm of the prose and the reversion to the 'archaic' plot form of the picaresque and adventure tales.[57]

If then we are to read McCrea's novel, along with those of Ridgway and Ó Conghaile, as novels of Celtic Tiger Ireland, their most powerful political intervention was not, *pace* Tóibín's account of *The First Verse*, to faithfully represent that 'new' Ireland to itself (whether in a mood of ambivalent celebration, cautious criticism or ironic satire). Their most powerful political intervention is to orchestrate an aesthetic and affective constellation that undermines the reader's assent to the dominant perception of human subjectivity – specifically, that reified conception of the separative, autonomous entrepreneurial individual reproduced by, while reproducing, neoliberal ideology. Thus, for instance, Ridgway's destabilising palimpsest of sharply contrasting tones – comic, ironic, satiric, tragic – and fragmented multiperspectival narration dislodged the primacy of the individual subject as the location of epistemological and moral certainty. The depiction of the human body and its various needs as wayward and disruptive serve in his fiction as a symbolic correlative of this dislodgement. Likewise, as we have seen, throughout these novels the narrative functions of social space reiterate the collective dimension in the novels' political imagination.

Their other powerful intervention is to affirmatively restore a utopian imaginary to contemporary Irish realism. To borrow David Lloyd's useful distinction, these novels are utopian but not *utopianist*; they offer no programmatic fantasy of the future or prescriptive vision of an achieved human freedom. As with the differential, counter-modern spaces of Irish oral culture beautifully illuminated by Lloyd, in these novels the utopian 'is projected from the damaged conditions of actual human existence as the realisation of abundance out of scarcity and of fulfilled pleasure out of the partial, threatened, yet irreducible pleasures of the present'. It is a form of utopian longing embedded 'in the texture of actual locations and the granular historicity of survival'.[58] Or, to adapt Kathi Weeks's definition of the utopian, these novels offer 'a variety of partial glimpses of and incitements towards the imagination and construction of alternatives'.[59] Drawing on Ernst Bloch, Weeks demonstrates that the cultivation of hope is indispensable for the utopian imaginary. Hope, she argues, is 'not something one either has or does not, but something that can be fostered and practiced by degrees.'[60]

Bloch's circuitously expansive philosophical mediations offer several key ideas for thinking about our novels as literary texts in which the most radical political effect is the projection of hope. Thus, Bloch reiterates that hope is always both cognitive and emotional, or more precisely affective; it merges the 'cold stream' of analysis with the 'warm stream' of imagination, thereby requiring us to challenge the ideological binary of cognition and affect. As we have noted, the representation of the body, as a site of varied, complex affects and needs in these novel gives imaginative form to this idea. Moreover, the cultivation of hope requires the cultivation of an alternative standpoint on reality than that promulgated by the rationality of capitalist realism. To be (politically) hopeful is to be alert not just to what is, but also to the 'not-yet-become' – those 'anticipatory elements which are a component of reality itself' – and to the 'not-yet-conscious', which, for Bloch, is the creative capacity that allows us to anticipate the 'not-yet-become' as an open possibility.[61] This requires a conception of the world as 'unenclosed', and therefore of reality as 'process', and of 'the widely ramified mediation between present, unfinished past and, above all, possible future'.[62] Hence, as Weeks argues, for Bloch hope is a mode of temporal reasoning in which 'thinking backward and thinking forward are necessary for the fullness of any moment in time ... hoping as an exercise in concrete utopianism does not ignore the present as it has come to be; it is not inattentive to history. On the contrary, it must be cognizant of the historical forces and present potentialities that might or might not produce different futures: the present as a fulcrum of latencies and tendencies.'[63] Or, as José Esteban Muñoz describes it, hope is 'a backward glance that enacts a future vision'.[64]

In what way do these novels cultivate the reader's 'capacity to think through time in both directions'?[65] Most obviously, as we have seen, through the rhythm of their plotting in which sequence and linearity is subordinated to juxtaposition, repetition and circularity. Moreover, the structure of the plots reinforces the thematic emphasis on contingency. This is particularly foregrounded in *The Parts* and *The First Verse*, in which the plot is predicated on the city as a space where the individual is at the mercy of random events, coincidences and synchronicities, while the protagonists aspire towards some mode of knowledge (the 'Fates'; bibliomancy) that might allow them to exercise agency over this. While this dialectic of contingency and control is melancholic – the desire for agency, for a less alienated mode of being, is currently impossible – it nevertheless generates a sense of hopeful futurity: the future not as a predictable evolution from the present but as ripe with possibilities for unforeseeable ruptures.

Homoerotic desire is a vector of utopian longing in these novels. In *Sna Fir* contingency, and thus the openness of time, is embedded in the plot through the structuring trope of cruising, with its thrilling excitement of uncertainty, speculation and risk. In *The First Verse*, Pour Mieux Vivre – 'To Live Better' – may be intended ironically, given the organisation's shattering effect on Niall, but it is still suggestive. The novel mistrusts this secular literary iteration of the religious impulse, while persuasively dramatizing the yearning for something beyond life as it is lived. Equally suggestive is the narration of the effects which the *sortes* rituals produce on Niall – hearing music, seeing visions – with their intimation of another sphere and of alternative possibilities. Thus, after Sarah's first experience of the ritual she 'knew she had succeeded in tearing open a tiny chink in the fabric of material reality'.[66] Before absconding to Paris, Niall presents to himself a life immersed in the *sortes* and a life with Chris as alternatives, enumerating the comforts and pleasure of the latter while melancholically allowing that he will invariably succumb to the temptations of the former. Niall begins to understand how one could passionately love Chris, appreciating those characteristics which

> would be transubstantiated from normal individuating characteristics, regular human habits and traits, into throbbing nuclei of longing: his fine body, for a start, his easy confident air, his dark skin, his big hands, his fussy, slightly feminine attention to clothes and appearance, his curiosity about the thoughts and lives of others, and with this, his natural acceptance of human difference and diversity, his working-class childhood on a rough enough street in the north inner city, his passion for French films. He would be the best of company, I thought, in body and spirit, always interested, always on the move.[67]

Chris is evoked in vibrantly lyrical prose. The concrete language is finely textured, delicately precise and suggestively erotic. But the prose is also disconcerting; seductively hypnotic rhythm, austere technical and metaphorical vocabulary ('transubstantiated'; 'individuating'; 'nuclei') and syntactical fragmentation of a human subject into an incongruous list. Thus, the syntax and tone echoes both the narration of Niall as *flâneur* and of the effects of the *sortes* ritual. The latter resemblance is accentuated by invoking transubstantiation – reminding us too of the linguistic playfulness, so that the choice of 'Chris' as forename for the beloved is at once ordinary, 'realistic', and imbued with potential symbolic resonances. In short, rather than Chris and the PMV standing as alternatives – the comforts of submitting to the reality principle against the treacherous seductions of questing after transcendence – these prose effects suggest a different reading, in which Chris emblematises what the PMV promises: an emblem of that potential, contained within the present, for creating in the future a holistic form of human life beyond reification, alienation and the performance principle.

In other words, Chris is both character and, what Bloch calls, a 'guiding image': a cultural figure or type imaginatively embodying an idealised form of human subjectivity to which we might aspire – an imaginative realisation of our potentialities. For Bloch, the most powerful guiding image of modernity is the '*citoyen*' first imagined by Marx, a figure that 'rose up in contrast to the egotistical individual member of bourgeois society'. By contrast with the ideal of bourgeois individualism, the *citoyen* 'was conceived as a member of a non-egotistical and therefore still imaginary *polis*. He was idealised as the other side of the bourgeois, and thus, in his non-egotistical dreamlike beauty, not subject to the division of labour and not reified, he was idealised with particular force.'[68] As we briefly noted in Chapter 1, Marcuse's alternative formulation for this idea is what he terms 'Orphic-Narcissistic' cultural images. In contrast with the 'Promethean cultural hero' that 'symbolises productiveness, the unceasing effort to master life' the images of Orpheus and Narcissus 'reconcile Eros and Thanatos. They recall the experience of a world that is not to be mastered and controlled but liberated – a freedom that will release the powers of Eros now bound in the repressed and petrified forms of man and nature. These powers are conceived not as destruction but as peace, not as terror but as beauty.'[69] Both figures, Marcuse notes, 'protest against the repressive order of procreative sexuality' and are associated with a form of homosexuality that expresses the demand for a 'fuller Eros'[70]. Given the long-standing neo-Freudian stigmatisation of male same-sex desire as 'narcissism' – still circulating in critiques of consumerism – Marcuse's reinterpretation of the myth of Narcissus is especially provocative. Paradoxically, Marcuse argues, the longing for images of self-identity, suggesting 'an egotistic withdrawal from reality', may actually 'contain the germ of a different reality principle: the libidinal cathexis of the ego (one's own body) may become the source and reservoir for a new cathexis of the objective world – transforming this world into a new mode of being'.[71]

In *The Parts* Kez is a complex figure – rather than character – around which human needs and desires cluster. As a guiding image, he simultaneously embodies the human form dominated by the rule of capitalist exchange and the persistent human yearning to transcend that domination. His is the desirable male body as commodity, and the human potential for sensuous pleasure and emotional intimacy starkly reified. Conventional responses to the cultural archetype of the sex worker, whether moralistic or as a 'social problem', situate that figure as exceptional and in need of rescuing – as one who has either failed morally or has been failed by society. In *The Parts*, however, the recurring references to Kez's relative prosperity, along with the comedy of Barry and Joe trying to locate Kez, negotiating the complex of communication technology used by contemporary male sex workers, prompts us to read the sex worker not as the exception but as the rule – as an ideal figure of the neoliberal entrepreneurial individual at its most flexibly resourceful.[72] But at the same time Barry, despite himself, falls in love with Kez, and it is an effect of the novel's tonal ambivalence that we are prompted towards both ironic scepticism and pleasurable romantic appreciation. In the melodramatic, comic-tragic unfolding of the plot they are lost to each other; nevertheless we are left with a glimpse that human connection – partial, flawed, fragile – is possible, or at least imaginable. Beyond this, we noted the lyrical cadences and distinctive tone of the prose in the sections of Kez narration. This gives a grandeur to Kez's naive dream of escaping 'the Fates' – a potent literary figuration of the dream of escaping our social and political conditions which can currently feel as unrelenting and uncontrollable as 'the Fates'.

In *Sna Fir* the location for glimpsing utopian potential is the gay sauna. In Ridgway's novels the narration of a gay man cruising the gloomy erotic possibilities of the sauna appears to emphasise the protagonist's feelings of squalor and self-loathing. In *The Parts* this association of the sauna, self-indulgence and guilt is literalised by the unfolding of the plot's web of coincidences – because Barry is in the sauna without his phone his effort to rescue Kez from Dr George is tragically delayed. Nevertheless, as we found, Ridgway's distinctive style – Gothic tropes, tonal ambivalence, comic irony, fluid perspective – allows us to read his depiction of the gay sauna straightforwardly as endorsing a sacramental critique of gay male sexual profligacy, or as a comic burlesque of such views; that these are equally plausible readings is an effect of that style.

By contrast, John Paul narrates his first visit to a gay sauna in precise descriptive language, with declarative sentences, parataxis and ellipsis creating a montage of images: 'Tá stócach óg i bpasáiste… Lámha fillte. Corp láidir storrúil matánach aige. Aghaidh dhearfa shocair … Breathnaíonn muid ar a chéile. Soicind. Siúlaim thairis.' ('A young lad in the passageway … Arms folded. Strong, broad, muscular body. Confident steady gaze … We glance at each other. Second. I walk across.')[73] This cinematic style omits Ridgway's *grand guignol* effects, while also removing any potential for moralising and pathologising self-reflection or for sacramentalising judgement. Instead, the rising percussive rhythm of the prose captures John Paul's pleasure keenly aroused by the speculative excitement of cruising as much as by the naked male body. However, there is one point in the episode where the style is briefly different. Having removed his clothes in the changing room, John Paul sits for a moment on the threshold of the cruising area. His mind is whirling, 'ar bís', with excitement, and he pauses to think about himself sitting completely naked apart from his little towel:

> Bhí an saibhir is an daibhir, an bocht is an nocht mar a chéile istigh anseo, fearacht na cille, a smaoinigh me. Bhraith mé ar mo chuid fola mar a bheadh saoirse iomlán aici rásáil trí mo chuisleachaí. Mhothaigh me mar a bheinn i saol eile, mo rútaí stoite amach as mo dhomhan oilte féin agus mé báite i mo dhomhan dúchais nua-aimsithe féin.
>
> Rich and poor, destitute and exposed were inside there together, as in the graveyard, I thought. I sensed my blood racing through my veins with absolute freedom. I felt that I was in another life, uprooted from the familiar world and thrown into my own newly created native place.[74]

As with Marcuse's revision of the Narcissus myth, John Paul's absorption in his naked body is a turning away from the collective

– perceiving physical nakedness as symbol of casting aside the markers and demands of social identity – that is actually precipitated by a deeper sense of democratically collective human belonging. Here Ó Conghaile evokes a familiar trope in American gay male writing in which the sauna offers a utopian glimpse into the imagined possibility of a Whitmanesque radical democracy. In post-AIDS gay male writing this vision is powerfully imbued with grief for the lost (imagined) sexual freedoms of the 1970s.[75] Strikingly, Ó Conghaile's allusion to Ó Cadhain's *Cré na Cille* (1949) marries this structure of feeling, adapted from American gay writing, with Irish-language literary modernism.[76] However, rather than a symptom of shame, John Paul's invocation of death in this context reiterates the inevitability of mortality underscoring the common vulnerability of human bodies; our perception of that common vulnerability and dependence is habitually distorted by reification and alienation. It is also striking that John Paul's sense of finding a new homeland takes place here in the sauna, rather than elsewhere in Dublin or the Dublin gay subculture. Rather than migrating from the social world of his birth to the social world of his adult identity he experiences freedom – that 'saoirse iomlán' ('absolute freedom'), which, strikingly, is felt viscerally, in his 'fola' ('blood'), rather than conceptually – in a space that is 'nowhere'. A socially and legally ambiguous space, tolerated so long as it remains invisible – an ambiguity literally expressed in the gap between what the building's exterior projects, how it presents itself to the public, and what happens within. This is at once a physical space and a transitory, contingent temporal experience, since it is the temporary occupation of that space by cruising and fucking male bodies that makes it a 'gay sauna.'

Of course, the lyrical evocation, in American writing, of the literary gay sauna as a glimpse of utopian democratic possibilities always foundered on the exclusions intrinsic to actual gay saunas. Most obviously, access to these spaces is, by definition, restricted to men. As its title alerts us, Ó Conghaile's novel situates the gay sauna on a continuum of homosocial spaces, such as the pub where men gather to watch all-male team sports. In the previous chapter we saw Lennon and Gregory confronting this central problematic of LGBT identity politics in their novels – that gay men *qua* men reap a patriarchal dividend. As we noted, the political valences of their novels varied, between conservative and radical, but they both framed the question through the optic of identity. In the 'liberal' society imagined in Lennon's fiction gay men would be interchangeable from their straight fellows; by contrast, in Gregory the comedy of authenticity troubled and then restored a clear distinction – more salient in cultural *habitus* than sexual desires – between 'gay' and 'straight'. By replacing the optic of identity with that of space, Ó Conghaile's novel allows for a more dialectical conception of the homosocial/homosexual continuum. The homosociality of the Dublin gay sauna and of the Connemara pub is, in both instances equally, both an expression of masculine, patriarchal power and of marginalised, subaltern lives.

Moreover, the novel depicts the gay sauna as emerging out of, and determined by, the same modes of domination which it simultaneously allows us to glimpse beyond. Before changing out of his clothes and reflecting on his nakedness, John Paul describes coming into the building and paying his 'deich punt' ('ten pounds') entry fee. Juxtaposing the prosaic depiction of a monetary transaction with the poetic evocation of liberation, the novel reiterates the paradox of the gay sauna – a place where sexual freedom is monetised. Then, in the paragraph immediately following on from his reflections, he describes television screens visible from every direction. As John Paul drily observes, if it were not for the type of programme being broadcast one would think they were in a shop selling electrical goods. Instead, the screens project, as John Paul describes it, a dazzling variety, and unceasing flow, of images showing 'buachaillí báire breátha bána' ('beautiful blond boys at play'). As Ó Conghaile's alliteration captures, the porn being projected on the screens is an image of the human form – its beauty, pleasures and needs – subject to the mechanised repetitive routine required by capitalist exchange; authentically recreating the spontaneity of sexual play in commodity form requires work, submission to the performance principle, that is as exhausting and alienating as any other form of labour. Likewise, the proliferation and inescapability of the television screens is an insistent, wearying technological incitement to sexual desire – a mundanely literal illustration of repressive incitement.

Does this undermine, or render naively mistaken, John Paul's transcendent moment? Ó Conghaile's style eschews any such connection, instead placing these divergent perceptions alongside each other as equally compelling insights into gay life at the turn of the twenty-first century, and into the condition of sexual freedom in late capitalism more generally. In all three novelists, their style – linguistic and syntactical exuberance; dynamic plotting; contrapuntal play of realist and non-realist or 'archaic' aesthetic modes – allows them to evade that disempowering pessimism to which Irish writing's naturalist dominant is prone (notwithstanding the redemptive impulse of that naturalism's signature 'fine writing').[77] By contrast, Ridgway's, Ó Conghaile's and McCrea's style engenders a political imagination that is at once dialectically 'realistic' – capturing the sexual freedoms of late capitalism as hopelessly compromised and yet, like cruising, not without moments of glamour and pleasure – and hopefully utopian: a political imagination in which history is open to the desire, and potential, for transforming present freedom into future liberation.

Notes

1 Mikhail Bakhtin, *The Dialogic Imagination*, trans. Caryl Emerson and Michael Holquist (Austin, TX: University of Texas Press, 1981), p. 84.
2 'It's not that what is past casts its light on what is present, or what is present its light on what is past; rather, image is that wherein what has been comes together in a flash with the now to form a constellation. In other words, image is dialectics at a standstill. For while the relation of the present to the past is a purely temporal, continuous one, the relation of what-has-been to the now is dialectical; is not progression but image, suddenly emergent. Only dialectical images are genuine images (that is, not archaic); and the place where one encounters them is language.' Walter Benjamin, 'Convolute N' in *The Arcades Project*, trans. Howard Eiland and Kevin McLaughlin (Cambridge, MA: Harvard University Press, 2002), p. 462.
3 Walter Benjamin, 'These on the Philosophy of History' in *Illuminations*, trans. Harry Zohn, ed. Hannah Arendt (New York: Shocken Books, 2007 [1969]), pp. 257 and 255.
4 Henri Lefebvre, *The Production of Space*, trans. Donald Nicholson-Smith (London: Blackwell, 1991 [1974]), p. 129.
5 Lefebvre, *The Production of Space*, p. 90.
6 David Harvey, *Spaces of Global Capitalism* (London: Verso, 2006), pp. 134–6.
7 Lefebvre, *The Production of Space*, p. 165.
8 Lefebvre, *The Production of Space*, p. 166.
9 Lefebvre, *The Production of Space*, p. 162.

10 Lefebvre, *The Production of Space*, p. 170.
11 Lefebvre, *The Production of Space*, p. 166.
12 Lefebvre, *The Production of Space*, p. 201.
13 Lefebvre, *The Production of Space*, p. 204.
14 Lefebvre, *The Production of Space*, p. 177.
15 Keith Ridgway, *The Long Falling* (London, Faber: 1998), p. 5
16 For discussion and analysis of this history see Stephanie Lord, 'The Eighth Amendment: planting a legal timebomb', Ivana Bacik, 'Abortion and the law in Ireland' and Sinéad Kennedy, 'Ireland's Handmaids' Tale' in A. Quilty, S. Kennedy and C. Conlon (eds), *The Abortion Papers Ireland, volume two* (Cork: Attic Press, 2015).
17 Ed Madden, '"Here of all places": geographies of sexual and gender identity in Keith Ridgway's *The Long Falling*', *South Carolina Review*, 43,1 (2010), 20–32, 26.
18 Ridgway, *The Long Falling*, p. 109.
19 Ridgway, *The Long Falling*, pp. 3–4.
20 Ridgway, *The Long Falling*, pp. 182–94.
21 Ridgway, *The Long Falling*, pp. 182 and 191.
22 Ridgway, *The Long Falling*, pp. 193–4.
23 Ridgway, *The Long Falling*, pp. 45–6.
24 Ridgway, *The Long Falling*, p. 122.
25 Ridgway, *The Long Falling*, p. 117.
26 Ridgway, *The Long Falling*, p. 122.
27 Keith Ridgway, *The Parts* (London: Faber, 2003), p. 256.
28 Ridgway, *The Parts*, pp. 117–22, 205 and 214.
29 Ridgway, *The Parts*, pp. 284–5.
30 For incisive analysis of the rhetorical tropes, political contradictions and vacuity of such commentary see Colin Coulter, 'Introduction' in C. Coulter and A. Nagle (eds), *Ireland Under Austerity: neoliberal crisis, neoliberal solutions* (Manchester: Manchester University Press, 2015), pp. 21–33 and Michael Cronin, 'Inside out: time and place in global Ireland' in E. Maher (ed.), *Reimagining Ireland Reader: examining our past, shaping our future* (Oxford: Peter Lang, 2018), pp. 281–3.
31 Sinéad Kennedy provides a cogent analysis of the rhetoric of austerity in Irish political discourse during the years after the 2008 crisis, in 'A perfect storm: crisis, capitalism and democracy' in Coulter and Nagel (eds), *Ireland Under Austerity*, pp. 86–109. On the ubiquity and currency of the phrase 'we all partied' and its synonyms, see Coulter, 'Introduction', p. 11.
32 Ridgway, *The Parts*, pp. 41–2.
33 Katherine O'Donnell, '*The Parts*: whiskey, tea and sympathy' in P. Vilar-Argáiz (ed.), *Literary Visions of Multicultural Ireland: the immigrant*

in contemporary Irish literature (Manchester: Manchester University Press, 2014), p 191. O'Donnell offers a particularly insightful reading of the novel's engagement with racism in neoliberal Ireland, and with the politically vital project of reimagining the 'native'–'migrant' relationship.
34 Rob Nixon, *Slow Violence and the Environmentalism of the Poor* (Cambridge, MA: Harvard University Press, 2011), p. 41.
35 Harvey, *Spaces*, p. 141.
36 Micheál Ó Conghaile, *Sna Fir* (Indreabhán, Conamara: Cló Iar-Chonnachta, 1999), p. 258. Translations from the novel are my own. Pádraig Ó Siadhial offers a useful discussion of the title's linguistic and cultural valences, along with a useful overview of the novel's place in contemporary Irish-language literature, in 'Odd man out: Micheál Ó Conghaile and contemporary Irish language queer prose', *Canadian Journal of Irish Studies*, 36,1 (2010), 143–61. For an incisive reading of Ó Conghaile's novel which overlaps with but also differs from that offered here, see Seán Mac Risteaird, 'Coming out, queer sex, and heteronormativity in two Irish-language novels', *Studi irelandesi: a journal of Irish Studies*, 10 (2020), 63–75.
37 Ó Conghaile, *Sna Fir*, p. 255.
38 Ó Conghaile, *Sna Fir*, pp. 14–16. The latter comments are from a group watching a football game between two English teams on television.
39 Sorcha de Brún, 'History repeating itself: men, masculinities and "his story" in the fiction of Micheál Ó Conghaile', *Eire-Ireland*, 52, 1&2 (2017), 17–48, 20. Along with Ó Siadhail's essay, this is the best critical introduction to Ó Conghaile's work.
40 de Brún, 'History repeating itself', pp. 32–3.
41 Ó Conghaile, *Sna Fir*, p. 40.
42 Ó Conghaile, *Sna Fir*, p. 43. Bakhtin, *The Dialogic Imagination*, pp. 87–110.
43 Barry McCrea, *The First Verse* (Dingle: Bandon Books, 2008), p. 13. The novel was first published in the US in 2005.
44 McCrea, *The First Verse*, p. 15.
45 McCrea, *The First Verse*, p. 17.
46 McCrea, *The First Verse*, p. 50.
47 McCrea, *The First Verse*, p. 71.
48 Daniel Soar, 'Amphibious green', *London Review of Books* (3 November 2005). www.lrb.co.uk/the-paper/v27/n21/daniel-soar/amphibious-green. Accessed 12 July 2021.
49 Flann O'Brien, *At Swim-Two-Birds* (London: Penguin, 2000 [1939]), p. 23.
50 Joseph Brooker, *Flann O'Brien* (Tavistock: Northcote House, 2005), p. 31.

51 In his classic study of the historical emergence of realist fiction Watt identified individualised characterisation, indexed by novel protagonists bearing a conventional 'ordinary' forename and surname, as a key development. Ian Watt, *The Rise of the Novel* (London: Pimlico, 2000 [1957]), pp. 19–20.
52 McCrea, *The First Verse*, p. 211.
53 McCrea, *The First Verse*, p. 143.
54 McCrea, *The First Verse*, p. 60.
55 McCrea, *The First Verse*, pp. 308–9.
56 The recurring Latin verses are extracts from *Miserere mei, Deus*, Gregorio Allegri's seventeenth-century choral setting of Psalm 50. The extract, with English translation, is included in the 'Preface', though without explaining the source – which is in keeping with the novel's style of incorporating intertextual quotations and allusions.
57 Here it is worth noting that as a critic McCrea has written about a queerly disruptive potential in the picaresque tradition in *In the Company of Strangers: family and narrative in Dickens, Conan Doyle, Joyce and Proust* (New York: Columbia University Press, 2011); see especially the Introduction.
58 David Lloyd, *Irish Culture and Colonial Modernity 1800–2000: the transformation of oral space* (Cambridge: Cambridge University Press, 2011), p 17.
59 Kathi Weeks, *The Problem with Work* (Durham, NC: Duke University Press, 2009), p. 176.
60 Weeks, *The Problem with Work*, p. 193.
61 Ernst Bloch, *The Principle of Hope*, vol. 1, trans. Neville Plaice, Stephen Plaice and Paul Knight (Cambridge, MA: MIT Press, 1986; original German-language publication, 1959), p. 197.
62 Bloch, *Principle of Hope*, vol. 1, pp. 246 and 195.
63 Weeks, *The Problem with Work*, p. 196.
64 José Esteban Muñoz, *Cruising Utopia: the then and there of queer futurity (10th anniversary edition)* (New York: New York University Press, 2019), p. 4.
65 Weeks, *The Problem with Work*, p. 195.
66 McCrea, *The First Verse*, p. 161.
67 McCrea, *The First Verse*, p. 233.
68 Bloch, *Principle of Hope*, vol. 3, p. 932.
69 Herbert Marcuse, *Eros and Civilisation* (New York: Vintage, 1962 [1955]), pp. 146 and 149.
70 Marcuse, *Eros and Civilisation*, p. 155.
71 Marcuse, *Eros and Civilisation*, pp. 153–4.
72 Paul Ryan's *Male Sex Work in the Digital Age* (London: Palgrave; 2019) is a richly textured sociological study of male sex work in contemporary

Ireland, and insightfully explores how the entrepreneurial sex worker distinctively embodies the neoliberal work ethic and its typical forms of consciousness.
73 Ó Conghaile, *Sna Fir*, p. 65.
74 Ó Conghaile, *Sna Fir*, p. 63.
75 This was the Barracks, this the divine rage
In 1975, that time is gone.
All here, of any looks, of any age,
Will get what they are looking for,
Or something close, the rapture they engage
Renewable each night.
　　　　　If, furthermore,
Our Dionysian experiment
To build a city never dared before
Dies without reaching to its full extent,
At least in the endeavour we translate
Our common ecstasy to a brief ascent
Of the complete, grasped, paradisal state
Against the wisdom pointing us away.

Thom Gunn, 'Saturday night' in *Boss Cupid* (London: Faber, 2000), pp. 45–6. For a comprehensive and searching analysis, alert to its political potential, contradictions and limitations, of the literary gay sauna ('bathhouse' or 'baths' in the US), see Dianne Chisholm, *Queer Constellations: subcultural space in the wake of the city* (Minneapolis, MN: University of Minnesota Press, 2004), pp. 63–100. See also Muñoz, *Cruising Utopia*, pp. 33–48.

76 In *Languages of the Night*, McCrea identifies four strands in Irish-language writing by writers who are native speakers (such as Ó Conghaile), as opposed to those who chose to write in Irish (such as Behan and Seán Ó Ríordán, a central figure in McCrea's study). Two strands were most prominent in the earlier twentieth century: autobiographies (most famously based on the oral storytelling of a group of Blasket Islanders) and realist novels and short stories, associated with such figures as Pádraic Ó Conaire and Liam O'Flaherty. The other two strands are still significant. One is a style of locally oriented poetic and ballad composition and the other is a style in which modernist literary techniques are adapted into Irish-language literary production. The latter was pioneered in mid-century by Ó Cadhain and the poet Máirtín Ó Direáin. Though McCrea does not address his work, it is within that latter modernist genealogy that we can situate Ó Conghaile's fiction. See Barry McCrea, *Languages of the Night: minor languages and the literary imagination in twentieth-century*

Ireland and Europe (New Haven, CT: Yale University Press, 2015), pp. 42–4.

77 Seamus Deane develops the idea of 'fine moments' – in which 'conflict is annulled and the distinction between deathly paralysis and total liberation is designedly and with great virtuoso skill cancelled' – in relation to Joyce's *Dubliners*. See Seamus Deane, 'Dead ends: Joyce's finest moments' in D. Attridge and M. Howes (eds), *Semicolonial Joyce* (Cambridge: Cambridge University Press, 2000), p. 36.

Conclusion

'After' equality

> We *must strive, in the face of the here and now's totalizing rendering of reality, to think and feel a then and there.*[1]

> *The body is given over to others in order to persist; it is given over to some other set of hands before it can make use of its own.*[2]

The cover of the October 2019 issue of *GCN* had an arresting image: a monochrome photograph of a late-medieval tower house, a cluster of trees around its base and in the foreground cattle grazing in a field.[3] There is a large-scale image, almost the full height of the building, fixed to the wall of the tower. The image is of two women embracing. One woman stands behind the other, while resting her head on the other's shoulder. Despite the tenderness of the gesture, the two women are rather ethereal. With their long flowing hair, and any signifiers of the contemporary absent from their style of dress and ornamentation, they seem deliberately abstracted from time. Invariably this temporal effect is reinforced by juxtaposing the image on the wall and its setting: an architectural residue of feudalism marooned in a pastoral space. The wilfully 'Celtic' connotations – is this Yeats's Thoor Ballylee? – combined with the women's enigmatic gaze evokes John Lavery's portrait of Hazel Lavery as Cathleen Ni Houlihan.[4] Like the *GCN* cover image, Lavery's painting merged contemporary and archaic styles, fusing the realism of fashionable society portraiture with the allegorical mode of political ballads and poetry. Since Lavery's image was intended to illustrate the new currency of the Irish Free State this stylistic fusion was overlaid with a historical irony. An image that had circulated within an insurrectionary political discourse would now circulate as that most emblematic token of a society's commitment to the primacy of exchange value, the alienation of human labour and the reification of human needs and potentialities.

The fourteen-metre-high mural in the photograph was erected on Caher Castle, in County Galway, by Joe Caslin in May 2015. It was a counterpart to Caslin's 'The Claddagh Embrace'. This was an image, similar in style and scale, of two men embracing, which Caslin created on the gable wall of a five-storey building at a prominent junction in Dublin city centre in April that year (see Figure 1). Together the images formed Caslin's intervention in support of the campaign for same-sex marriage rights, and, more specifically, in support of a 'yes' vote in the referendum held on 22 May 2015. The Dublin image developed a very significant media currency – in Ireland and internationally – as a key signifier of the marriage equality campaign.[5] In 2016 he also created a large-scale mural, portraying two women, in more recognisably contemporary dress, kissing, on a wall in Belfast to draw attention to the ongoing campaign for marriage equality in Northern Ireland.

Caslin describes his artistic practice as explicitly political and activist. In 'Our Nation's Sons', for instance, he created a series of portraits of working-class boys and young men in various urban locations around Ireland, and in Edinburgh. The project, created over five years, addressed the media stereotyping of these young men and the prevalence of mental health disorders, self-harm and suicide among them. In 2016 one of his largest murals – on a seven-storey vacant hotel overlooking Waterford city – also addressed the prevalence of male suicide. 'Ar scáth a chéile a mhaireann na daoine' ('We live protected under each other's shadow') shows a bearded male figure with downcast eyes and outstretched arms; each of his hands is clasped by the hands of unseen figures whose arms stretch from the margins of the mural. The central figure is also being embraced from behind, and again we only see the arms of this embracing figure clasped tightly across the man's naked torso (see Figure 2).

Likewise, Caslin has collaborated on 'The Volunteers', a multimedia project 'highlighting the importance of volunteerism in tackling some of Ireland's most pressing issues: drug addiction, mental health, and direct provision'.[6] In the first part of the project Caslin created a mural on a building at Trinity College, in 2017, specifically addressing

1 Joe Caslin, 'The Claddagh Embrace' (2015)

the criminalisation of drug use, and the attendant diversion of resources from care and treatment. There are four figures: three women (Rachel Keogh and Fiona O'Reilly, who work in the field, and Senator Lyn Ruane, who introduced legislation to decriminalise drug use) and a male figure representing a doctor turning away from the women. One of the women is dressed as a nurse, but the style of her uniform is reminiscent of the early twentieth-century. Likewise, the doctor's formal clothes (hat, overcoat, wing-collar and tie) are vaguely Edwardian. The historical allusions play on the references to 1916 in the project title. This idea, contemporary

Conclusion: 'After' equality

2 Joe Caslin, 'Ar scáth a chéile a mhaireann na daoine' ('We live protected under each other's shadow') (2016–present)

political activists as heirs to the spirit of the Easter Rising, is foregrounded more directly in the short video on which Caslin collaborated. Over a montage (Caslin working on his drawing; the mural being erected; drug use; inner city neighbourhoods; Glasnevin cemetery) an actress, Ally Ni Chiaran, recites a poem – 'We Will Let No Life be Worth Less' – written for the project by Erin Fornoff: 'The new volunteers/a nation reflected/its warrior creed: "We will be fierce in our compassion and believe".'[7]

A second mural in 'The Volunteers' project was erected on the wall of the National Museum of Ireland at Collins Barracks in Dublin. It shows two young men, facing each other in a crouched position. One looks out at the viewer, while holding the other man; the latter's gaze is towards the ground as he leans his head against the other's chest and supports his arms on the other's shoulders (see Figure 3). Caslin identified the men 'as 20-year-old GAA athlete and volunteer Cormac Coffey and Eanna Walsh, a 28-year-old man who in 2014 was diagnosed with bipolar disorder'.[8] One assumes that Cormac is the figure gazing outward, his unflinching gaze indexing the physical and emotional strength he can impart to the suffering Eanna. However, the awkward physical position in which they are posed means that the two men are literally supporting each other to stay upright. In other words, the pose suggests mutuality and connection, rather than a paternalistic flow of support from 'carer' to 'client'.

Caslin's posing of the lovers in 'The Claddagh Embrace', along with their anxious mood, explicitly referenced Frederic William Burton's 'Hellelil and Hildebrand, the Meeting on the Turret Stairs' (1864), a Pre-Raphaelite-style watercolour depicting a scene from a medieval Danish ballad. In a 'poll' conducted by the National Gallery of Ireland in 2012, this painting was 'voted' 'the nation's favourite' and this popularity was one reason Caslin choose to allude to it.[9] In 2017–18 Caslin had a residency at the National Gallery, in conjunction with an exhibition of Burton's work, and the result of this was a project entitled 'Finding Power'. This included a sequence of seven photographic portraits. Those portrayed included: a politician, a comedian, two people who had come to Ireland as an asylum seeker and a refugee respectively; an academic and disability rights activist; a queer activist/writer; a drag performer. Each portrait incorporates a plinth and various gold-coloured accessories or objects, and the stylised poses echo motifs and conventions of classical statuary and post-Renaissance portraiture. Caslin reproduced one of these photographs, of Stephen Moloney, as a highly finished graphite and ink drawing, which was then installed as a large-scale mural in the gallery.[10]

Thus there are manifest critical and progressive political commitments in Caslin's work. These are expressed through his choice of subjects, his collaborations and his framing of the work in media interviews and public talks. At the same time, there is a more radical political perspective latently embedded in his form and style. This radical potential takes shape through the recurring dialectic of power and vulnerability. Caslin's monochrome line drawings are delicate, refined and sparse, and yet the murals confront the viewer forcefully because of their size; intimate images of the human form are projected on a startlingly inhuman scale. The murals are aesthetically disconcerting. The realist style – reminiscent of early Soviet-era social realism, with its 'ordinary' figures posed heroically – is undermined by the expressionism of contorted bodies and enigmatic gazes. The realism is further distorted by the scale and puzzling hybridity of the form (neither fresco nor poster nor digital projection but adapting some

Conclusion: 'After' equality

3 Joe Caslin, 'The Volunteers – Collins Barracks' (2017)

texture from each). This discombobulating affect is reiterated through the positioning of the murals. The viewer does not go looking for them in spaces designated for contemplating art. Instead, the murals find their viewers, and surprise them, as they go about their daily lives. Like Benjamin's revolutionary memory flashing up at a moment of danger, Caslin's murals rise up unexpectedly from the city- and landscape.[11] In this way the content of the images portrays the human form as vulnerable, while their form – monumental scale; hybrid styles; unexpected appearance – makes the viewer viscerally conscious of their own vulnerability. And, recalling Lefebvre's terms discussed in the previous chapter, by wresting a space of aesthetic experience and political contemplation from the dominated space of capitalism, Caslin engages in the potentially revolutionary act of appropriating space by resituating the human body in a dynamic and relational encounter with the space it creates.

Caslin's portraits of the male body – a significant motif in his work – engage directly with those cultural ideals framing hegemonic masculinity as aggressively competitive and autonomous, and with the damage these discourses inflict on young men specifically. Thus, for instance, the images comprising 'Our Nation's Sons' repeatedly show the young men wearing a hooded sweatshirt or hoodie. Their clothing acts as a signifier of their stigmatised lack of respectability and of how they, and those of their class, are perceived as dangerous – the hoodie's potential to provide anonymising disguise for criminality. Yet the posture of the young men shows them wearing those hoodies less as armour, an assertive gesture of aggression, than as a protective shield: a cocooning, womblike space in which to hide. In 'Ar scáth a chéile a mhaireann na daoine' ('We live protected under each other's shadow') and the 'Finding Power' image of Stephen Moloney magnified for the gallery installation, this vulnerability is conveyed through the contorted posing of the body: disproportionate outstretched arms; awkwardly arranged limbs; twisted torso. But that vulnerability merges with a mood of resilience and powerfulness that is not conveyed as assertiveness but as easeful contemplation (closed eyes; averted gaze) and as dependence (the restful body supported by the arms of the other – in the other's hands, to recall Butler's phrase). Strikingly, these images depict the beauty and erotic energy of the male body, but not a male body armoured in musculature. Caslin's images reject that signifier of male desirability, circulating everywhere in contemporary visual culture, through which the performance principle is erotically embodied: sculpted bodies as the exchange value extracted from the relentless labour to 'produce' such results. Moreover, the vulnerability inhering in his images of the male body remind us how the expectation that one should inhabit an aggressively competitive autonomy is not just specific to masculine identity, but is woven into the hegemonic conception of subjectivity as such, the ideal of the entrepreneurial self, valorised in neoliberal culture. More than just signifiers of an alternative masculine identity Caslin's male bodies are guiding images of a radical humanism – gesturing towards the radical potential of vulnerability and dependence to reorientate our political imaginary.

In creating his murals Caslin affixes the drawings to the building using biodegradable materials. This intentional transience weaves vulnerability, such a key symbolic element in the imagery and aesthetic, into the material fabric of the work. This material transience of the artwork encodes a revolutionary perspective on history – a sense of time as open, and of present and future as dynamic and plastic. Likewise that open historical perspective is reiterated through Caslin's incorporation of allusions to political and art history, and, most notably, his incorporation of structures of feeling that take their coordinates from religious iconography (the Waterford mural alluding to crucifixion scenes, for instance) and anticolonial nationalism. This is daring, since in the liberal and progressive Irish political discourse that embraces Caslin, and from which he takes his coordinates, those 'traditional' structures of feeling are conventionally held to be irredeemably discredited by their association with conservative and oppressive institutions.

Looking again at the *GCN* October 2019 cover, the arrangement of the slogan – 'Love' placed over 'Equality' – invites reflections on just these revolutionary perspectives in Caslin's work. Could it be an exhortation to love the political objective of equality? That is, challenging us to love (value; commit ourselves to) the ideal of a social order where human needs are met, exploitation is absent and freedom and human potentiality find expression. Alternatively, is the challenge to think about the connection between love and equality? What is the political relationship between how we might fulfil those human needs encoded in the word 'love' (nurture, connection, intimacy, pleasure, excitement, glamour, affirmation) and various other, related, human needs? Is love even possible in a social order where the whole spectrum of human needs go unmet by so many, and where the means through which to fulfil those needs are so inequitably distributed? Can there be love where there is no freedom from necessity? The adjacent image of Caslin's mural proffers one optimistic historical perspective on this question. A hierarchical feudal order – violent; exploitative; extractive – that was once dominant, as its architecture dominated the landscape, is now residual, archaic and merely 'picturesque'. That which seems unavoidably real is subject to transformation – another world is possible.

However, where Caslin's technique underscores the openness of history, it is striking how this issue of *GCN* using his image worked to stifle any such radical possibilities. The issue contains an interview with Caslin about his work, where he discusses creating a mural in New York to mark the fiftieth anniversary of the Stonewall riots. While it was important to remember Stonewall, he observed, it was also important that 'that sense of rebellion, or that sense of revolt, is still active in the community'.[12] The interviewer then asserts that each of Caslin's murals 'is born within the fight for social equality rather than from the perspective of commemoration'. Arguably, this is a distorting simplification of Caslin's view. Unlike his interviewer, Caslin does not distinguish between commemoration and political commitment. Rather he implicitly recognises that commemoration is always political; the political valences of any specific commemorative act can be either conservative or radical – as has been evident from the Irish State's Decade of Commemoration since 2012. Bringing forth the radical potential of commemoration requires creating artistic modes through which to reconnect us imaginatively with utopian energies once visible in the past, and with, as David Lloyd describes it, 'social movements whose potential and formative effects have not been exhausted simply because they were not victorious'.[13] Moreover, the interviewer's phrase 'social equality' achieves contradictory effects. While ostensibly praising Caslin's political commitments, the phrase actually subverts the idea Caslin is quoted expressing. Qualifying 'equality' with 'social' implies there are different types of equality, and further suggests that some types – such as something we might, following this linguistic logic, call 'economic equality' – are quite distinct and not of any concern for Caslin's work. While wholly appreciative and affirmative of Caslin's art and politics, the interviewer's prose unconsciously reprimands Caslin's unseemly recourse to outmoded political categories and feelings – 'rebellion'; 'revolt' – using the blandly bureaucratic, contractual connotations of 'social equality' to neutralise the danger he presents.

Aside from the Caslin interview almost the entire publication was given over to what the editorial describes as the 'ninth annual wedding issue'. In other words, where Caslin's art conveys a sense of history as open and transformable, his imagery is being used to signify a sense of history as accomplished. 'Equality' is not imagined as a dynamic process but as a punctual event, and as having been definitively achieved in the Irish Republic on 22 May 2015.[14] This is reiterated by the reminder that, in this world view, 'equality' is only open in so far as it is yet, at this point in 2019, to be fully achieved in Northern Ireland.[15]

This terminal conflation of 'equality', as a political objective, with the achieved reality of access to legal marriage is illustrated by the content of the magazine – inadvertently illuminating the contradictions and ironies of what this contractual model of equality might actually mean in an individualised, consumerist neoliberal culture. A series of interviews with various couples about their lives together – but heavily concentrated on how they planned and celebrated their weddings, or are planning to do so – were surrounded by advertising and advertorial from hotels and wedding venues, along with florists, wine suppliers and charities (promoting charitable contributions as 'wedding favours').This includes an advertisement for the 'Viva School of Dance' where one can pay for lessons to ensure that one's wedding dance is 'magical'. In addition, there was advertorial copy written by an estate agent (whose company also placed a paid advert) offering advice to 'first-time buyers'. This unacknowledged assumption, that the typical readership of a *GCN* 'wedding issue' can afford to buy a home in a society where meeting our human need for shelter is so starkly subordinated to a profit-seeking market logic, grimly illustrates the material reality undermining that ideological distinction between 'social' and 'economic' equality.

The *GCN* 'wedding issue' literalises Marcuse's observation that, in the form of capitalist society taking shape as he wrote, 'sexual liberty is harmonised with profitable conformity'.[16] As David Alderson and Finn Bowring argue, notwithstanding that Marcuse was analysing postwar Western societies characterised by Fordism and welfare capitalism, we can distil from his work a conceptual framework that remains powerfully operative for understanding the hegemonic ideology and forms of consciousness in our post-Fordist, neoliberal societies. As we have seen, what he terms 'sexual liberty' does not align with liberation as he conceptualises it. For Marcuse, 'sexual liberation' is not a meaningful term, since liberation – forms of human consciousness and freedom enabled by a non-repressive culture – requires the transformation of sexuality into Eros, which in turn requires a transformation in the entire structure of social relations. Nevertheless, it is notable that he considers that this existing sexual liberty is in some way autonomous from capitalism – it is harmonised *with* rather being an effect *of* the logic of the market. In other words, there has been some historical change and some form of freedom or liberty, however compromised, has been achieved. As Bowring summarises, 'Marcuse was mindful of the fact that sexual freedoms were increasing along with living standards, and the critique of moral puritanism was beginning to sound antiquated. This is why he insisted on distinguishing the socially organised release of suppressed sexuality from the free self-sublimation of libido. The latter presupposes fundamental social change; the former merely assimilates sexual relations to the existing social relations.'[17] Moreover, Marcuse's formulation excludes any suggestion of 'false consciousness', of people condescended to as hapless dupes unable to distinguish between authentic and inauthentic emotions or 'real' and 'false' needs.

The *GCN* marriage issue usefully illuminates these points. It is not that those stories of shared love recounted by the couples in the articles are invalidated or exposed as inauthentic by the surrounding advertisements and advertorial. On the contrary, it is precisely the profound depth of feeling – reservoirs of human need and relationality – expressed in those stories that the neoliberal market strives to reify, commodify and profitably monetise. We could say that the 'wedding issue' stages a dichotomy between two distinct, contradictory but equally resonant meanings of marriage.

One is marriage as it exists now. Firstly, a social ritual with deep roots in the heterosacramentalism of Judeo-Christian and post-Enlightenment bourgeois culture, powerfully propelled by a long-standing and persistent belief that 'sexual pleasure stands in need of redemption, whether conceived in religious or humanistic terms, and that this endows the sacramental relationship with a qualitative moral and emotional superiority over all others'.[18] Secondly, a form of legal contract – again, with deep roots in premodern aristocratic alliance and modern bourgeois property rights – which is expected to counterbalance the inherent instability and disorientating flux engendered by capitalism. In its contemporary form, this contract conceptualises human relationships as aggregative and individualist rather than relational and collective; two individuals merge to function as an individual. As Alison Shonkwiller argues, 'the modern family serves as a larger new unit of "selfhood" within the terms of liberal individualism. In this sense, the development of the gay family cannot be separated from the development of the family in general as a way to organise consumption.'[19] The intensified privatisation of neoliberal culture, and the dismantling of the socialised supports of welfare capitalism in recent decades, makes the family the location to which we are increasingly forced to turn to sustain ourselves, to negotiate the marketplace and to manage our lives with some degree of security. Thirdly, marriage and the family as a privatised resource for the reproduction of labour and the principle mechanism through which the physical and affective work of sustaining human life is naturalised as the responsibility of women in bourgeois gender ideology. As Rosemary Hennessy argues, the production of surplus value in capitalism is accompanied by the 'outlawing' of human needs, since the 'price' paid to a worker for his or her labour excludes many of the worker's potentials and needs as the unnamed price of the exchange.[20] Gender ideology displaces the meeting of human needs on to the domestic labour of feeding, clothing and caring that is marked, and devalued, as woman's 'natural' role and either unpaid or, increasingly in contemporary middle-class households, exploitatively underpaid.

Confronting this reality is marriage as, to adapt Bloch's terms discussed in the last chapter, a guiding image; not marriage as such, as it is now, but as offering a glimpse of future possibilities – of what human consciousness might be like in transformed conditions, where the relations of production were directed towards the collective meeting of human needs. The idea of 'marriage', and its mediating social rituals, is so emotionally resonant and compelling – and, conversely, the reality of 'being married' so exhausting to sustain – because such a variety of 'outlawed' human needs are condensed within it. Pleasure, sustenance, nurture, creativity, shelter, security – an elastic, historically contingent continuum of needs; needs that are corporeal, necessary for physical survival, but not 'natural', since they can only ever be met in and through social relations. The stories from the couples in the *GCN* 'wedding issue' articulate a hopeful faith in the imagined potentialities emblematised in 'marriage': potential forms of human relationships in which human need, vulnerability and interdependence might be a potent solvent of self-interested, entrepreneurial individualism and a source of collective solidarity. In 'marriage' we glimpse a not-yet-become freedom that is not predicated on the autonomy of the sovereign individual but on the vulnerability of a dependent human body; we glimpse a world where all human relationships resemble what we ideally, and under current conditions unsustainably, expect of 'marriage'.

Looking at the *GCN* 'wedding issue', it is tempting to use a colonial metaphor to describe what is being done to this utopian potential represented by marriage. The capitalist market is moving into a new territory and striving to extract profit from the previously untapped resource of same-sex desires and relationships. However, as Katherine Sender argues, that metaphor underestimates marketing discourse as an ideological dynamic which is actively constituting and shaping sexual and other identities; marketing, as she observes, 'does not merely represent gay and lesbian people, but produces recognisable – and sellable – definitions of what it means to be gay or lesbian'.[21] Or, in Marcuse's terms, the needs and potentialities condensed within our ideal of marriage are being restructured in conformity with the performance principle, where our 'erotic performance is brought into line with [our] societal performance'.[22] Thus, for instance, the recurring imagery in the *GCN* special issue conflates the visible performance of 'happiness' with the performance of 'success', where such success is in turn conflated with affluence. The 'Viva School of Dance' advertisement – two handsome men in tuxedos dancing for their assembled guests and a photographer – particularly exemplifies the cruel paradox that in this economy of romance spontaneous affection will 'fail' if it is not assiduously rehearsed.

One possible response to this conjunction is to redouble our commitment to the politics of identity, diversity and recognition. For instance, this is the position adopted by Emer O'Toole in her critique of the campaign for same-sex marriage rights in Ireland. O'Toole offers a perceptive account of the evolving discussion of 'gay marriage' in Irish media discourse in the years leading up to the referendum in 2015. Paradigmatic here was the media persona of the drag-activist Panti Bliss. That persona, O'Toole argues, could be simultaneously transgressive and persuasively reassuring for an Irish audience. O'Toole underscores how the framing of homophobia in Irish media discourse illustrates that the ideological lacunae of liberalism can provide succour for conservatives – in this case, a group of conservative activists very handsomely compensated, out of public money, for the 'injury' of being named as homophobic. Her central criticism of the 'Yes' campaign is that it did not counter the pervasive imagery of heterosexual families circulated by the 'No' campaign, and so it secured its victory through complicity with the homophobia prevalent in the society.

The principal difficulty with O'Toole's analysis is that it displaces ideology with recognition. The neoliberal politics of marriage rights is reducible to the liberal politics of representation. Thus, the 'Yes' campaigners are culpable because they 'disguised queer subjectivities and queer kinship, and by extension they disguised queer politics'.[23] The emphasis here is on visibility and marginalisation, and 'queer' solidifies into actuality, an existing form of identity, rather than remaining a potentiality. As José Esteban Muñoz asserts, queer 'is not yet here' but instead exists for us as an 'ideality that can be distilled from the past and used to imagine a future'.[24] As is common in contemporary critical theory the category of queer in O'Toole's usage is contradictory: a radical standpoint on identity as such, or constituting in itself another category of identity. In an ironic twist, queer, once a tool for deconstructing what Butler in *Gender Trouble* famously termed the 'metaphysics of substance', has somehow become a guarantor of authenticity – those categorising themselves as queer being more authentic than those who, being 'merely' lesbian or gay, find themselves hopelessly inauthenticated by their unthinking aspiration to 'homonormativity'.[25]

Strikingly this vanguardism coexists in O'Toole's analysis with a strategic temporal lag. In a telling aside, she notes that after a few days Caslin's 'The Claddagh Embrace' bore traces of an egg which was thrown at it. For O'Toole, this is yet another instance of the censorship which Panti Bliss was subjected to on RTÉ. In an Irish context formulating a political question in terms of censorship, and resistance to it, is to implicitly evoke the mid-twentieth-century decades when censorship legislation was very actively and oppressively used by the post-Independence state to supress intellectual life and, in particular, to supress discussion of sexuality. The implication is that nothing really has changed. This may be demoralising – or it may be remarkably reassuring. If our political positions can be formulated in familiar terms of oppressive institutions and oppressed or marginalised minorities we are spared the difficult, challenging work of thinking dialectically about the actual hegemonic norms shaping our lives, political perspectives and identities.

The narrative arc of O'Toole's analysis elides the very significant gap in cultural capital between the person who threw the egg – by any standards a hostile but impotent gesture – and those with control over, and access to, cultural and political institutions such as the national broadcaster, RTÉ. Thus, politics is framed in statically minoritarian terms – an homogenously oppressive majority of 'them' aligned against an equally homogenised minority of 'us' – in which the dynamic structure of class relations, and the neoliberal ideology underpinning contemporary capitalism, disappear from view. We might note two ironies here. One is that Panti Bliss (and her creator, Rory O'Neill) is, in this view, an exemplary figure of the marginalised minority, and yet, as O'Toole's discussion illustrates, has considerable access to institutions such as RTÉ and the Abbey Theatre. In short, has access to considerably greater cultural capital and power than the anonymous egg thrower, who is nevertheless, in O'Toole's schema, exemplary of that powerful majority. The second irony is that the anonymous egg thrower was, in all probability, somebody very like the alienated boys and young men whose lives Caslin so sympathetically evoked in 'Our Nation's Sons'. The point, of course, is not to reverse the polarities – Panti Bliss is 'really' powerful; the anonymous egg thrower is 'really' marginalised – but to note how this minor instance illustrates more generally the futility of this calculus of *ressentiment* to which minoritarian identity politics can lead.

Focusing on the hostility directed towards Caslin's mural, O'Toole frames this image of two men embracing as expressive of, and defined by, injury. By contrast, adapting the literary critical practice formulated throughout this book, I essayed a way of framing Caslin's murals in terms of vulnerability, where the latter is an affective and aesthetic mode encoding a radical political imaginary into the work. In turn, that divergence in aesthetic interpretation represents in microcosm the defining choice confronting sexual politics in contemporary Ireland: to persist with the form of politics which culminated in the securing of marriage rights for same-sex relationships, along with the various other forms of recognition and protection secured since 1993, while making that politics just a bit more queer and diverse by reformulating the vocabulary but not the political grammar of the demand for recognition. Or to grasp those achievements dialectically – neither the ultimate apotheosis of 'equality' nor a betrayal to the forces of homophobia, but a paradoxical victory that simultaneously makes the society more equal and more unequal – as way of looking beyond them to a different form of politics: a politics universal and radically humanist in its imaginative scope, and anticapitalist and revolutionary in its objectives. Literature and art do not provide solutions to that dilemma, nor roadmaps for the political future – nor should we require them to do so. What art and literature can provide are guiding images prompting us towards imagining less alienated, more humane and sustainable ways of being human – imagining 'a mode of being that has absorbed all becoming, that is for and with itself in all otherness'.[26] Above all, art and literature provide 'ironic points of light' to guide us hopefully in dark and hopeless times.[27]

Notes

1 José Esteban Muñoz, *Cruising Utopia: the then and there of queer futurity (10th anniversary edition)* (New York: New York University Press, 2019), p. 1.
2 Judith Butler, *The Force of Non-Violence* (London: Verso, 2020), p. 49.
3 The cover image can be found at gcn.ie/magazine/love-equality [accessed 12 July 2021]. *GCN* (formerly *Gay Community News*) is an Irish not-for profit publication which has been published by a voluntary organisation, the National Lesbian and Gay Federation (NXF), continuously since 1988.
4 Painted in 1927, this painting now hangs in the National Gallery of Ireland. It can be viewed online at http://onlinecollection.nationalgallery.ie/objects/11919 [accessed 12 July 2021].

5 Una Mullally, 'Joe Caslin installs second mural on the side of a castle', *Irish Times* (19 May 2015) www.irishtimes.com/news/ireland/irish-news. Oisin Kenny, 'Conversations in monochrome', *GCN* (October 2019), www.gcn.ie/magazine/love-equality. 'Joe Caslin's new mural gets pride of place in Belfast', *GCN* (3 August 2016), https://gcn.ie/joe-caslins-new-mural-gets-pride-place-belfast/. Accessed 29 July 2021.
6 Peter Carboy, 'Joe Caslin interview: the Irish teacher using street art for social change', www.designboom.com/art/joe-caslin-interview-irish-street-art-06-29-2017/ (29 June 2017). Accessed 29 July 2021.
7 The video can be viewed at www.joecaslin.com. Accessed 8 July 2020.
8 The details are available on the National Museum of Ireland website. See '"Mental health difficulties are still fraught with stigma" – new mural challenges Ireland's attitudes', www.thejournal.ie/mental-health-mural-national-museum-3594543-Sep2017/. Accessed 29 July 2021.
9 'Interview with Joe Caslin', www.thebridgetcd.com/2016/02/02/joe-caslin. Accessed 9 July 2020.
10 For details on the project see 'Finding Power, by Joe Caslin' on the National Gallery of Ireland website at www.nationalgallery.ie/finding-power-joe-caslin. Accessed 9 July 2020. As you will see, the image used in the installation is reproduced on the cover of this book.
11 Walter Benjamin, 'These on the Philosophy of History' in *Illuminations*, trans. Harry Zohn, ed. Hannah Arendt (New York: Shocken Books, 2007 [1969]), p. 255.
12 Kenny, 'Conversations in Monochrome', pp. 34–5.
13 David Lloyd, *Ireland After History* (Cork: Cork University Press/Field Day, 1999), p. 25–6.
14 For detailed accounts of the political evolution of the campaign for marriage rights in Ireland see: Una Mullally, *In the Name of Love: the movement for marriage equality in Ireland, an oral history* (Dublin: The History Press of Ireland, 2014), Sonja Tiernan, *The history of marriage equality in Ireland: a social revolution begins* (Manchester: Manchester University Press, 2020) and Gráinne Healy, Brian Sheehan and Noel Whelan, *Ireland Says Yes: the inside story of how the vote for marriage equality was won* (Sallins Co Kildare: Merrion Press, 2016). As its subtitle implies, the latter was written by three leading figures in the Yes campaign. For an astute and thoughtful critical analysis of the campaign, sharply perceptive about its neoliberal undertones, see Ann Mulhall, 'The Republic of Love', https://bullybloggers.wordpress.com/?s=the+republic+of+love (20 June 2015). Accessed 5 July 2021. Likewise, Aidan Beatty, in his response to the referendum result, criticised the focus on the political objective of marriage rights as a victory for reformism over liberation in 'From Gay Power

to Gay Rights', *Jacobin* (29 May 2015), www.jacobinmag.com/2015/05/ireland-gay-marriage-referendum-rights-movement. Accessed 29 July 2021.
15 Love Equality is a campaigning organisation for marriage rights in Northern Ireland, where equal marriage came into law in January 2020.
16 Herbert Marcuse, *Eros and Civilisation* (New York: Vintage, 1962 (1955)), p. 86.
17 Finn Bowring, 'Repressive Desublimation and Consumer Culture: re-evaluating Herbert Marcuse', *new formations*, 75 (2012), 8–24, 16.
18 David Alderson, *Sex, Needs and Queer Culture: from liberation to the post-gay* (London: Zed Books, 2016), p. 71.
19 Alison Shonkwiller, 'The Selfish-Enough Father: gay adoption and the late capitalist family', *GLQ; a journal of lesbian and gay studies,* 14:4 (2008), 537–67, 550.
20 Rosemary Hennessy, *Profit and Pleasure: sexual identities in late capitalism* (London: Routledge, 2000), p. 215–16.
21 Katherine Sender, *Business, Not Politics: the making of the gay market* (New York: Columbia University Press, 2005), p. 11.
22 Marcuse, *Eros and Civilisation,* p. 42.
23 Emer O'Toole, 'Guerrilla Glamour: the queer tactics of Dr Panti Bliss', *Eire-Ireland* 52:3&4 (2018), 104–21, 117.
24 Muñoz, *Cruising Utopia,* p. 1
25 Judith Butler, *Gender Trouble: feminism and the subversion of identity* (London: Routledge, 1990), pp. 1–34.
26 Marcuse, *Eros and Civilisation,* p. 118.
27 'Defenceless under the night/our world in stupor lies;/Yet, dotted everywhere,/Ironic points of light/Flash out wherever the Just/Exchange their messages.' W.H. Auden, 'September 1, 1939' in *Another Time* (London: Faber, 2007 (1940)), p. 106.

Select bibliography

Abelove, Henry, Michele Aina Barale and David M. Halperin (eds). *The Lesbian and Gay Studies Reader* (London: Routledge, 1993).
Adorno, Theodor W. *The Culture Industry*, ed. J. M. Bernstein (London: Routledge, 2001).
Alderson, David. *Sex, Needs and Queer Culture: from liberation to the post-gay* (London: Zed Books, 2016).
Allen, Kieran. *The Celtic Tiger: the myth of social partnership in Ireland* (Manchester: Manchester University Press, 2000).
Altman, Dennis. *Homosexual: oppression and liberation* (London: Serpent's Tail, 1971).
Amin, Kadji. 'Anachronizing the penitentiary, queering the history of sexuality'. *GLQ: a journal of lesbian and gay studies* 19,3 (2013), 301–40.
Arrighi, Giovanni. *The Long Twentieth Century: money, power and the origins of our time* (London: Verso, 1994).
Auden, W.H. *Another Time* (London: Faber, 2007 [1940]).
Bacik, Ivana. *Kicking and Screaming: dragging Ireland into the twenty-first century* (Dublin: O'Brien Press, 2004).
Bacik, Ivana. 'Abortion and the law in Ireland' in Aideen Quilty, Sinéad Kennedy and Catherine Conlon (eds), *The Abortion Papers Ireland, volume two* (Cork: Attic Press, 2015), pp. 104–17.
Bakhtin, Mikhail. *The Dialogic Imagination*, trans. Caryl Emerson and Michael Holquist (Austin, TX: University of Texas Press, 1981).
Barron, Michael. 'Advocating for LGBT youth: seeking social justice in a culture of individual rights', *Irish University Review*, 43,1 (2013), 23–30.
Beatty, Aidan. 'From Gay Power to Gay Rights', *Jacobin* (29 May 2015).
Behan, Brendan. *Borstal Boy* (London: Corgi, 1958).
Behan, Brendan. *After the Wake*, ed. Peter Fallon (Dublin: O'Brien Press, 1981).
Behan, Brendan. 'I become a Borstal Boy' in Sean McMahon (ed.), *The Best from The Bell* (Dublin: O'Brien Press, 1978), pp. 83–8.
Benjamin, Walter. *The Arcades Project*, trans. Howard Eiland and Kevin McLaughlin (Cambridge, MA: Harvard University Press, 2002).

Benjamin, Walter. *Illuminations*, trans. Harry Zohn, ed. Hannah Arendt (New York: Shocken Books, 2007 [1969]).
Bersani, Leo. *Homos* (Cambridge, MA: Harvard University Press, 1995).
Bloch, Ernst. *The Principle of Hope*, 3 volumes, trans. Neville Plaice, Stephen Plaice and Paul Knight (Cambridge, MA: MIT Press, 1986).
Bowring, Finn. 'Repressive desublimation and consumer culture: re-evaluating Herbert Marcuse', *new formations*, 75 (2012), 8–24.
Boxall, Peter. *The Value of the Novel* (Cambridge: Cambridge University Press, 2015).
Boyer, Susannah. 'Queer patriots', *Cultural Studies*, 24,6 (2010), 801–20.
Brannigan, John. *Brendan Behan: cultural nationalism and the revisionist writer* (Dublin: Four Courts Press, 2002).
Brannigan, John. 'Bohemian Behan: late modernism, sexual politics and the "great awakening" of Brendan Behan' in McCourt (ed.), *Reading Brendan Behan*, pp. 58–60.
Bravmann, Scott. *Queer Fictions of the Past: history, culture and difference* (Cambridge: Cambridge University Press, 1997).
Broderick, John. *The Pilgrimage* (London: Weidenfeld and Nicolson, 1961).
Broderick, John. *The Fugitives* (London: Weidenfeld and Nicolson, 1962).
Broderick, John. *The Waking of Willie Ryan* (London: Weidenfeld and Nicolson, 1965).
Brooker, Joseph. *Flann O'Brien* (Tavistock: Northcote House, 2005).
Brookes, Les. *Gay Male Fiction since Stonewall: ideology, conflict, and aesthetics* (London: Routledge, 2009).
Brown, Wendy. *States of Injury: power and freedom in late modernity* (Princeton, NJ: Princeton University Press, 1996).
Brown, Wendy. *Edgework: critical essays on knowledge and politics* (Princeton, NJ: Princeton University Press, 2005).
Brown, Wendy. *Undoing the Demos: neoliberalism's stealth revolution* (New York: Zone Books, 2015).
Butler, Judith. *Gender Trouble: feminism and the subversion of identity* (London: Routledge, 1990).
Butler, Judith. *Bodies that Matter: on the discursive limits of 'sex'* (London: Routledge, 1993).
Butler, Judith. *Precarious Life: the powers of mourning and politics* (London: Verso, 2004).
Butler, Judith. *The Force of Non-Violence* (London: Verso, 2020).
Carboy, Peter. 'Joe Caslin interview: the Irish teacher using street art for social change', www.designboom.com/art/joe-caslin-interview-irish-street-art-06-29-2017/ (29 June 2017). Accessed 29 July 2021.
Carlson, Julia (ed.) *Banned in Ireland: censorship and the Irish writer* (London: Routledge, 1990).
Casey, Maurice. 'Radical politics and gay activism in the Republic of Ireland, 1974–1990', *Irish Studies Review*, 26, 2 (2018), 217–36.
Chisholm, Dianne. *Queer Constellations: subcultural space in the wake of the city* (Minneapolis, MN: University of Minnesota Press, 2004).

Chitty, Christopher. *Sexual Hegemony: statecraft, sodomy and capital in the rise of the world system*, ed. Max Fox (Durham, NC: Duke University Press, 2020).

Cleto, Fabio. 'The spectacles of camp' in Andrew Bolton, Fabio Cleto, Karen Van Godtsenhove and Amanda Garfinkel (eds), *Camp: notes on fashion* (New York and New Haven, CT: Metropolitan Museum of Art and Yale University Press, 2019).

Conrad, Kathryn. *Locked in the Family Cell: gender, sexuality and political agency in Irish national discourse* (Madison, WI: University of Wisconsin Press, 2004).

Corber, Robert T. 'Nationalising the gay body: AIDS and sentimental pedagogy in *Philadelphia*', *American Literary History*, 15,1 (2003), 107–33.

Costello-Sullivan, Kathleen. *Mother/Country: politics of the personal in the fiction of Colm Tóibín* (Bern: Peter Lang, 2012).

Coulter, Colin and Steve Coleman (eds). *The End of Irish History?: critical approaches to the 'Celtic Tiger'* (Manchester: Manchester University Press, 2001).

Coulter, Colin and Angela Nagle (eds). *Ireland Under Austerity: neoliberal crisis, neoliberal solutions* (Manchester: Manchester University Press, 2015).

Crimp, Douglas. *Melancholia and Moralism: essays on AIDS and queer politics* (Cambridge, MA: MIT Press, 2002).

Cronin, Michael. 'Inside out: time and place in global Ireland' in Eamon Maher (ed.), *Reimagining Ireland Reader: examining our past, shaping our future* (Oxford: Peter Lang, 2018), pp. 281–3.

Cronin, Michael G. 'What we talk about when we talk about sex: modernization and sexuality in contemporary Irish scholarship', *boundary 2*, 45,1 (2018), 231–52.

Deane, Seamus. 'Dead ends: Joyce's finest moments' in Derek Attridge and Marjorie Howes (eds), *Semicolonial Joyce* (Cambridge: Cambridge University Press, 2000), pp. 21–36.

de Brún, Sorcha. 'History repeating itself: men, masculinities and "his story" in the fiction of Micheál Ó Conghaile', *Eire-Ireland*, 52, 1&2 (2017), 17–48.

Delaney, Paul (ed.) *Reading Colm Tóibín* (Dublin: The Liffey Press, 2008).

DiBattista, Maria. 'Lessons of detention' in McCourt (ed.), *Reading Brendan Behan*, pp. 33–44.

Dollimore, Jonathan. *Sexual Dissidence* (Oxford: Oxford University Press, 1991).

Dowling, Linda. *Hellenism and Homosexuality in Victorian Oxford* (Ithaca, NY: Cornell University Press, 1994).

Eagleton, Terry. *Heathcliff and the Great Hunger* (London: Verso, 1995).

Eagleton, Terry. 'Mothering', *London Review of Books* (14 October 1999), p.8.

Earls, Brian. 'Oscar and the Irish' (January 2013) and 'Oscar Wilde and the Irish' (February 2013), *Dublin Review of Books*, www.drb.ie/essays/

oscar-and-the-irish and www.drb.ie/essays/oscar-wilde-and-the-irish. Accessed 5 July 2021.
Epstein, Steven. 'Gay politics, ethnic identity: the limits of social constructionism' in Edward Stein (ed.), *Forms of Desire* (London: Routledge, 1990), pp. 239–93.
Esty, Jed. *Unseasonable Youth: modernism, colonialism and the fiction of development* (Oxford: Oxford University Press, 2012).
Fanon, Frantz. *The Wretched of the Earth*, trans. Constance Farrington (London: Penguin, 1991).
Federici, Silvia. *Caliban and the Witch: women, the body and primitive accumulation* (London: Autonomedia, 2004).
Felski, Rita. *The Gender of Modernity* (Cambridge, MA: Harvard University Press, 1995).
Fisher, Mark. *Capitalist Realism: is there no alternative?* (Hants: Zero Books, 2009).
Fisher, Mark and Jeremy Gilbert. 'Capitalist realism and neoliberal hegemony: a dialogue', *new formations*, 80/81 (2013), 89–101.
Floyd, Kevin. *The Reification of Desire: towards a queer Marxism* (Minneapolis, MN: University of Minnesota Press, 2009).
Freud, Sigmund. *Civilisation and its Discontents*, trans. David McLintock (London: Penguin Modern Classics, 2002).
Genet, Jean. *Miracle of the Rose*, trans. Bernard Frechtman (London: Faber, 1973).
Gibbons, Luke. *Gaelic Gothic: race, colonialism and Irish culture* (Galway: Arlen House, 2004).
Giffney, Noreen. 'Quare theory' in Wanda Balzano, Anne Mulhall and Moynagh Sullivan (eds), *Irish Postmodernisms and Popular Culture* (Basingstoke: Palgrave Macmillan, 2007), pp. 197–209.
Gilbert, Jeremy. 'What kind of thing is "neoliberalism"?', *new formations*, 80/81 (2013), 7–22.
Gillespie, Michael Patrick (ed.) *The Picture of Dorian Gray (Norton Critical Edition)* (New York: W.H. Norton, 2006).
Gramsci, Antonio. *Selections from the Prison Notebooks*, trans. Quintin Hoare and Geoffrey Nowell Smith (London: Lawrence and Wishart, 1971).
Greenwald Smith, Rachel. *Affect and American Literature in the Age of Neoliberalism* (Cambridge: Cambridge University Press, 2015).
Gregory, Jarlath. *Snapshots* (Dublin: Sitric Books, 2001).
Gregory, Jarlath. *G.A.A.Y.: one hundred ways to love a beautiful loser* (Dublin: Sitric Press, 2005).
Gunn, Thom. *Boss Cupid* (London: Faber, 2000).
Halperin, David. *One Hundred Years of Homosexuality* (London: Routledge, 1990).
Halperin, David. 'Pal o' me heart', *London Review of Books* (22 May 2003).
Hand, Derek. 'Brendan Behan's *Borstal Boy*: the public persona and the delicate art of deceit' in McCourt (ed.), *Reading Brendan Behan*, pp. 15–43.

Hansen, Jim. *Terror and Irish Modernism: the Gothic tradition from Burke to Beckett* (Albany, NY: SUNY Press, 2009).
Harte, Liam (ed.) *The Oxford Handbook of Modern Irish Fiction* (Oxford: Oxford University Press, 2020).
Harvey, David. *A Brief History of Neoliberalism* (Oxford: Oxford University Press, 2005).
Harvey, David. *Spaces of Global Capitalism* (London: Verso, 2006).
Hennessy, Rosemary. *Profit and Pleasure: sexual identities in late capitalism* (London: Routledge, 2000).
Holohan, Conn and T. Tracy (eds). *Masculinity and Irish Popular Culture: tiger tales* (Basingstoke: Palgrave Macmillan, 2014).
Jeffers, Jennifer M. *The Irish Novel at the End of the Twentieth Century: gender, bodies, and power* (London: Palgrave, 2002).
Kavanagh, Declan. *Effeminate Years: literature, politics and aesthetics in mid-eighteenth-century Britain* (Lewisburg, PA: Bucknell University Press, 2017).
Kearney, Colbert. *The Writings of Brendan Behan* (Dublin: Gill and Macmillan, 1977).
Kehoe, Denis. *Nights Beneath the Nation* (London: Serpent's Tail, 2005).
Kennedy, Maurice. 'Middle-class morality?', *Irish Times* (28 January 1961), p. 6.
Kennedy, Sinéad. 'A perfect storm: crisis, capitalism and democracy' in Coulter and Nagel (eds), *Ireland Under Austerity*, pp. 86–109.
Kennedy, Sinéad. 'Ireland's Handmaids' Tale' in Aideen Quilty, Sinéad Kennedy and Catherine Conlon (eds), *The Abortion Papers Ireland, volume two* (Cork: Attic Press, 2015), pp. 275–83.
Kennedy, Sinéad. 'Ireland's fight for choice', *Jacobin* (25 March 2018).
Kennedy, Sinéad. '"#Repealthe8th": Ireland, abortion access and the movement to remove the Eighth Amendment', *Anthropologia*, 5,2 (2018), 13–31.
Kenny, Oisin. 'Conversations in monochrome', *GCN* (October 2019).
Kingston, Madeline. *Something in the Head: the life and work of John Broderick* (Dublin: Lilliput Press, 2004).
Kingston, Madeline (ed.) *Stimulus of Sin: selected writings of John Broderick* (Dublin: Lilliput Press, 2007).
Kirby, Peadar. 'Contested pedigrees of the Celtic Tiger' in Peadar Kirby, Luke Gibbons and Michael Cronin (eds), *Reinventing Ireland: culture, society and the global economy* (London: Pluto, 2001), pp. 21–37.
Klein, Naomi. *The Shock Doctrine: the rise of disaster capitalism* (London: Allen Lane, 2007).
Lefebvre, Henri. *The Production of Space*, trans. Donald Nicholson-Smith (London: Blackwell, 1991 [1974]).
Lennon, Tom. *When Love Comes to Town* (Dublin: O'Brien Press, 1993).
Lennon, Tom. *Crazy Love* (Dublin: O'Brien Press, 1998).
Lloyd, David. *Ireland After History* (Cork: Cork University Press/Field Day, 1999).

Lloyd, David. *Irish Culture and Colonial Modernity 1800–2000: the transformation of oral space* (Cambridge: Cambridge University Press, 2011).

Lord, Stephanie. 'The Eighth Amendment: planting a legal timebomb' in Aideen Quilty, Sinéad Kennedy and Catherine Conlon (eds), *The Abortion Papers Ireland, volume two* (Cork: Attic Press, 2015), pp. 90–103.

Love, Heather. *Feeling Backward: loss and the politics of queer history* (Cambridge, MA: Harvard University Press, 2007).

Lukács, Georg. *The Historical Novel*, trans. Hannah and Stanley Mitchell (Lincoln, NE: University of Nebraska Press, 1983 [1937]).

Mac Risteaird, Seán. 'Coming out, queer sex, and heteronormativity in two Irish-language novels', *Studi irelandesi: a journal of Irish Studies*, 10 (2020), 63–75.

Madden, Ed. '"Here of all places": geographies of sexual and gender identity in Keith Ridgway's *The Long Falling*', *South Carolina Review*, 43,1 (2010), 20–32.

Maher, Eamon. 'Representations of Catholicism in the twentieth-century Irish novel' in Louise Fuller, John Littleton and Eamon Maher (eds), *Irish and Catholic?: towards an understanding of identity* (Dublin: Columba Press, 2006), pp. 103–19.

Maher, Eamon. 'John Broderick (1924–89) and the French "Roman Catholique"' in Eamon Maher, Eugene O'Brien and Grace Neville (eds), *Reinventing Ireland through a French Prism* (Frankfurt: Peter Laing, 2007), pp. 245–61.

Maher, Eamon. 'John Broderick: "a fugitive from a superior civilisation"', *Irish Times* (23 February 2018).

Marcuse, Herbert. *Eros and Civilisation* (New York: Vintage, 1962 [1955]).

Marcuse, Herbert. *One-Dimensional Man* (London: Sphere Books, 1968).

Marx, Karl. *Selected Writings*, ed. Lawrence H. Simon (Indianapolis, IN: Hackett Publishing, 1994).

Matterson, Stephen. 'Dreaming about the dead: *The Master*' in Delaney (ed.), *Reading Colm Tóibín*, pp. 131–48.

McCarthy, Conor. 'Geographies of liberalism: the politics of space in Colm Tóibín's *Bad Blood: a walk along the Irish border* and *The Heather Blazing*' in Glenn Hooper (ed.), *Landscape and Empire 1720–2000* (Aldershot: Ashgate, 2005), pp. 220–35.

McCourt, John (ed.) *Reading Brendan Behan* (Cork: Cork University Press, 2019).

McCrea, Barry. *The First Verse* (Dingle: Bandon Books, 2008).

McCrea, Barry. *In the Company of Strangers: family and narrative in Dickens, Conan Doyle, Joyce and Proust* (New York: Columbia University Press, 2011).

McCrea, Barry. *Languages of the Night: minor languages and the literary imagination in twentieth-century Ireland and Europe* (New Haven, CT: Yale University Press, 2015).

McDonagh, Patrick. '"Homosexuals are revolting": gay and lesbian activism in the Republic of Ireland 1970s-1990s', *Studi irelandesi: a journal of Irish Studies*, 7 (2017), 65-91.

McGuinness, Frank. 'Saint Behan', *Irish University Review*, 44,1 (2014), 78-91.

Medd, Jodie. '"Patterns of the possible": national imagining and queer historical (meta)fictions in Jamie O'Neill's *At Swim, Two Boys*', *GLQ: a journal of lesbian and gay studies*, 13,1 (2007), 1-31.

Mendos, Lucas Ramon. *State-Sponsored Homophobia 2019* (Geneva: ILGA [International Lesbian, Gay, Bisexual, Trans and Intersex Association], 2019).

Mould, Oli. *Against Creativity* (London: Verso, 2018).

Mullen, Patrick. *The Poor Bugger's Tool: Irish modernism, queer labour and postcolonial history* (Oxford: Oxford University Press, 2012).

Mulhall, Ann. '"Deviant" filiation and the (un)holy family' in Lisa Downing and Robert Gillett (eds), *Queer in Europe* (Farnham: Ashgate, 2011), pp. 122-35.

Mulhall, Ann. 'The Republic of Love', https://bullybloggers.wordpress.com/?s=the+republic+of+love (20 June 2015). Accessed 5 July 2021.

Mulhern, Francis. 'Critical revolution', *New Left Review*, 110 (2018), 39-54.

Mullally, Una. *In the Name of Love: the movement for marriage equality in Ireland, an oral history* (Dublin: The History Press of Ireland, 2014).

Mullally, Una. 'Joe Caslin installs second mural on the side of a castle', *Irish Times* (19 May 2015).

Muñoz, José Esteban. *Disidentifications: queers of colour and the performance of politics* (Minneapolis, MN: University of Minnesota Press, 1999).

Muñoz, José Esteban. *Cruising Utopia: the then and there of queer futurity (10th anniversary edition)* (New York: New York University Press, 2019).

Murray, Patrick. 'Athlone's John Broderick', *Eire-Ireland*, 27, 4 (1992), 20-39.

Ngai, Sianne. *Ugly Feelings* (Cambridge, MA: Harvard University Press, 2005).

Ní Fhrighil, Ríona. 'Brendan Behan's Irish-language poetry' in McCourt (ed.), *Reading Brendan Behan*, pp. 93-116.

Nixon, Rob. *Slow Violence and the Environmentalism of the Poor* (Cambridge, MA: Harvard University Press, 2011).

Nolan, Emer. *Five Irish Women: the second republic, 1960-2016* (Manchester: Manchester University Press, 2019).

North, Joseph. *Literary Criticism: a concise political history* (Cambridge, MA: Harvard University Press, 2017).

North, Joseph. 'Two paragraphs in Raymond Williams', *New Left Review*, 116/117 (2019), 161-87.

Nowlan, David. 'Novelists speak about writing: realists without realism', *Irish Times* (28 August 1970).

O'Brien, Flann. *At Swim-Two-Birds* (London: Penguin, 2000 [1939]).

O'Brien, Gearoid (ed.) *Proceedings of the Second John Broderick Weekend* (Athlone: The John Broderick Committee, 2001).

Ó Conghaile, Micheál. *Sna Fir* (Indreabhán, Conamara: Cló Iar-Chonnachta, 1999).
O'Donnell, Katherine. 'The Parts: whiskey, tea and sympathy' in Pilar Vilar-Argáiz (ed.), *Literary Visions of Multicultural Ireland: the immigrant in contemporary Irish literature* (Manchester: Manchester University Press, 2014), pp. 188–200.
O'Neill, Jamie. *At Swim, Two Boys* (London: Scribner, 2001).
Ó Siadhial, Pádraig. 'Odd man out: Micheál Ó Conghaile and contemporary Irish language queer prose', *Canadian Journal of Irish Studies*, 36,1 (2010), 143–61.
O'Sullivan, Michael. *Brendan Behan: a life* (Dublin: Blackwater Press, 1997).
O'Toole, Fintan. 'An interview with Colm Tóibín' in Delaney (ed.), *Reading Colm Tóibín*, pp. 183–208.
O'Toole, Fintan. 'Brendan Behan: playwright, novelist, terrorist', *Irish Times* (6 September 2014), p.B8.
O'Toole, Emer. 'Guerrilla glamour: the queer tactics of Dr Panti Bliss', *Eire-Ireland*, 52, 3&4 (2018), 104–21.
Peach, Linden. *The Contemporary Irish Novel* (London: Palgrave, 2004).
Quinn, Vincent. *Reading* (Manchester: Manchester University Press, 2020).
Ridgway, Keith. *The Long Falling* (London: Faber, 1998).
Ridgway, Keith. *The Parts* (London: Faber, 2003).
Rose, Kieran. *Diverse Communities: the evolution of lesbian and gay politics in Ireland* (Cork: Cork University Press, 1993).
Rowbotham, Sheila. *Edward Carpenter: a life of liberty and love* (London: Verso, 2009).
Rubin, Gayle. 'Thinking sex: notes for a radical theory of the politics of sexuality' in Carol S. Vance (ed.), *Pleasure and Danger: exploring female sexuality* (London: Kegan Paul, 1984), pp. 267–319.
Ryan, Matthew. 'Abstract homes: deterritorialisation and reterritorialisation in the work of Colm Tóibín', *Irish Studies Review*, 16,1 (2008), 19–32.
Ryan, Paul. 'Coming out of the dark: a decade of gay mobilisation in Ireland, 1970–80' in Linda Connolly and Niamh Hourigan (eds), *Social Movements in Ireland* (Manchester: Manchester University Press, 2007), pp. 86–105.
Ryan, Paul. 'The pursuit of gay and lesbian sexual citizenship rights, 1980–2011' in Máire Leane and Elizabeth Kiely (eds), *Sexualities and Irish Society: a reader* (Dublin: Orpen Press, 2014), pp. 101–26.
Ryan, Paul. *Male Sex Work in the Digital Age* (London: Palgrave, 2019).
Scheible, Ellen. 'Imperialism, aesthetics and Gothic confrontation in *The Picture of Dorian Gray*', *New Hibernia Review*, 18,1 (2014), 131–50.
Schultz, Matthew. *Haunted Historiographies: the rhetoric of ideology in postcolonial Irish fiction* (Manchester: Manchester University Press, 2014).
Seaton, Lorna. 'The ends of criticism', *New Left Review*, 119 (2019), 105–32.
Sedgwick, Eve Kosofsky. *Between Men: English literature and male homosocial desire* (New York: Columbia University Press, 1985).

Sedgwick, Eve Kosofsky. *The Epistemology of the Closet* (London: Penguin, 1990).

Sender, Katherine. *Business, Not Politics: the making of the gay market* (New York: Columbia University Press, 2005).

Shonkwiller, Alison. 'The selfish-enough father: gay adoption and the late capitalist family', *GLQ: a journal of lesbian and gay studies*, 14, 4 (2008), 537–67.

Shrank, Bernice. 'Brendan Behan's *Borstal Boy*: politics in the vernaculars', *Irish University Review*, 44,1 (2014), 129–48.

Sinfield, Alan. *Faultlines: cultural materialism and the politics of dissident reading* (Oxford: Oxford University Press, 1992).

Sinfield, Alan. *The Wilde Century* (London: Cassell, 1994).

Sinfield, Alan. *Literature, Politics and Culture in Post-War Britain* (London: Continuum, 3rd edn, 2004).

Sinfield, Alan. *On Sexuality and Power* (New York: Columbia University Press, 2004).

Smyth, Gerry. *The Novel and the Nation: studies in the new Irish fiction* (London: Pluto Press, 1997).

Soar, Daniel. 'Amphibious green', *London Review of Books* (3 November 2005).

Soper, Kate. 'Alternative hedonism, cultural theory and the role of aesthetic revisioning', *Cultural Studies*, 22, 5 (2008), 567–87.

Tiernan, Sonja. *The History of Marriage Equality in Ireland: a social revolution begins* (Manchester: Manchester University Press, 2020).

Tóibín, Colm. *The Trial of the Generals: selected journalism 1980–1990* (Dublin: Raven Arts Press, 1990).

Tóibín, Colm. *The Story of the Night* (London: Picador, 1996).

Tóibín, Colm. *The Blackwater Lightship* (London: Picador, 1999).

Tóibín, Colm. *Love in a Dark Time: gay lives from Wilde to Almodovar* (London: Picador, 2001).

Tóibín, Colm. *The Master* (London: Picador, 2004).

Treichler, Paula A. *How to do Theory in an Epidemic: cultural chronicles of AIDS* (Durham, NC: Duke University Press, 1999).

Valente, Joseph. 'Race/sex/shame: the queer nationalism of *At Swim, Two Boys*', *Eire-Ireland*, 40,3&4 (2005), 63–5.

Vogel, Lise. *Marxism and the Oppression of Women: toward a unitary theory* (Chicago, IL: Haymarket Books, 2014 [1983]).

Walshe, Eibhear. 'The vanishing homoerotic: Colm Tóibín's gay fictions', *New Hibernia Review*, 10,4 (2006), 122–36.

Walshe, Eibhear. '"This particular genie": the elusive gay male body in Tóibín's novels' in Delaney (ed.), *Reading Colm Tóibín*, pp. 115–30.

Walshe, Eibhear. *Oscar's Shadow: Wilde, homosexuality and modern Ireland* (Cork: Cork University Press, 2011).

Walshe, Eibhear. *A Different Story: the writings of Colm Tóibín* (Dublin: Irish Academic Press, 2013).

Watt, Ian. *The Rise of the Novel* (London: Pimlico, 2000 [1957]).

Weeks, Kathi. *The Problem with Work* (Durham, NC: Duke University Press, 2009).
Weeks, Kathi. *Constituting Feminist Subjects* (London: Verso, 2018 [1998]).
Wilde, Oscar. *De Profundis, The Ballad of Reading Gaol and Other Writings* (London: Wordsworth Classics, 1999).
Wilde, Oscar. *The Picture of Dorian Gray*, ed. Joseph Bristow (Oxford: Oxford University Press, 2006).
Wilde, Oscar. *The Decay of Lying and Other Essays* (London: Penguin, 2010).
Williams, Raymond. *Marxism and Literature* (Oxford: Oxford University Press, 1977).
Wisenfarth, Joseph. 'An interview with Colm Tóibín', *Contemporary Literature*, 50,1 (2009), 1–27.

Index

Note: literary works can be found under authors' names. 'n.' after a page reference indicates the number of a note on that page.

Abbey Theatre 210
Abortion Referendum (2018) 29
   see also Eighth Amendment (1983); X case (1992)
Adorno, Theodor W. 23
AIDS, see HIV/AIDS
Alderson, David 20–2, 24, 50–1, 205–6
Altman, Dennis 120
Amin, Kadji 52
anticapitalism 28, 119, 124–5, 211
   Behan, Brendan and 41
   O'Neill, Jamie and 147–8
   Wilde, Oscar and 18
anticolonialism 11, 118, 119
   Behan, Brendan and 13, 41, 43, 48, 58
   Caslin, Joe and 203
   O'Neill, Jamie and 147–8
   Wilde, Oscar and 13–14, 18, 43
Argentina *see* Tóibín, Colm *The Story of the Night*
Armagh (Women's Prison) 40
Arrighi, Giovanni 34n.40

Bacik, Ivana 149n.4
Bacon, Francis 163
Bakhtin, Mikhail 153, 174
Baldwin, James 95

ballad (Irish political) 6, 11, 33n.27, 43–4, 143, 146, 194n.76, 196
Barry, Sebastian 11, 32–3n.26, 94
Beatty, Aidan 212–13n.14
Behan, Brendan 13, 24
   'After the Wake' 46, 48, 51
   Borstal Boy 24, 37–48 *passim*, 49, 50, 51–2, 56–9, 84
   Irish language and 58, 62n.58, 194n.76
   'The Courteous Borstal' 46
   The Hostage 41
   The Quare Fellow 41
   see also anticapitalism; anticolonialism; *bildungsroman*; Dublin; injury; perversion; republicanism; vulnerability
bildungsroman (narrative)
   Behan, Brendan and 41–2
   Lennon, Tom and 127, 129, 130
   Ó Conghaile, Micheál and 171, 174
   O'Neill, Jamie and 142, 147
   Tóibín, Colm and 91–2
   Wilde, Oscar and 7
Benjamin, Walter 49, 154, 190n.2, 202

Index

Bersani, Leo 61n.39
Bliss, Panti 209–10
Bloch, Ernst 207
  the *citoyen* and 185
  hope (concept) and 27, 182–3
Bowring, Finn 22, 23, 205–6
Boyne, John 28
Brannigan, John 43
Bravmann, Scott 139
Brecht, Bertolt 104
Brehon Laws 118
Broderick, John
  Athlone, background in 63
  in writings of 64
  Catholicism in writings of 25, 63–4, 78, 85, 86, 87
  The Fugitives 65, 70, 71, 81–6, 87
  The Pilgrimage 65, 69, 70–3, 78–9
  The Trials of Father Dillingham 88n.7
  The Waking of Willie Ryan 65, 70–1, 73–81
  see also perversion; realism; republicanism; vulnerability
Brooker, Joseph 178
Brookes, Les 26–7, 122
Brown, Wendy 28–9, 108–9, 123–7
  see also injury; neoliberalism
Burton, Frederic William 200
Butler, Judith 51, 202, 209
  see also vulnerability

Carpenter, Edward 32n.23, 145
Carson, Edward 144
Casement, Roger 43, 144
Caslin, Joe 197–211
  'Our Nation's Sons' 197, 202, 210
  'Ar scáth a chéile a mhaireann na daoine' 197, 199, 202
  'Finding Power' 200, 202
  'The Claddagh Embrace' 197, 198, 200, 209–10

'The Volunteers' 197–200, 201
  see also anticolonialism; injury; neoliberalism; realism; vulnerability
Cathleen ni Houlihan 86, 196
Catholicism *see* Broderick, John
Celtic Tiger 17, 122, 182
  Gregory, Jarlath and 136
  Kehoe, Denis and 142
  Lennon, Tom and 132
  Ridgway, Keith and 158, 167–8
  McCrea, Barry and 177, 180
Chile *see* Tóibín, Colm
Chitty, Christopher 34n.40
Christ (male body of)
  Lennon, Tom and 130
  Marcuse, Herbert and 55
  Wilde, Oscar and 24, 49–50
Civil War (American), *see* Tóibín, Colm, *The Master*
Civil War (Spanish), *see* Kehoe, Denis *Nights Beneath the Nation*
Clarke, Thomas 43
Cleto, Fabio 135
Coffey, Cormac 199
colonialism *see* anticolonialism
'coming-out' novels 8, 12, 26, 105, 127–39 *passim*, 157, 171–4
Connolly, James 144, 147
Conrad, Joseph 65
  The Secret Agent 81
Costello-Sullivan, Kathleen 113n.4

Davis, Thomas 145
decriminalisation (of homosexuality in Ireland) 25, 117–8, 120, 127, 158, 165
D'Emilio, John 18–19
DiBattista, Maria 40–1
Dollimore, Jonathan 65–9
Donoghue, Emma 12
Dorcey, Mary 12

Douglas, Alfred 49
Doyle, Roddy 94
Dublin
  Behan, Brendan and 37, 46, 57–8
  gay subculture in 128, 140, 157–8, 188
  Irish gay male fiction set in 130–1, 134, 136, 138, 139–40, 153–90 *passim*
  see also gay saunas

Eagleton, Terry 14, 113n.4
Earls, Brian 14–15
Easter Rising, see Rising (Easter 1916)
Eighth Amendment (1983) 157
Emmet, Robert 43
Enright, Ann 11, 94, 95
Equality Authority 120
Equal Status and Employment Equality Acts 125
Esty, Jed 7, 16–17
European Court of Human Rights 118

Family Solidarity 118
Famine (Irish) 15
Fanon, Frantz 24, 58, 59
feminism 2, 12, 19, 29, 105, 119, 123, 150n.6, 158
Fenians 42
Fianna Fáil 95, 118
Finucane, Marian 128
Fisher, Mark 110
Floyd, Kevin 32n.24
Fornoff, Erin 199
Forster, E.M. 143
Foucault, Michel 67, 68, 108
Freud, Sigmund 22, 53, 67, 156
  Civilisation and its Discontents 62n.53
  self-formation narrative 54, 56
  psychoanalysis 69
  see also perversion
Friedman, Milton 107

Gays Against Imperialism 119, 149–50n.6
Gays Against the Amendment 149–50n.6
Gay and Lesbian Equality Network
  see GLEN
Gay Collectives (Cork, Dublin, Galway) 119, 149n.6
Gay Community News
  see GCN
Gay Defence Committee 149n.6
Gay Rights Movement (Irish) 117
gay saunas (in literature) 153, 164–5, 171, 186–9
GCN 196, 203, 204, 205–6, 208
Genet, Jean 24, 53
  Miracle of the Rose 51–2
Geoghegan-Quinn, Máire 118
Gilbert, Jeremy 110–11, 112
GLEN 119, 120, 121
Gonne, Maud 86
Gramsci, Antonio 34n.40, 115n.43
Greenwald Smith, Rachel 5–6, 103–4
Greenwell, Garth 28
Gregory, Jarlath 26, 133–8 *passim*, 188–9
  Snapshots 134–5, 137
  G.A.A.Y: one hundred ways to love a beautiful loser 21, 134–6
  see also Celtic Tiger; injury; neoliberalism; republicanism; vulnerability
Guantánamo (prison) 39
Gunn, Thom 95, 194n.75

Hand, Derek 37
Harris, Frank 42, 44, 58
Harvey, David 107, 108, 155, 171
H-Blocks (prison) 40
Hellenism 8–9, 17, 32n.23, 145–6
Hennessy, Rosemary 11–12, 31, 207

HIV /AIDS 117, 149–50n.6
  Lennon, Tom and 128
  Tóibín, Colm and 92–3, 95, 98–9
  Ó Conghaile, Micheál and 188
Home Rule 14, 99, 144
hope *see* Bloch, Ernst
hunger strikes 40
Hyde, Douglas 143

injury (narrative) 27–8, 30–1, 129
  Brown, Wendy and 28, 124, 127
  Caslin, Joe and 210
  Gregory, Jarlath and 136, 139
  Kehoe, Denis and 141–2
  McCrea, Barry and 179
  O'Neill, Jamie and 145
  Wilde, Oscar and 49–50
IRA (Irish Republican Army) 38, 41, 70, 81, 134
Irish Council for Civil Liberties 118

James, Henry 65, 95–6
Jameson, Fredric 5
Jesus *see* Christ
Jowett, Benjamin 145
Joyce, James 14, 33n.27, 65, 143, 195n.77
  A Portrait of the Artist as a Young Man 142

Kavanagh, Patrick 111
Kearney, Colbert 41, 43
Kehoe, Denis
  Nights Beneath the Nation 139–42, 148
  see also Celtic Tiger; injury; neoliberalism; realism
Keogh, Rachel 198
Kennedy, Maurice 87
Kennedy, Sinéad 36n.62, 191n.16, 191n.31
Kettle, Thomas 144
Kirby, Peadar 121

Klein, Naomi 107, 112n.2
Knights of Columbanus 118

Lavery, Hazel 197
Lavery, John 197
Law Reform Commission 118
Leavis, F.R. 4
Le Fanu, Sheridan 15
Lefebvre, Henri
  social space and 154–6
Lennon, Tom 26, 136, 153, 172, 188–9
  Crazy Love 127, 129–33
  When Love Comes to Town 127–9
  see also bildungsroman; Celtic Tiger; Christ; HIV/AIDS
LGBT (political movement) 12, 119, 122, 123–4, 126, 136, 188, 196
Lloyd, David 39–40, 61n.35, 182, 204
Lockout, the (Dublin 1913) 143
Lorca, Federico García 140
Louis, Édouard 28, 36n.61
Love, Heather 53
Lukács, Georg 32n.24, 41, 106, 140

McCracken, Henry Joy 85
McCrea, Barry 27
  In the Company of Strangers 193n.57
  Languages of the Night 62n.58, 194n.76
  The First Verse 153, 171, 175–86 *passim*
  see also Celtic Tiger; injury; neoliberalism; realism
McGahern, John 94, 131
McKeon, Belinda 11
MacLíammóir, Micheál 14
Mangan, James Clarence 86
Magdalene Laundries 78
Maher, Eamon 63–4
Manchester Martyrs 43

Mann, Thomas 95
Marcuse, Herbert 3, 119, 205–6
  Eros and 23, 59, 185
  Eros and Civilsation 22, 53–5, 185–6
  Narcissus and 55–6, 185–6, 187–8
  One-Dimensional Man 23
  Orpheus and 55, 185
  'performance principle' and 22–4, 53–6, 208
  repression and 22–3, 53–5
Marlowe, Christopher 46
marriage equality 105, 125, 165, 197, 212n.14
  see also same-sex marriage
Marxist theory 2, 3, 12, 21, 36n.62, 119, 120, 126, 156, 185
Mauriac, François 64
Medd, Jodie 147
Milton, John 66
Moloney, Stephen 200, 202
Mulhern, Francis 4–5
Mullen, Patrick 147
Muñoz, José Esteban 11, 183, 194n.75, 209
Murray, Patrick 65

neoliberalism 2–5, 19, 21–9 *passim*, 39–40, 107–8, 110–11, 121, 123, 124, 154, 206–7
  Brown, Wendy and 108–9, 125
  Caslin, Joe and 203, 205
  Gregory, Jarlath and 135, 138–9
  Kehoe, Denis and 142
  McCrea, Barry and 179
  O'Neill, Jamie and 147
  Ridgway, Keith and 182, 186
  Tóibín, Colm and 91–112 *passim*
Ngai, Sianne 110
Ni Chiaran, Ally 199
Ní Fhrighil, Rióna 48

Nietzsche, Friedrich 28, 124, 156
North, Joseph 4–5
Norris, David 118

O'Brien, Edna 63, 94
O'Brien, Flann 142
  At Swim-Two-Birds 177–8
O'Brien, Kate 12
Ó Cadhain, Máirtín 173, 188
Ó Conaire, Pádraic 14, 194n.76
Ó Conghaile, Micheál 27
  Connemara and 171, 173, 189
  Sna Fir 153, 171–4, 181–2, 184, 186–90
  see also bildungsroman; HIV/AIDS; vulnerability
O'Connor, Maureen 15
Ó Direáin, Máirtín 194n.76
O'Donnell, Katherine 170
O'Flaherty, Liam 194n.76
O'Neill, Jamie 13, 26, 32n.23, 153
  At Swim, Two Boys 1, 139, 142–9
  see also anticapitalism; anticolonialism; *bildungsroman*; injury; neoliberalism; perversion; realism; republicanism
O'Neill, Rory *see* Bliss, Panti
O'Reilly, Fiona 198
Orwell, George 176
O'Sullivan, Michael 37
O'Toole, Emer 208–10
O'Toole, Fintan 39, 40–1, 43, 95
Orientalism 16–17

Parnell, Charles Stewart 42
Pater, Walter 145
Pearse, Patrick 144
'performance principle' 155, 164–5, 185, 189, 203
  see also Marcuse, Herbert
perversion (theme)
  Behan, Brendan and 51–2
  Broderick, John and 10, 25, 65–71, 79, 81, 86–8

Freud, Sigmund and 53, 56
  Marcuse, Herbert and 56
  O'Neill, Jamie and 148
  Ridgway, Keith and 164
  Wilde, Oscar and 25
  see also Dollimore, Jonathan
Philadelphia (film) 99
Plunkett, James 143
political song see ballad
Programme for National Recovery (1987) 120
psychoanalysis, see Freud, Sigmund
Puig, Manuel
  The Kiss of the Spider-Woman 50

realism 182–3
  Broderick, John and 65, 72, 77, 78, 82, 84, 86
  Caslin, Joe and 200
  McCrea, Barry and 178
  O'Neill, Jamie and 143
  Ridgway, Keith and 160, 166
  Tóibín, Colm and 26, 91, 110–11
  Wilde, Oscar and 15
republicanism (Irish) 6, 11, 40, 59, 117, 149–50n.6
  Behan, Brendan and 25, 38–9, 42–4, 49–50
  Broderick, John and 25, 85–6
  Gregory, Jarlath and 137
  O'Neill, Jamie and 147–8, 153
  Wilde, Oscar and 13, 50, 60–1n.28
repression, see Marcuse, Herbert
Rich, Adrienne 12
Richards, I.A. 5
Ridgway, Keith 27, 182, 190
  Monaghan (county) in writings of 156, 159–60
  The Long Falling 153, 156–66, 169, 173–4
  The Parts 153, 166–71, 183, 186–7

  see also Celtic Tiger; neoliberalism; perversion; realism; vulnerability
Rising (Easter 1916) 143, 144, 199
Robinson, Mary 105
Romanticism 9, 20, 79, 80
Rose, Kieran 117–9, 121
RTÉ (Raidió Teilifís Éireann) 209, 210
Ruane, Lynn 198
Rubin, Gayle 98
Ryan, Matthew 112–3
Ryan, Paul 149n.5

Saint Augustine 66, 143
Saint Paul 65
same-sex marriage 209
  see also marriage equality
Sands, Bobby 61n.35
saunas see gay saunas
Scheible, Ellen 16
Sedgwick, Eve Kosofsky 5, 9, 13, 45, 89n.11, 127, 139
Sender, Katherine 208
September 11 (attacks on US, 2001) 29
Shakespeare, William 7, 8, 9, 46
Shanks, Bernice 38
Shonkwiller, Alison 207
Sinfield, Alan 5, 10, 52, 89n.17, 122, 133
Soar, Daniel 177
social space 17, 27, 153, 169–70, 174, 181, 182
  see also gay saunas; Lefebvre, Henri
Socrates 46
'Speranza' (Lady Jane Wilde) 15, 42
spéirbhean 86
Stoker, Bram 15
Stonewall (riots) 25, 52, 79, 119, 122, 204
Symonds, John Addington 146

The Last September (Elizabeth Bowen) 142
Tóibín, Colm 13, 25–6, 159, 179–80, 182
   Chile 107–08
   Love in a Dark Time 95
   The Blackwater Lightship 91, 93–4, 98, 105–6, 108, 156, 157, 161, 172
   The Heather Blazing 94, 95, 106
   The Master 91, 96, 99–103, 104
   The South 94
   The Story of the Night 25, 91, 92–3, 96–8, 99, 106–10
   see also *bildungsroman*; HIV/AIDS; neoliberalism; realism; vulnerability
Tone, Wolfe 38, 43, 85
Treichler, Paula 99
Trilling, Lionel 4

Valente, Joseph 142, 147
vulnerability (narrative) 27, 36n.61, 40, 50, 56, 154
   Butler, Judith and 29–31
   Behan, Brendan and 56
   Broderick, John and 80–3, 85
   Caslin, Joe and 200, 202–3, 208, 210–11
   Gregory, Jarlath and 133, 135, 138–9
   Marcuse, Herbert and 55–6
   Ó Conghaile, Micheál and 188
   Ridgway, Keith and 164

Tóibín, Colm and 98, 102, 103, 112
Wilde, Oscar and 7, 24

Walsh, Eanna 200
Walshe, Eibhear 113n.4, 114n.20
   Oscar's Shadow: Wilde, homosexuality and modern Ireland 13–14
Weeks, Kathi 2, 182–3
Whitman, Walt 145, 32n.23
Wilde, Oscar 1–18 *passim*, 42–3, 44, 53, 55–6, 58, 68, 96, 100, 143, 144–5
   De Profundis 24, 48–9, 50
   'Indivdualism' and 2–3
   'The Portrait of Mr W.H.' 6, 7–9
   The Ballad of Reading Gaol 48–9
   The Picture of Dorian Gray 6, 7–9, 15, 16–18, 56
   'The Soul of Man under Socialism' 1–2, 7, 49–50
   see also anticolonialism; anticapitalism; *bildungsroman*; Christ; injury; perversion; realism; republicanism; vulnerability
Williams, Raymond 4, 5, 104
Woolf, Virginia 65
   Orlando 38

X case (1992) 156–7, 158

Yeats, William Butler 14, 86, 196
Young Ireland 14, 42

EU authorised representative for GPSR:
Easy Access System Europe, Mustamäe tee 50,
10621 Tallinn, Estonia
gpsr.requests@easproject.com

www.ingramcontent.com/pod-product-compliance
Lightning Source LLC
Chambersburg PA
CBHW070347240426
43671CB00013BA/2432